Nature, Science, and Religion

Publication of this book and the SAR seminar from which it resulted were
made possible with the generous support of Eric and Barbara Dobkin through their
commitment to scholarly enterprises that foster positive social change in our world.

School for Advanced Research
Advanced Seminar Series

James F. Brooks
General Editor

Nature, Science, and Religion

Contributors

Andrea Ballestero
School of Human Evolution and Social Change, Arizona State University

Marthinus L. Daneel
School of Theology, Boston University, Massachusetts

Anne Motley Hallum
Department of Political Science, Stetson University, Florida

Adrian J. Ivakhiv
Rubenstein School of Environment and Natural Resources, University of Vermont

Colleen M. Scanlan Lyons
Center for the Study of Conflict, Collaboration, and Creative Governance &
Department of Anthropology, University of Colorado, Boulder

Andrew S. Mathews
Department of Anthropology, University of California, Santa Cruz

Kristin Norget
Department of Anthropology, McGill University, Montreal, Canada

Joel Robbins
Department of Anthropology, University of California, San Diego

Scott Schnell
Department of Anthropology, University of Iowa

Catherine M. Tucker
Department of Anthropology, Indiana University

Nature, Science, and Religion

Intersections Shaping Society and the Environment

Edited by Catherine M. Tucker

SAR
PRESS

School for Advanced Research Press

Santa Fe

School for Advanced Research Press
Post Office Box 2188
Santa Fe, New Mexico 87504-2188
www.sarpress.org

Managing Editor: Lisa Pacheco
Editorial Assistant: Ellen Goldberg
Designer and Production Manager: Cynthia Dyer
Manuscript Editor: Cecile Kaufman
Proofreader: Kate Whelan
Indexer: Margaret Moore Booker

Library of Congress Cataloging-in-Publication Data

Nature, science, and religion : intersections shaping society and the environment / edited by
Catherine M. Tucker.
    p. cm. – (Advanced seminar series)
  Includes bibliographical references and index.
  ISBN 978-1-934691-52-6 (alk. paper)
1. Philosophy of nature. 2. Nature–Religious aspects. 3. Religion and science. 4. Religion and
sociology. 5. Anthropology of religion. I. Tucker, Catherine M.
  BD581.N373 2012
  201'.65–dc23

                              2011043066

Library of Congress Catalog Card Number 2011043066
International Standard Book Number 978-1-934691-52-6
First edition 2012.

All photos by individual chapter authors unless otherwise noted.

All maps by Molly O'Halloran unless otherwise noted.

Cover illustration: Hugo Florencia Camey Calaj, a farmer in Xiquin Sanai, Guatemala, after a
ceremony asking forgiveness for cutting trees and blessings for the work of replanting, 2010.
Photograph by Anne Motley Hallum.

Dedicated to
Marthinus "Inus" L. Daneel
Environmental activist, inspiration, and friend

Contents

Figures

Tables

Acknowledgments

Working with the contributors of this volume has been a remarkably productive and enjoyable process. They have shared their insights and good humor without fail, and patiently supported numerous stages of manuscript development and revisions. Due to the contributors' enthusiastic participation and insights, the advanced seminar that led to this volume ranks as one of the most outstanding experiences in my professional career. Many thanks go to the School for Advanced Research on the Human Experience (SAR) and the Latin American Studies Association for generously sponsoring the seminar. Douglas W. Schwartz, founder of the advanced seminar program, deserves great credit for creating this unique opportunity for scholars to meet and discuss intellectual puzzles and challenges. We are indebted to the SAR staff, who enhanced the seminar experience through their attentive assistance. James Brooks, president, provided excellent insights and feedback at key moments in the planning process, and was a gracious host. Nancy Owen Lewis, then director of Scholar Programs, offered invaluable logistical support. All of us greatly appreciated the wonderful meals prepared by Leslie Shipman, Guest Services manager, and a gifted team of cooks, as well as their cheerful responses to our requests.

The chapters benefited from insightful comments from two anonymous reviewers; the book is better due to their suggestions. The preparation of a manuscript for publication requires dedication and an eye for detail; I thank Joanna Broderick for her patient and thorough editorial assistance. I am also grateful to Lisa Pacheco, managing editor, and other staff at SAR Press, who have given excellent support throughout the process. It has been a privilege to be part of a project that has involved so many talented and gracious people.

Nature, Science, and Religion

1

Intersections of Nature, Science, and Religion

An Introduction

Catherine M. Tucker and Adrian J. Ivakhiv

Nature, science, religion. Each term carries with it claims to truth: *nature* inasmuch as it conveys our beliefs of how things naturally are and should be; *science* in and through its methods, evident results, and institutional prestige; and *religion* in its objects and the commitments they generate among devotees. When these terms become objects of contention—as when claims to truth are questioned—each emits a great deal of heat and light, rather like a small-scale atomic explosion. They are, to use Douglas's (1975) term, "trump cards," terms customarily deployed to win arguments. But they are much more than that; where they meet, at those intersections where each of them is unsettled by the others, very interesting things happen. This book examines such spaces of intersection. The relations among the three terms are not symmetrical. Science and religion have been at odds with each other for centuries in the West, while nature has been, in a certain sense, the terrain they have struggled over. In our time of ecological risks and crises, it is the relationship between humans and nature that seems most at stake. Science is frequently (but not always) seen as the crucial ally by people who would wish to address environmental issues; religion has come to play the role of ally only belatedly, and then only in some circumstances. But things are rarely as simple as this, especially once one gets out into "the field," where most social and cultural researchers get their proverbial hands dirty.

This book is about some of the ways these three terms and the domains they refer to—science, religion, and nature—intersect in challenging, provocative, and complicated ways, in real settings where people attempt to live in some semblance of harmony with their physical environments. The research presented in these chapters explores how scientific knowledge and religious–spiritual beliefs may interact, conflict, or be used to shape natural resource management, environmental activism, and political processes.

Scholars of philosophy, religious studies, and science and technology studies have been at the vanguard of considering and critiquing the roles of religion and science in human–environment interactions. Researchers in the environmental (and related) sciences, by contrast, encounter disciplinary barriers to examining the possibility that religious beliefs influence social-ecological behaviors and processes, because the issue resists quantitative assessment. In one of our cases (Tucker's, chapter 6, this volume), the possible role of spiritual beliefs and values was at first disregarded in research on community forest management. However, with each successive period of fieldwork, Tucker encountered more and more farmers whose agricultural and forest-use practices engaged religious understandings along with indigenous knowledge and current technical information. These encounters made her wonder how the diverse arenas intersected and influenced social-ecological processes. When the Latin American Studies Association and the School for Advanced Research on the Human Experience (SAR) offered the panel competition "Nature, Science, and Religion in Latin America," Tucker saw the opportunity to organize a panel with researchers who were exploring similar puzzles. She posted the proposal to an environmental studies listserv, and four other Latin Americanists—three environmental anthropologists and a political scientist—volunteered papers. The proposed panel won the prize, which included the opportunity to hold a week-long advanced seminar at SAR. The panelists shared a goal of interacting with scholars from a variety of backgrounds who worked in different regions of the world. Toward this end, the seminar assembled ten scholars who represented a range of strengths and interdisciplinary experiences. Three of the anthropologists had training in the natural sciences (Mathews, Schnell, and Tucker); a fourth, Ballestero, had been a lawyer, while political scientist Hallum and missiologist Daneel came as environmental activists and established scholars. Norget, Robbins, and Scanlan Lyons had broad anthropological experience, and Ivakhiv's work on environment and culture drew on multiple disciplines. Together, our diverse backgrounds encompassed science and technology studies, forestry, natural resources planning, biology, East Asian literature, history, religious studies, and missiology, in addition to political science and anthropology.

When we arrived in Santa Fe for the seminar, we barely knew one another, and most of us felt some uncertainty as we sat down to introductions the first morning. We began to discuss our work, experiences, and perspectives and discovered that we shared more than anticipated. By the end of the week, we had exchanged ideas and contrasting interpretations that stretched our understanding. We experienced a moment of community, nourished by shared intellectual adventures, respect, camaraderie, delicious food, and the tranquil beauty of the SAR campus. Laughter punctuated intense discussions, and lively conversations kept us awake into the night.

Our work resonates with the question that has animated the field of "religion and ecology" since White's 1967 classic *Science* article "The Historic Roots of Our Ecological Crisis." The question White implicitly raised—*Does religion shape or affect environmental practice, and if so, how?*—has echoed through debates, uneasy alliances, and continuing tensions among environmentalists, religious–spiritual groups, and natural and social scientists concerned with environmental problems. Our research encompasses contrasting case studies and theoretical perspectives, which suggests that current interactions of science and religion have opened new frontiers for exploring and understanding local human-natural environments and global social-ecological systems. We found no clear answers to White's question; neither have others. As Ivakhiv summarized during the seminar,

> to the extent that there are reliable results, these have been mixed and probably more negative than positive, in the sense that, if anything, *most societies—no matter what their beliefs are—are prone to overdrawing on their natural resource base.* With small-scale indigenous societies, there's a stronger argument that locally based, adaptively evolved knowledge-belief-practice complexes —as Berkes, for instance, defines traditional ecological knowledge—have tended to result in longer-term sustainability of human–environment interactions. But even if that's true, the conditions in which those societies developed are not the conditions they find themselves in today. So we cannot look to them in any simple way for answers to the environmental challenges that we face. We need a more complex understanding of all these questions. [Ivakhiv, recorded presentation, August 20, 2009, emphasis added]

We concurred that "a more complex understanding" of human inter-actions with the environment requires considering human experience holistically; this means an integrative examination of the historical, eco-nomic, political, sociocultural, institutional, and spiritual dimensions of human experience. Toward this goal, our work applies ethnographic and related approaches to investigate how specific groups interact with their natural environments (which are always culturally co-constituted) and the larger-level contexts they engage when realizing experiences and responses. Reversing or mitigating environmental problems implies trans-formations that implicate the full range of human experience and organi-zation. Therefore, our discussions explored possible patterns and synthetic approaches for understanding the ways that empirical–scientific, religious–spiritual, and political–economic endeavors sway societies and transform human relationships with their socionatural and built environments.

In the process, we discovered contrasting viewpoints. Our differences proved productive and provocative and compelled us to question conclu-sions about our own work and anyone else's. In the process, we moved toward more complex and nuanced understandings.

ANTECEDENTS AND ADVANCES

In White's 1967 article, he famously argued that the Judaeo-Christian tradition shared a heavy burden of responsibility for the crisis in relations between humans and the natural world. In the article's aftermath, histori-ans, theologians, and social scientists responded in one of three predomi-nant ways: by trying to prove White wrong, whether about the ecological "disvirtues" of Christianity or Judaism or about the presumable virtues of other religions; by agreeing with him and calling for an alternative to replace the Judaeo-Christian worldview; or by taking up the charge to research the matter in greater depth. Thus was born the field of "religion and ecology," and thus began what R. Nash (1996) has called the "green-ing of religion" (Foltz 2003, 2005; Gottlieb 2004, 2006b; Hessel and Reuther 2000; Kinsley 1995; Palmer and Finlay 2003; Sponsel 2007; M. Tucker and Grim 2001, 2007; Watling 2008). The results of these trends are evident in a series of international meetings and publications, including the gathering of religious leaders sponsored by World Wildlife Fund (WWF) in Assisi, Italy, in 1986 (WWF 1986); the Religions of the World and Ecology conferences held at Harvard University in the late 1990s and the ensuing book volumes (for example, Foltz, Denny, and Baharuddin 2003; Grim 2001; M. Tucker and Williams 1997); the publication of *The Encyclopedia of Religion and Nature* (B. Taylor 2005); and initiatives like the

Earth Charter, a global values statement endorsed to date by more than eight thousand organizations around the world (see also Kellert and Farnham 2002; Oelschlaeger 1994; E. Wilson 2006). Religious–environmental alliances have proliferated in recent years. These range from broad-based international efforts to local grassroots initiatives: they include WWF's Network on Conservation and Religion, now the Alliance for Religions and Conservation (ARC), Conservation International's Faith-Based Initiatives Program, the Earth Island Institute's Sacred Lands Films Project, the International Union for the Conservation of Nature (IUCN) task force on cultural and spiritual values of protected areas, Sacred Sites International, the Green Pilgrim Cities Network (launched in late 2010), and groups like the "Redwood Rabbis," the Sisters of Earth, the African Earthkeepers of Zimbabwe (Daneel, chapter 10, this volume), the Sarvodaya Movement of Sri Lanka, the Tzu-Chi Foundation of Taiwan, the Interfaith Global Climate Change Network, and the Evangelical Environmental Network, famous for its "What would Jesus drive?" anti-SUV campaign (Daneel 2001; Dudley, Higgins-Zogib, and Mansourian 2005, 2009; Gardner 2006; Gottlieb 2006a; Lee and Schaaf 2003; Posey 2002; C. Taylor 2007).

Scholarly responses to White's challenge can be distinguished as two main types (see Derr 1975; Livingstone 1994; Minteer and Manning 2005; Whitney 1993). The first has focused on ideas, beliefs, and cultural resources—texts, narratives, rituals, images and iconographies, psalms and sutras, and other religious materials—with an eye to interpreting their ecological significance or using them to generate ecologically productive meanings. These efforts can be called "ecotheological" or "religious–ecological" in that they interpret inherited elements of religion in the direction of a constructive project of helping religious communities meet the ecological needs of our time. They constitute a kind of religious turn to ecology.

The second type of response has been to undertake empirical assessments of the ecological practices of particular societies to determine how those societies' religious–cultural beliefs and worldviews shaped their environmental practices. Analogous inquiries motivated the quantitatively focused work of cultural ecologists such as Rappaport (1984), Vayda (1969), and Reichel-Dolmatoff (1976), but recent research has shown the relationship between beliefs and ecological outcomes to be rather complicated. Indigenous peoples and others with seemingly organic or holistic worldviews have overhunted, deforested, eroded, and otherwise altered their habitats to their own detriment (Burkert 1996; Denevan 1992; Diamond 2005; Gomez-Pompa and Kaus 1992; Krech 1999; Pyne 1997; Redman 1999; Tuan 1968). The relationship between worldviews and behavior is, in any case, less predictable than social scientists had once hoped. Besides religious motivations, behavior is recognized to depend on economic, social-structural, technological, and intergroup factors, among others (Kempton, Boster, and Hartley 1995; Minteer and Manning 2003; Proctor and Berry 2005). That said, some examples suggest a connection between religion and a society's ability to respond to environmental challenges. The fates of Classic Mayan and Greenland Norse cultures are two that come to mind, if only because of Diamond's (2005) popularization of how religion—that is, culturally sanctified and ritualized practices and the vested, institutional interests associated with them—may have played a mal-adaptive role in each group's ability to meet environmental challenges. On the other hand, the growing discourse of traditional ecological knowledge, or TEK, makes a reasonable prima facie case that locally based, adaptively evolved "knowledge-practice-belief complexes" (Berkes 1999) result in rel-ative sustainability.

Debates over "noble savages," "ecological Indians," and theories of "Pleistocene overkill" are unlikely to be settled anytime soon (Harkin and Lewis 2007; Krech 1999), but even if some measure of authority is granted to a sophisticated TEK version of the "ecological Indian" hypothesis, the conditions in which such societies developed (as pointed out already) are dramatically different from those of the past, making any lessons from the past elusive in the present. In real-world situations involving indigenous groups, it is difficult to disentangle the religious factors from others: mate-rial and environmental factors, such as the perception of a shared environ-mental emergency, as in the Zimbabwean case study discussed by Daneel (chapter 10, this volume); social and psychological factors, such as the role of charismatic personalities, organizations with their needs for growth and expansion, social movements, interest groups, and social-structural condi-tions; and so on. Research on the roles of religion, ritual, belief, mythic narrative, and the like, within institutions of cultural-ecological practice remains important and perhaps essential—a point made or assumed by most of the authors in this volume—but the precise relationships among any of these pieces (ritual, myth, and so forth), like their definitions, remain elusive.

Having broached the question in this way, let us take a few steps back and think about the three terms of our title: *nature, science,* and *religion.*

CONCEPTIONS OF NATURE AND ENVIRONMENT

In a historical overview of the meanings of *nature,* Raymond Williams (1976:219) calls it "perhaps the most complex word in the [English] language." He traces out three general "areas of meaning": nature as "(i) the essential quality and character of something; (ii) the inherent force which directs either the world or human beings or both; (iii) the material world itself, taken as including or not including human beings." Ecophilosopher Evernden (1992:20–21) points out that once we have articulated a concept of nature as distinct from "all things" or "the world as a whole," it becomes possible to speak of some things as belonging to nature or being natural and of other things as being unnatural (or supernatural). *Nature* has therefore come to function as a boundary term demarcating a primary realm (which can consequently be elevated or downgraded) from a secondary realm of the human, cultural, or unnatural. It is a term that denotes value and that, as Douglas (1975) and others have shown, is often used as a discursive trump card (Cronon 1996; Franklin 2001; Glacken 1967; Horigan 1988; Ivakhiv 2002; Soper 1995; Urry and Macnaghten 1996).

A genealogy of Western concepts of nature would include the following: nature conceived as a divinely ordained system of norms and rules, rights and obligations; a book to be read, divined, and studied; a motherly female, nurturing and providing for the needs of her children (or punishing them at whim); a body-like organism whose features mirror those of the human body; a clock-like object or machine to be studied dispassionately, taken apart, and used for human benefit; a ruthless and harsh kingdom from which humans should distance themselves through the social contract of civilization; a flourishing web of life; a storehouse of resources; an Edenic garden to be set aside in protected areas and visited periodically for the replenishment of one's soul; a museum or theme park for curiosity seekers or an open-air gymnasium for trials of masculinity; a cybernetic system or data bank of circulating information; a spirit or divinity or a locus for the residence of many spirits; and an avenging angel, capriciously and unpredictably meting out its inhuman justice to a humanity that has transgressed its natural order. Each of these concepts and images carries assumptions about what kinds of action are appropriate in relation to it, from subjugation, control, measurement, prediction, and management to aesthetic contemplation, protection, and active resistance on its behalf (Ivakhiv 2001:36ff.).

Environmental movements have drawn strategically on scientific and popular understandings of nature. Since the 1960s, environmentalists have made effective use of the ecological idea that nature, when left to its own devices, tends towards exhibiting a dynamic balance or equilibrium among species, ideally leading to climax ecosystems of maximum diversity (for a given climate), harmony, and stability. This image of nature, however, has been all but rejected within the ecological science of the past four decades. Instead of a balance of nature, the natural world is more typically seen as an unstable and nonlinear one characterized by a ceaseless movement of individual organisms, species, and communities, whose overall trajectory is directionless and in many ways unpredictable, even chaotic (Worster 1996 [1994], 1997). Even tropical ecosystems—the paragons of nature's flourishing and harmonious balance—have been shown to have undergone extensive climatic and ecological change and to have been influenced for millennia by human beings through hunting and fire (Balée and Erickson 2006; Denevan 1992). If nature, as ecologists like Botkin (1990) point out, is always changing and always being remade by human activities, then how can it function as a "transcendental signified"—a source of values, direction, and religious inspiration or guidance? Other scholars have countered that a nature as complex and unpredictable as this one needs all the more to be treated carefully: in situations not fully controllable, we must apply the precautionary principle and the tools of adaptive management, not only of our resources but of ourselves as well.

SCIENCE AND ENVIRONMENTAL PROBLEMS

If nature presents uncertainties as a guide to human behavior, then science, as the enterprise that seemingly deciphers nature for us, presents its own uncertainties when viewed through a historical prism. Even specifying what science *is* can be challenging. Science can be thought of as a form of inquiry (the scientific method), as what scientists do (including their errors, human faults, and ideological stances), as established or verified truths resulting from those methods and activities (such as the First Law of Thermodynamics), as popular science (Bill Nye the Science Guy, children's science museums, kits, and fairs), or as high technology and socially and environmentally transformative Big Science (space travel, nanotechnology, the Green Revolution). In addition, anthropologists have pointed to "ethnoscience," or locally based and long-enduring pragmatic knowledge practices, as empirically tested understanding comparable to that of Western science (González 2001; Malinowski 1992[1925]; Nazarea 2003). Indigenous science, however, can be couched within worldviews that Western scientists fail to comprehend (Nadasdy 2007; Verran 2001).

From a historical perspective, science arguably has been less about finding truths as it has been working with interpretations of observed reality that seem to perform well at the time but that are replaced or reinterpreted as new paradigms and evidence emerge. Science thus involves evolving ideas and perspectives, and over time it has proven to be a self-correcting enterprise. It is equally true that the efficacy of science to discover specific facts does not ensure that scientists will follow scientific principles in asking questions or interpreting their results. Kuhn (1970) and Young (1972) noted contradictions between the ideals of the scientific method and the reality that scientists tend to work unquestioningly within the dominant paradigms of their time. In some ways, belief in a scientific paradigm bears similarity to religious faith (Kuhn 1970). In one telling example, anthropologist Nader (1996) served on a committee charged with examining energy use and policy, and she observed scientists ignoring data that suggested the possibility of a "low energy, high technology" society. By faithful adherence to the dominant ideology and "group-think," the scientists reinforced an unsustainable "high energy, high technology" economic model (Nader 1996). Intentionally or not, scientists at times have been complicit with powerful political and economic interests.

Environmental problems have presented new conundrums for considering the relationships among the sciences, politics, and economics. Scientific investigation has made some progress in identifying drivers of environmental degradation and climate change (Friedlingstein and Solomon 2005; Geist and Lambin 2001; Malhi et al. 2008; Peters et al. 2006). But scientific findings have not transformed the confounded political, socioeconomic, and institutional relationships that propel these drivers (Ascher 1999; Caddy and Seijo 2005). Moreover, complex social and ecological systems present thorny challenges for scientific investigation, due to the difficulties of examining numerous interactions and linkages among climatological, biophysical, and socioeconomic processes (Dessai, O'Brien, and Hulme 2007). From a scientific perspective, climate change science appears to be proceeding as it should: results and projections have been revised as data accumulates, while flawed analyses have been reexamined and rejected. By contrast, the media often represent scientific consensus, such as the Intergovernmental Panel on Climate Change, as exaggerating the risks of climate change. Interestingly, recent work on the social construction of science suggests that scientists have accommodated political and social opposition by underestimating climate change risks (Freudenburg and Muselli 2010).

A different situation exists for conservation biology and environmentalism, which have found political allies in their efforts to protect endangered animals and habitats. Governments have used conservation science to justify the forcible removal of native populations from areas designated as parks or nature reserves, even where inhabitants have shaped and maintained these "natural" environments (Brockington 2002; see also Brandon, Redford, and Sanderson 1998). In North America, environmentalism and protected area creation have rested on romanticized visions of untouched wilderness and overlooked the degree to which human activity has transformed and created nature (Cronon 1996; Denevan 1992). Tsing (2005) points out that conservation biologists have been motivated by an understanding of nonhuman life-forms, therefore overlooking human influence. At the same time, social scientists and activists have emphasized human rights over biodiversity conservation and viewed plants and animals as resources to be exploited. Accumulating evidence has found a strong correlation between cultural diversity and biological diversity (Ayres 2003; Cocks 2006; Stepp, Castaneda, and Cervone 2005), but neither the natural nor social sciences have adequately grasped the interdependence of humans, plants, wildlife, and landscapes (Tsing 2005). Instead, naturalists and philosophers writing in the humanist tradition, from Thoreau (1995[1854]) and Leopold (1970) to E. Wilson (2006) and Lopez (1978, 2001[1986]), and others, have made greater advances in conceptualizing human interdependence with the natural environment.

By recognizing the shortcomings of science, we do not deny the utility of the scientific method, or more broadly, empirical investigation to extend certain realms of knowledge. Indeed, we ground our work on careful observation. We nevertheless recognize that science has multiple expressions and manifestations. Similar to any other human endeavor, science is subject to vagaries of context and perception, as well as political and economic expedience. A genuine commitment to knowledge—whether scientific or humanistic—requires us to question our assumptions, or we could reproduce biases that prevent us from recognizing alternative interpretations or discovering unexpected patterns (Cronon 1996).

Because science has become increasingly influential and authoritative through the twentieth century (Nader 1996), many groups (even the marginalized) have found it strategically advantageous to present themselves or their positions as scientific in their struggles against opposing groups, which also claim scientific justifications for their own positions. Just as science means different things to different people, the information and ideas that it produces can be distorted or appropriated for diverse purposes. Chapters 3 and 4 by Robbins and Mathews, respectively, examine how groups can make claims of scientific ideas for their own purposes, regardless of their actual scientific credence. Similarly, chapters 2, 4, and 5 by Scanlan Lyons, Mathews, and Norget, respectively, examine novel alliances that emerged as different groups identified common environmental concerns and terms to act on their predicaments. By contrast, P. West (2006) found that an environmental alliance in Papua New Guinea worked because different groups misunderstood one another's terms of reference. The polyvocality of scientific knowledge intrigues many of the researchers who participated in the SAR seminar as we endeavor to understand how humans interrelate with their natural, or not-so-natural, environments.

RELIGION AND THE ENVIRONMENT

How, then, do we fit religion into this already complicated picture? Just as nature and science have varying definitions, scholars have defined religion in various ways: according to the objects of devotional practice and belief, such as deities or superhuman entities or powers; the moral systems or answers to questions of "ultimate concern" (Tillich 1959) arising from narratives about superhuman or exemplary figures; the cosmological or other propositions to which believers give assent; the rituals and cultic practices that provide a community with a sense of social solidarity (Durkheim 1976[1912]) or of belonging to a particular "chain of belief" (Hervieu-Léger 2001); or the "webs of significance" connecting human thought and behavior and providing both with the "aura of factuality" that makes life meaningful (Geertz 1973). Both *religion* and *the sacred* are terms that emerged historically as categories distinguishing certain things from others: religion from magic and superstition or from science, politics, and the secular; *a* religion as an identifiable system of related beliefs and practices that is clearly distinguishable from other such systems; the sacred as against the profane or secular; and so on (Asad 1993; Beyer 2006; Dubuisson 2003; Fitzgerald 1997, 2000, 2007; Latour 1993; Luhmann 1995; McCutcheon 1997; Styers 2004). In the encounter between Western and non-Western societies, the concept of religion has evolved from being a tool of measurement and speciation (Do Amerindians have souls?) to one of comparative evaluation (Where on the ladder of evolution do they fall?) to one of cultural management (How do we make room for them?). As Lambek (2008) points out, religion emerged as a category that circumscribed Western or European forms of religion within discourses of politics and statecraft and simultaneously inscribed and institutionalized these forms of religion as normative and universal.

Several features of religion are given heightened examination in the chapters of this book. Religion's function or role within a cultural or social-ecological system is a prominent and recurrent theme. As popularized in the cultural ecology of Steward (1955), Rappaport (1984), and others, as well as the TEK paradigm, ritual practices might be seen as institutionalized, belief-practice complexes that maintain stability, order, and reciprocity in relations between humans and the perceived or conceived transhuman world. Although cultural ecology is thought to have foundered on its functionalist and quantitative assumptions, some people continue proposing variants of cultural–ecological–religious holism (Anderson 1996; E. Messer and Lambek 2001; Peet and Watts 1996; P. Robbins 2004). Such is Parajuli's (1998, 2001) notion of "ecological ethnicities." According to this, religious or cultural sensibilities tie together shared values, cosmological ideas, social-organizational principles, and some relationship to land or territory and to identity. Roughly analogous is Dasmann's (1988) distinction between "ecosystem people" and "biosphere people." The postcolonial literature features a range of interesting, if not uncritical, engagements with this kind of distinction, from Mignolo's (2000) "border gnoseology" to Escobar's (2008) "territories of difference." In this spirit, Norget's contribution to this volume (chapter 5) proposes that such terms as *cosmovision*, *moral ecology*, and *ecological cosmology* carry a useful sense of the continuity between a small-scale society's lived cultural phenomenology and its non-human environment.

Some of the authors here, including Robbins, Tucker, Hallum, and Schnell (chapters 3, 6, 7, and 8, respectively, this volume), appear to be probing the usefulness and the limitations of the model articulated by White (1967). In this, traditional or indigenous beliefs and practices place constraints on people's behavior—constraints that shape the environmental efficacy, or ecological footprint, of a given community, whether or not they are intended as such. Traditional peoples live within animate worlds of mutual obligations with spirits or nonhuman beings, and their beliefs constrain the behavior of members of the communities, ideally limiting their environmentally destructive behavior. Modernization processes, on the other hand, disenchant and despiritualize those worlds to enable life without the constraints and obligations.

More commonly, however, religion is seen in this volume as a set of mobile references. Ritual, in Robbins's chapter 3 on the Urapmin of Papua New Guinea, is a traveling set of artifacts that takes on new functions in new contexts. The ecorituals developed by the African-instituted churches and the Shona Traditionalists in Zimbabwe, in Daneel's account (chapter 10, this volume), are generative; they forge new relations even as they revive broken ones. Other chapters articulate religion more diffusely, as religiosity, spirituality, and the sorts of things that scholars have referred to as "diffuse" or "implicit religion," "nature religion," and the like (Ivakhiv 2006). Ballestero (chapter 9, this volume) speaks of "faith" in similarly diffuse terms, without any reference to the trappings or practices of religion per se. This apparent shift toward a diffuse sense of religiosity, spirituality, or faith might be taken as evidence of a desire for a more open-ended alternative to the religious–secular duality. But perhaps more so, it demonstrates a desire for a broadened understanding of science, knowledge, and practice, a way of articulating the shared space in which people, lacking the firm and final knowledge that science always promises but never quite delivers, can make do with a politics of a world-to-come that always remains a not-yet—a "cosmopolitics," as Stengers (1996–97) calls it, that grows in the gaps between rival knowledge systems, rival cultures, and (crucially) rival natures. Ivakhiv develops this argument in the concluding chapter to this volume.

OVERVIEW OF THE VOLUME

The case studies that compose this volume examine instances in which scientific and religious perspectives overlap, interact, and become entangled with specific human-environmental challenges. With the exception of Ivakhiv's synthetic closing chapter, each explores a different social-ecological context, with particular experiences of people facing environmental issues. All of us share a commitment to ethnographic research, and our discussions rely variously on participant observation, interviews, surveys, and archival research. As a general rule, we use pseudonyms for individuals unless they are public figures. We also found that our participation in the SAR seminar influenced our thinking, so we refer to one anothers' work and our joint explorations of the constructions of nature, science, and religion as they played out in our research.

Scanlan Lyons examines how threats to the natural environment spurred unlikely alliances across environmental and religious groups in Bahia, Brazil (chapter 2, this volume). The poverty-stricken region encompasses one of the world's biodiversity hotspots, and conservationists motivated to protect the endangered Atlantic Forest have long been at odds with social and religious groups struggling to address social injustice. The dual threats of an open-pit mine and construction of a deep-sea port beside a marine protected area motivated groups to join forces in hopes of preventing the adverse environmental consequences. Shared experiences of suffering and economic deprivation helped to unify people around ideals of environmental and social justice and servant leadership. Many religious leaders in the region see the natural environment as integral to their spiritual well-being, and many environmentalists are faithful churchgoers and recognize that human suffering and environmental degradation are connected. Religious and environmental motivations for action have interacted and merged, creating a dynamic social movement that recognizes the linkages among social, economic, and ecological problems and the need to address them collaboratively. In this context, the merging of religious values with a scientifically grounded environmentalism empowered new understandings and action.

The merging of religion and science takes a very different turn in the cases presented by Robbins, who explores the development and implementation of spiritual warfare among charismatic Christians in the USA and the Urapmin people of Papua New Guinea (chapter 3, this volume). In the USA, charismatic Christians adapted ideas from the social sciences to develop more effective means of converting people. Central to their mission was the idea of spiritual geographies, in which certain spaces are dominated by demons. To bring people to Christianity, demons had to be ousted through spiritual warfare. When the animist Urapmin people encountered charismatic Christianity, they welcomed spiritual warfare as a way to end their obligations to spirits of the forest that limited their use of forest resources. By liberating themselves from the spirits, they intended to end taboos on forest use and attract a mining company, jobs, and wealth. Thus, charismatic Christians pursued a path that enchanted science, whereas the Urapmin endeavored to disenchant nature. The case of the Urapmin reveals the flaws in idealistic perceptions of indigenous groups living happily and sustainably with their traditional visions of nature. Indigenous peoples may wish to change their lives and beliefs and adopt Western religion and science to conquer nature.

Mathews presents another case in which indigenous groups link religious practice and scientific claims to achieve specific purposes (chapter 4, this volume). Unlike the Urapmin, the indigenous Mexicans studied by Mathews merged traditional religious ideas with desiccation theory in an effort to protect valued natural resources and resist an interventionist state. Desiccation theory posits linkages among climate, forests, and water flows, proposing that deforestation leads to higher temperatures and less water. In the early twentieth century, the Mexican state used the theory to justify its opposition to traditional agricultural practices that included forest clearing. Although desiccation theory fell from favor among foresters, it was embraced by rural communities as providing a scientific justification to defend their forests from state logging. By appropriating desiccation theory, indigenous groups built alliances with culturally distinct urban populations that share concerns for water availability. Thus, desiccation theory transmuted from a tool of the state to protect forests and criticize rural practices into a tool for rural communities to oppose the state and its forest policies as immoral and irresponsible. Mathews's analysis delves into the malleability of scientific knowledge and its vulnerability to dispute, along with the fluidity of social boundaries as people from very different cultural and environmental contexts seek alliances to challenge state authority and defend deeply felt needs and beliefs.

Efforts to protect land and resist the state also motivate the rural peoples studied by Norget (chapter 5, this volume), whose research in Oaxaca, Mexico, finds synergies and contrasts with Mathews's work. Norget posits the existence of moral ecologies, which serve to express and confirm people's relationships with their land and empower them to resist state hegemonies. In her study site, state intervention in indigenous communities, including the construction of a dam that displaced many people, provided motivations for them to unite against the state. They refer to sacred, spiritual powers in claiming supernatural justification for their environmental activism. She points out that some Oaxacan peoples have come together around Catholic and traditional ideas to express their linkages to a landscape inscribed with sacred significance. In the process, they are affirming moral ecologies that lend meaning and motivation to their social, environmental, and political endeavors. Their struggles reveal alternative ways of perceiving and living in the world, with ramifications for their cultural and ecological futures.

Whereas the rural Oaxacans endeavor to recapture and affirm their ecological and religious heritage, Tucker discusses how the Lenca people of western Honduras are forming syncretic beliefs that reformulate traditional conceptions of their land and its resources (chapter 6, this volume). Traditional indigenous practices and Western science meet and merge as the Lenca apply traditional agricultural rituals to new contexts, transform forests to shaded, highly biodiverse coffee plantations, and maintain a communal cloud forest reserve. Catholic and Evangelical churches have opposed traditional beliefs and rituals, but these traditions have not been abandoned as much as driven into hiding, transformed into new expressions, and adapted to fit new realities. After testing and rejecting state-supported technical advice to adopt sun-grown coffee, Lenca farmers now receive recognition for sustainable coffee production as scientific advances and market demands acknowledge the advantages of traditional shade-grown coffee. By contrast, community efforts to create a watershed reserve reveal the influence of Western conservationist ideals and national environmental rhetoric. Thus, syncretism can entail creative adaptations, not simply a decline of traditional practices and knowledge, as social, economic, and environmental contexts evolve.

Hallum's study offers a contrasting experience that emphasizes the resilience and power of indigenous beliefs as she relates her work in Guatemala with the Alliance for International Reforestation (AIR), a nongovernmental organization (NGO) (chapter 7, this volume). She analyzes the relationships between religion and conservation she encountered while working with Maya peoples on reforestation projects. The integration of traditional beliefs and rituals added meaning to tree planting and constructing efficient wood-burning stoves. She argues that the vivid power of symbols contained in syncretic Catholic and Mayan beliefs and practices reinforced the scientific knowledge involved in reforestation, making tree planting a meaningful endeavor that dovetailed with cultural values. AIR's successes point to the value of participatory, grassroots efforts that involve local people as leaders from the beginning, and she argues that other NGOs could benefit by incorporating local religious rituals and indigenous knowledge in their projects.

Local knowledge and ritual also offer provocative insights in Japan, where Schnell explores the affective dimensions of ritual in human cognition of the natural environment (chapter 8, this volume). He focuses on two models of mountain climbing that reveal dramatically contrasting perceptions of nature. The dominant model is exemplified by Walter Weston, a late nineteenth-century English clergyman who gained fame in Japan for his popularization of mountain climbing as a purely recreational activity. The alternative model derives from the example of Banryū, an early nineteenth-century Buddhist monk who climbed mountains as a spiritual endeavor to experience nature and merge with it directly. Whereas the Weston model emphasizes human mastery over the physical landscape, the increasingly popular Banryū model favors veneration and respect for nature as a vital presence. Both models can be seen as carrying ritual dimensions that express values about human relationships with the natural environment and influence cognition and behavior. The Banryū model, however, has greater potential to encourage environmentally conscious and sustainable practices.

Human cognition of the environment and conflicting models of nature play very different roles in Ballestero's examination of water politics in Brazil and Costa Rica (chapter 9, this volume). In both nations, scientific modeling, legal frameworks, and public experiences with water scarcity create incommensurable knowledge and convictions. Nevertheless, people with opposing convictions return again and again to the negotiating table with minimal expectations of an agreement. Yet representatives of state powers refrain from imposing their will, and those representing public concerns patiently persist in identifying and questioning weaknesses in the scientific models. Ballestero discovers in these cases a generative, inexplicable faith in the value of process and the possibility of unforeseeable innovations despite manifest uncertainties. She avoids the tendency to see faith as a religious form of conviction and proposes a nonreligious faith that allows surrender to uncertainty and tolerance of possible failure. Faith unexpectedly becomes a key to negotiation, political process, and active engagement with social, economic, and ecological conundrums.

The hopeful outlook of Ballestero contrasts with Daneel's account of Zimbabwe's Earthkeepers movement (chapter 10, this volume). Unique in this volume, Daneel contributes the perspective of an environmental-activist Christian lay-minister, missiologist, and scholar. For more than a decade, he helped to lead an ecumenical reforestation movement of traditional African and Christian churches. The creation of tree-planting rituals that honored both religious traditions provided a context for new understanding and cooperation. Then Zimbabwe's political and economic situations deteriorated dramatically, which exacerbated internal, organizational weaknesses and drove the movement to collapse. The experience points to the great potential for environmental restoration and group alliances when people actively integrate spiritual and environmental values and practices. The subsequent disintegration reveals the vulnerability of grassroots movements to outside pressures and internal shortcomings. Daneel reflects on the difficult lessons of faithfulness and failure in a seemingly intractable situation and embraces Ballestero's vision of a generative faith that tolerates uncertainty and allows for the emergence of unforeseeable possibilities.

In the final chapter, Ivakhiv reflects on the case studies presented, synthesizing their insights into the role and meaning of religion amidst social-ecological challenges for which science may be necessary but not sufficient (chapter 11, this volume). He points to three broader shifts in the relations among science, religion, and nature: a turn to ecology within communities of faith, a turn to religion among environmentalists, and a return of prominent intellectuals to the vitality of religion in the post–Cold War and post–September 11, 2001, world. Citing Bruno Latour's argument that modernity has segregated science from politics, authorized science alone to speak on behalf of nature, and relegated religion to the realm of private belief and morality, Ivakhiv argues that the case studies reveal a science, a religion, and a nature that are much more plural, hybrid, and entangled with one another than our formal conceptions of them suggest. He advocates that these hybridities be viewed not as exceptions but as the rule, that what counts as science, as knowledge, as religion, and as nature be thought of as active "co-articulations" of people and material relations—"cosmopolitical" propositions negotiated among multiple players. The future, he suggests, lies in a willingness to enter into spaces of uncertainty, in which novel articulations make possible new relations among scientists, environmental activists, policy makers, religious believers, indigenous people, and others.

OPENNESS TO UNCERTAINTY

The gritty and sometimes grim realities of the social-environmental problems we discussed at the seminar could have been depressing. Most of us had worked with impoverished and marginalized peoples, and we had witnessed processes that harmed human lives along with the natural environment. Through our conversations, we found glimmers of hope and cause for encouragement. Inus Daneel, who has witnessed tragedies that most of us could barely imagine, shared his struggle with despair and then inspired us with the conviction that failure can provide fertile ground for renewal. Scott Schnell brought deep knowledge of Asian religious traditions and ritual, along with an unshakeable patience and a lucid perspective that kept discord and confusion at bay. Andrea Ballestero applied her insight that faith can embrace uncertainty, revealing a remarkable ability to gently deconstruct our analyses and offer alternative interpretations. Colleen Scanlan Lyons analyzed the ways that shared religious convictions and sensed connections with nature might inspire creative, collective action, simultaneously enlivening our conversations with her irrepressible enthusiasm. Anne Hallum reminded us that traditional societies may have much to teach the modernized world about human interdependence with nature and convincingly argued that respectful activism can empower marginalized peoples to address their social-ecological challenges. Kristin Norget called attention to the complexities of power relations and encouraged closer examination of the struggles over religious beliefs, cultural values, and knowledge claims that play out in social-ecological problems. Andrew Mathews examined how science can be transformed as it is appropriated to support diverse political agendas, and he thoughtfully challenged attempts to generalize about human–environment interactions. Joel Robbins pointed out that religion and science can imitate each other and be crafted in unpredictable ways to shape social and environmental processes, imparting an upbeat outlook. We, co-authors of this introductory chapter, brought our own strengths to the table: Adrian Ivakhiv's knowledge of theories of nature, environment, science, and religion and his careful reading of each contribution grounded our discussions in a rich philosophical heritage. Catherine Tucker's attentive facilitation, coupled with an anthropological appreciation for diverse perspectives and an environmental scientist's pragmatism, steered us on a productive course.

On the last night of the seminar, we all sat on the patio sipping wine and talking as if we had been lifelong friends. We began to share our favorite memories and songs. Joel taught us the "bighead time" song that the Urapmin had created in their enthusiastic move to accept Christianity, vanquish the forest spirits, and attract development. Halfway around the world, here we were, also endeavoring to challenge established ways of knowing and encounter new ways of understanding. Unexpectedly, we shared much in common with the Urapmin. The song dissolved into laughter and the silence that friends share when words are unnecessary. It ended a week in which we all contributed diverse experiences and reflections. As our conversations concluded, we had not found answers to the conundrums that drew us together. Instead, we affirmed that embracing uncertainty proves requisite to understanding and navigating the mutable landscape of nature, science, and religion that our own and other scholarship begins to map. We acknowledged that this landscape, already rife with conflicts, is also rich with possibilities. This embrace of uncertainty encourages us to explore a full range of interpretations and responses as social-ecological-ideational systems undergo transformation. We share hopes for unforeseeable emergences, perhaps for radically new natures, that might allow for social justice, environmental sustainability, and cultural and biological diversity to co-exist and flourish. These hopes may seem fleeting and ungraspable even as we anticipate and envision them. The chapters that follow, while divergent in their social-ecological contexts and to some extent in their focal concerns, reflect our shared engagement with this terrain of uncertainty and possibility at the intersections of nature, science, and religion.

2

Suffering, Service, and Justice

Matters of Faith and How Faith Matters to the Environmental Movement in Brazil's Atlantic Forest

Colleen M. Scanlan Lyons

In December 2008, a group of people gathered in a small town in the state of Bahia, Brazil, in a region known as Southern Bahia (figure 2.1), to oppose a large-scale mining and infrastructure development project. The group united around a common fear that the mining operation would bring environmental and social catastrophe to the place where they lived. They worried that mining would divert water from the already heavily impacted regional source, the San Francisco River, while leaving tailings in the remaining water that countless people, plants, and animals depended on. They also feared that mineral transport would harm their air quality as iron ore and other products traveled across the state in open-air railcars. They anticipated that plans for massive export of these minerals would hurt their coastline, because a proposed deep-sea port was to be constructed in a relatively pristine area abutting land designated to preserve rare plants and animals. They foresaw that this megaproject would change their economy and community, because the jobs that were promised would either quickly end or be given to more specialized labor from outside the region, creating more poverty in and migration to an already poor area. The likelihood of each of these future scenarios inspired priests, environmentalists, and other social movement activists to come together. Their speeches, banners, and chants articulated a common conception of the suffering they

FIGURE 2.1

Map of Southern Bahia, in the state of Bahia, Brazil. This is the location of the Atlantic Forest study site. Proposed mining and infrastructure projects in this region have caused concerns among social activists and prompted alliances between environmental and religious leaders who largely oppose the projects.

would face, cried for sound leadership against this project, and called for concrete actions that would promote social and environmental justice throughout the region.

The threat of this project still looms large, but another reality has also taken root in Southern Bahia. Alliances between religious leaders and prominent environmentalists around projects such as this mining and infrastructure intitiative are becoming increasingly common as people break down divisions between the secular and the sacred to unite in a common vision of place and life.

Although there are long-standing ideological connections between the environment and the major world religions (M. Tucker 2003), the environmental movement, globally and in Brazil, has historically derived its credibility from science and biology and worsening environmental crises (Escobar 1998; Nasr 2003; Tsing 2005) rather than from faith and spirituality. However, we are increasingly confronting the shortcomings of that approach (Shellenberger and Nordhaus 2004) and sometimes see the distrust between religious people–institutions and environmentalists–scientists (Gardner 2006). Particularly in the global South, an environmentalism that people viewed as divorced from the realities of their daily lives is failing (McKinley 2008).

In many ways, the Brazilian environmental movement has united around the ideal of social environmentalism (Esterci and Telles do Valle 2003; Hochstetler and Keck 2007; Santilli 2005), which lies at the core of what has grown in the past twenty-five years to be a distinctly "Brazilian environmentalism." This movement emerged as environmentalists joined with indigenous and river peoples (Santilli 2005:32), and "environmentalism allied with the social movements, and social movements turned more environmentalist" (Crespo cited in Santilli 2005:51). Organizations like the Social-Environmental Institute (Instituto Socioambiental, ISA) and the Center for Social-Environmental Assistance (Centro de Apoio SócioAmbiental, CASA) were founded to make a clear distinction between their work and the environmentalism that had failed to devote attention to the social issues associated with environmental degradation. Furthermore, distinctly social movements, like the land reform movement, also consider themselves to be aligned with core environmental conservation values, blurring the boundaries between environmental and social movements.

As priests and nuns join environmentalists against mining and development projects, the long-standing separation and distrust are gradually breaking down. In 1986, the World Wildlife Fund (WWF) invited five of the major world religions—Buddhism, Christianity, Hinduism, Islam, and Judaism—to Assisi, Italy, the birthplace of the Catholic patron saint of animals and ecology, St. Francis. The purpose of this meeting was to examine the intersections between religion and environmental conservation (Palmer and Finlay 2003). In turn, the meeting inspired the founding of the Alliance of Religions and Conservation (ARC) ten years later. Since then, Baha'ism, Daoism, Jainism, Shintoism, Sikhism, and Zoroastrianism have joined ARC, and countless other groups have begun to explore ways in which religion can merge with what are often conceived of as secular concerns of environmental conservation, thus taking a "theophilosophical turn" (Ivakhiv, chapter 11, this volume) in a way that benefits both (Palmer and Finlay 2003). The WWF-ARC alliance has inspired a series of conferences and discussions involving top scientists and religious leaders (B. Taylor 2005) and resulting in policy actions. For example, in 2005, WWF and ARC co-published a list of one hundred sacred and biodiverse places in the world in an effort to put religiously important places on the environmental conservation map (Dudley, Higgins-Zogib, and Mansourian 2005:40–71).

While connections between religion and environmentalism appear to be growing through meetings and declarations of alliance, we still know little about how these relationships are taking place in practical ways. Furthermore, the union of religion and environmentalism is still somewhat awkward and surprising, even to the people involved. A declaration issued by a 2007 initiative of Harvard University that brought these different interests together opens with this statement: "Scientific and evangelical leaders recently met to search for common ground in the protection of the creation. We happily discovered far more concordance than any of us had expected, quickly moving beyond dialogue to a shared sense of moral purpose" (SEI 2007:1).

What happens when we take a deeper look at this apparent shift "beyond dialogue to a shared sense of moral purpose"? How is the discourse of the growing integration between environmental conservation and religion made real? Furthermore, is religion instrumental for environmentalism, and is the environmental movement pushing religious communities to become more involved in salient issues that affect our world? To better understand such questions, I argue that the emerging relations between religion and environmentalism in Brazil are being concretely articulated in three ways that prove beneficial to both: (1) common conceptions of suffering, (2) common approaches to leadership that focus on service, and (3) actions that work toward justice. Each articulation is instrumental in bridging the divide between religion and environmentalism. First, the suffering experienced by environmentalists as subjects and activists within this movement brings a human face to a movement that, particularly in Brazil, can be seen as more concerned with animals and plants than with people. Second, servant leadership provides a concrete mechanism for crossing boundaries between science and religion as environmentalists act in ways that incorporate others and as religious leaders become engaged with important ecological issues that affect people every day. Finally, the notion of justice advocates an approach that incorporates social justice and environmental justice and therefore can be a force for mobilizing people to action. In sum, I aim to reveal how suffering, servant leadership, and justice are articulated through religion and environmentalism separately and how these articulations indicate important areas of intersection that suggest how these movements might be even more powerful together.

In making these arguments, I draw from the work of Hall to reveal the ways in which relations between two entities can be instrumental for both. Hall (1996; Hall and Grossberg 1996:141) considers articulation as a two-sided, relational process. He notes, "The term has a nice double meaning because 'articulate' means to utter, to speak forth, to be articulate. It carries that sense of language-ing, of expressing, etc....An articulation is...the form of the connection that can make a unity of two different elements, under certain conditions. It is a linkage which is not necessary, determined, absolute and essential for all time." Extending Hall's ideas, I aim to show how the power of articulation transforms religion and environmentalism. I align with Li (2000:153), who points out that one of Hall's contributions to understanding articulation lies in his description of its ability "to define broad constellations of shared or compatible interests, and mobilize social forces across a broad spectrum." Articulation characterizes the process through which each author in this volume thought through the myriad connections among religion, science, and nature. Conceptions of faith are articulated within Brazilian and Costa Rican water politics (Ballestero, chapter 9, this volume), environmental degradation is expressed through moral ecologies (Norget, chapter 5, this volume), Western science joins with traditional spiritual beliefs to inspire environmental conservation initiatives (Tucker, chapter 6, this volume), and local practices and religious traditions become woven into the conservation initiatives of nongovernmental organizations (NGOs) (Hallum, chapter 7, this volume). This list goes on, the point being that articulation has power to help us better understand the ways in which these forces are coming together in various cultural, geographical, political, and environmental contexts.

I begin this chapter with a brief description of how the intersections between religion and environmentalism emerged during the course of my research in Bahia, followed by an explanation of the background necessary to understand these growing relations in Bahia, as well as in the broader context of Brazil. I then turn to the ways in which "collective suffering" fosters solidarity across different religions and environmental groups in Bahia today and examine how ideologies and practices of servant leadership arise in response to perceptions of suffering. I conclude by discussing how justice is articulated to bring moral and ethical issues to the fore and, ideally, to inspire collective action across diverse groups of people. I particularly incorporate the perspectives of Raul, an NGO leader with a profound religious life, but also draw from the views of other environmental, religious, and social movement leaders in Southern Bahia.

STUMBLING UPON THE SPIRITUAL

In May 2006, I attended a meeting in Bahia organized by a local environmental NGO and an agrarian reform community it was working with. Everyone in the room formed a circle as the man in charge began the meeting with a fervent prayer. Everyone present seemed to join in, some uttering expressions of agreement when appropriate. I soon learned that this community meeting in the Atlantic Forest was similar to many others. Like countless environmental and other social movement gatherings I attended, it began with God.

The process of merging prayer with secular activities is increasingly accepted throughout Brazil. As Birman (2006:58) notes, "the inclusion of prayers has become a standard and expected feature of public events.... Religious language is being disseminated as a form of changing the world by acting positively within social circles." Prayers also extend to other methods of communicating the role of religion within social and environmental activism. For example, one regional environmental NGO opened a report with the dedication "To God, for the internal strength and understanding that faith and good work generate solutions, open roads, clear our vision, and also fulfill us spiritually" (Floresta Viva 2008:3).

I went to Southern Bahia, midway along the state of Bahia's coastline in Brazil's northeast region, to learn how different social movements were negotiating with one another around land management issues in one of the most biodiverse places in the world. As my interactions with the people involved in environmental and social issues grew, however, I found myself continually confronted with the prominent presence of religion in people's lives. For example, one small town has a population of less than two thousand yet supports a staggering variety of worship places—Baptist, Church of God and Love, the Church of Rebirth in Christ, Pentecostal, Jehovah's Witnesses, Seventh Day Adventist, the Universal Church of King of God, and others. This modest community also has worshippers of Santo Daime,[1] an Afro-Brazilian Candomblé *terreiro* (worship house) (figure 2.2) (Bastide 2007; Harding 2003; P. Johnson 2005; Voeks 1997), and a devout Catholic community.

In addition to this overtly religious character, which permeates much of the region, many social movement leaders of NGOs and other groups (for example, Landless Rural Workers Movement [MST] and *quilombo* communities composed of descendants of former slaves, called *quilombolas*) had vibrant personal religious identities that seemed instrumental in their broader activist work. The active environmental and social movement context in Bahia mirrors Brazil's national characteristic of strong movement mobilization (Escobar and Alvarez 1992; Hochstetler and Keck 2007; Keck and Sikkink 1998; Petras and Veltmeyer 2005; Viola 1992, 1997; Wright and Wolford 2003). My conversations with leaders in Bahia regularly reached beyond environmental politics and the broad strategies of the movements,

FIGURE 2.2

Building that serves as a Catholic church and Candomblé terreiro in a quilombo community in Southern Bahia, Brazil, reflecting the syncretic religious traditions throughout the region.

to people's personal lives: My calls for interviews often interrupted people's participation in evening church services or self-organized weekend retreats. I sometimes found people's properties bearing names like "The Quiet Corner of Our Lord," and I was constantly blessed, prayed for, and told to "go with God."

Many environmentalists' professional and spiritual lives were deeply integrated in a way that was surprising even to me, having been raised in a devout Catholic family. Of the semi-structured interviews I conducted with environmental leaders, twenty-one out of twenty-seven (77 percent) expressed a strong religious or spiritual identification. Furthermore, nearly half of the environmental events had a religious component within their broader work. While I was aware that dialogue between religious and environmental communities was growing throughout the world, sweeping claims to growing alliances often lacked detail that would have made the relationships come alive more fully. I wondered *how* religion and environmentalism were merging in the context of people's lives and why.

CONTEXTUALIZING ENVIRONMENTALISM, SOCIAL MOVEMENTS, AND RELIGION IN BAHIA AND BRAZIL

Southern Bahia provides a particularly rich location for exploring the hows and whys of the religion-environmentalism alliances. Brazil's Atlantic Forest, designated a World Biosphere Reserve in 1992 and 2002 (Diegues 1995; UNESCO 2008), is one of the most endangered natural areas on the planet. Although less than 8 percent of the original Atlantic Forest remains (Leal and Câmara 2003; Tabarelli et al. 2005), parts of it have more floral and faunal diversity than the more globally famous Amazon Forest (Morellato and Haddad 2000:786; Saatchi et al. 2001). The Atlantic Forest is also commonly characterized as a global "hotspot," a term coined by Conservation International (CI 2007) and now widely used to describe "areas featuring exceptional concentrations of endemic species and experiencing exceptional loss of habitat" (Myers et al. 2000:853). The Atlantic Forest in Southern Bahia, moreover, is called a "hot-point within a hotspot" (Martini et al. 2007), designating it as one of the most ecologically critical forest fragments in all of Brazil (see CI 2007, ELI 2008, Myers 1988, Myers et al. 2000 for global hotspots and their impacts).

The region's rich biodiversity, however, contrasts with the economic needs of many people who live here. Bahia has more economic inequality than Brazil as a country, which is infamous for having one of the world's greatest income disparities (Caldeira 2000; Page 1996; Ribeiro 2000). This disparity between environmental wealth and economic poverty must be considered when questioning the relations between religion and environmentalism. Environmentalists must increasingly incorporate their causes into the daily realities of people's lives, because considerations of flora and fauna are often not the top priority for many of the people living here. As Beto, an environmentalist in the region, noted, "it doesn't do any good to take care of nature without taking care of people" (personal communication, March 8, 2006, Itacaré, Bahia), meaning that a narrow, biologically focused environmentalism is divorced from people's hunger, poverty, and joblessness.

The religious context of Bahia must also be considered as a backdrop to emerging environmental–economic relations. The case of Bahia aligns with two broader religious characteristics in Brazil, syncretism and the recent Evangelical transformations that have increased throughout the country, particularly over the past twenty years (Bastide 2007; Birman 2006; Burdick 1993, 2004; Clarke 2006; Dawson 2007; Greenfield and Droogers 2005; Pierucci and Prandi 2000; C. Smith and Prokopy 1999). The pervasiveness of syncretism and the growth of Evangelicism are also evident across the Latin American region (Hallum 1996; Steigenga and Cleary 2008; Willems 2008). Since the 1950s, the number of people who self-identify as Catholic has consistently fallen. According to the 2000 Brazilian census, Catholicism composes 73 percent of the population and Evangelicism 15 percent (IBGE n.d.). The 2010 census data will likely show more of a decline in Catholicism and a rise in Evangelicism.

Given these realities of religion in Brazil, it is difficult to draw strict affiliations between particular environmental groups and particular religions. One Catholic church in my study region has a vibrant youth group oriented toward environmental issues, and the pastor of the region's Catholic cathedral tells of nuns and priests who incorporate social-environmentalism into their religious work. On the other hand, some of the region's most prominent environmentalists happen to be strong leaders within Evangelical churches. One regional church, the Vale do Amanhecer (Valley of Rebirth), has plans to start an organic farming community. Furthermore, other environmentally oriented agrarian reform settlements that adhere to organic farming practices comprise Catholics and Protestants. Other groups, such as quilombos (Leite 2000:333), that increasingly identify with environmentalism and work with more formal environmental NGOs reveal similarly diverse religious identities. Cloildo, a quilombola leader, observed when asked about religion in his community: "There are some people who are Catholics. There are others who are Evangelicals. Some follow Candomblé...others don't have a formal religion. To each his own." (personal communication, March 30, 2007, Itacaré, Bahia) It is important to consider these hybrid and dynamic realities to better understand how the cross-religious concepts and practices of suffering, service, and justice are articulated across religion and environmentalism today.

ARTICULATING SUFFERING: CRIES OF THE EXCLUDED

> The force of knowledge is arriving at its limit. There is a monumental production of knowledge, many publications, many academic productions, and at the same time a diminution of the power of this knowledge in reality. It is separated from people, with other realities that mark the lives of people. [Personal communication, Raul, October 2009, Southern Bahia]

One of the realities present across different lives in Southern Bahia is the notion of o grito (the cry), a phrase that is often uttered. This cry hints at the ways in which histories of social exclusion and ecological catastrophe have created present-day suffering for the people and the natural environment and blur the boundaries between environmentalism and social issues. The environmental movement here, perhaps more so than in other urban environments of Brazil, draws a distinct connection between the natural environment and the people who depend on it for their livelihoods. For example, in 2006, Minister of the Environment Marina Silva came to one of the region's main towns to celebrate Earth Day. In an effort to catch her attention, environmentalists highlighted the interconnected ecological and economic crises in the region. They wore brightly colored shirts emblazoned with the words *O Grito do Cacau* (The Cry of Cocoa), referring to the witches broom disease (from the fungus *Crinipellis perniciosa*) that had been wiping out nearly all of the region's cacao crop for the prior two decades. The effects of this disease, however, extended beyond unproductive cacao crops, leaving farmers without their livelihoods and the remaining Atlantic Forest more susceptible to illegal hunting and logging. Thus, suffering is rooted in concrete and complex political, social, and environmental issues, such as the spread of a disease that curtails farming or livelihood options, which then causes people to scramble for ways to make a living and eat, thus exerting pressure on the region's surrounding forests.

Suffering can also extend to the emotional and psychological realm. Padre Oswaldino, a priest who has been active in opposition to the mining project mentioned at the opening of this chapter, describes the people in the region: "The feelings of people in the municipalities of Lagoa Caetité and Real [the mining sites] seem to be of silence and indifference, perhaps the result of the imposition of the [name of the company]....When the company appears, people are apprehensive with fear and even terror." This priest knows the situation well; he has been a leading public figure against this project, emotionally noting, "Mining and environmental preservation don't go together...[this company] is using the politics of sustainability and social responsibility as a 'slogan' and business card. I'll put my opinion on the table—I'm against [this]!" (Pacheco 2009). However, these public statements have resulted in lawsuits against him by the mining company that the environmental organizations say are meant for pure intimidation. Furthermore, although environmentalists working in the Atlantic Forest of Bahia have not reached the levels of personal danger faced by people in the Brazilian Amazon—the murders of Chico Mendes in 1988 and Sister Dorothy Stang in 2005—they still face the threat of assaults. In 2003, local activist Amilton survived an attack by loggers that left deep scars on his hands and arms from knife wounds. Caio, another local environmentalist, described his own efforts: "We were fighting for the beaches....Bruno [an activist] had to leave the city. He stayed hidden, Bela [another activist] was threatened, I was threatened. This brought out a lot of enemies, a lot of enemies" (personal communication, March 5, 2007, Itacaré, Bahia).

Finally, other groups in this region who often interact with environmental and religious leaders experience similar and arguably more insidious forms of suffering. Gustavo, an environmentally focused agrarian reform leader, described how the land reform group he works with was inspired by "a cry from the countryside....The large landowners threw people off the land, and there weren't options. There were a few with a lot of land and so many without any land at all." He continued, "A month ago, we had a companion assassinated....We know he was linked to the [agrarian reform] movement. The large landowner lived near the agrarian reform settlement, and he wanted to put his son on the land....Later, in [a nearby town], two [agrarian reform settlers'] tents were burned" (personal communication, March 21, 2006, Itabuna, Bahia). One quilombola leader, a feisty young woman named Joana, aptly described a blatant form of physical suffering during a meeting meant to unite groups and interests connected to the natural environment: "Forest and water, forest and water, no one speaks of my hunger" (personal communication, July 22, 2008, Itacaré, Bahia). Environmental activism and environmentally related issues of livelihood development—even hunger—are intricately intertwined as conceptions of suffering sweep across the social landscape of Bahia.

Religious communities in this region are also attuned to these realities—the demise of cacao and livelihoods, the threats to people's psychological and even personal beings. Padre Oswaldino noted, "We instituted a Parish Commission on the Environment to try to implement our demands," which include requiring the state and federal governments to work for human rights, to monitor the health of people in this region, and to ensure independent investigation of the level of radioactivity in water consumed by these people (Contaminação 2009). Padre Emilio, another local Catholic priest, echoes this intersection between environmental and human rights issues, noting how the church plays a prominent role in the annual, nationwide Grito dos Excluidos (Cry of the Excluded), which is meant to draw attention to myriad environmental and social issues. In 2009, in fact, the theme of the Grito dos Excluidos invoked a widespread vision of environmentalism through the theme "Life in First Place: The Force of Transformation Is in Organizing the People."

In an interesting way, this broad theme reflects anthropologist Escobar's (2008:25) call for the use of the term *life* "instead of 'nature' or the 'environment'...since it seems...that what is involved...is the under-standing and defense of life itself, in all of its complex manifestations." As in the outcry against mining, the local participants in the Grito dos Excluidos, who hail from many religious groups and environmental and social organizations, are advocating for alternative development that can be supported by the organizations and popular participation and has as its principles living sustainably within biomes, food security, economic soli-darity, and gender, ethnic, and generational equality, among others (for a similar account of community mobilization, see Norget, chapter 5, this vol-ume). Such views of integration are also reflected in Brazilian theologian Boff's (1997) book *Cry of the Earth, Cry of the Poor*, which breaks down dif-ference and stresses the connections among ecology, social justice, and spirituality.

This linkage between social–environmental issues movements and the recognition of human suffering across the various religions in this region may be hinting at a broader change. Burdick (1993) draws a clear distinc-tion between the different approaches to suffering taken by Catholicism, Pentecostalism, and Umbanda, an Afro-Brazilian religion. He argues that even progressive Catholicism has generally judged suffering as something that people bring on themselves whereas Pentecostalism and Umbanda offer people relief from the worldly suffering they endure by attributing it to nonhuman forces, such as the devil, rather than to people's actions (Burdick 1993:67). In Bahia today, the realities of environmental degrada-tion put forth by the environmental movement appear to be minimizing religious distinctions and, instead, bringing together people of different religions and environmentalists through a common conception of human suffering. Daneel (chapter 10, this volume) shows how this transition also happened in Zimbabwe. In this way, articulations of suffering are instru-mental in broadening environmentalism by tethering it to social justice and cross-religious issues and may also be breaking down long-standing religious differences on the important realities of people's lives. Further-more, these realities may, in fact, represent an emerging "re-engagement" of the Catholic Church in social activism. Whereas Catholicism in the 1950s had been characterized by Ecclesial Base Communities united around social justice causes (Mainwaring 1986), over the past few decades, the Catholic Church in Brazil (and elsewhere in Latin America) was grow-ing more conservative, often eschewing involvement in controversial issues that shape people's lives, such as birth control and abortion (Burdick and Hewitt 2000:viii; see also Adriance 1995). Could it be that the more recent articulations of suffering connected to environmentalism are indicative of a resurgence in progressive church politics, tying it once again to salient issues of social and environmental justice?

ARTICULATING LEADERSHIP: SERVICE, TOLERANCE, AND RENEWAL THROUGH NATURE

Not only does suffering forge solidarity between environmental and religious issues, but it also provides the foundation for an approach to leadership that mirrors the tenets of world religions in general and, in particular, religious leaders such as Jesus Christ. Across the board, environmental and religious leaders throughout Southern Bahia articulate a common leadership style predicated on service and tolerance. Furthermore, many of these leaders experience a deep sense of personal renewal through connections with nature.

Environmentalists who work with NGOs, agrarian reform settlements, and communities like quilombos often articulate leadership by serving others. As one environmentalist who has long interacted with farmers and land reform activists throughout the region stated, "the best way to lead is to serve others." Even more specifically, many of the region's environmentalists use the term *servant leadership* to describe their style. It is unlikely that they draw the term directly from Greenleaf (1977:13), who coined it in 1970 to describe "the natural feeling that one wants to serve, to serve first. Then conscious choice brings one to aspire to lead. This is sharply different from the person who is leader first, perhaps to assuage a power drive or to acquire material possessions." Some leaders are moved by a need to serve others in eradicating injustices, which brings them to leadership. One woman, a well-known environmentalist, land reform activist, community leader, and quilombola representative, noted that "people lived on the earth for years and then others would come in and be able to take the land. Land is a common right." She continued, "I would go to the fields and fight [for this right]" (personal communication, June 2, 2006, Itacaré, Bahia).

Environmental leaders in Southern Bahia often stress service by bringing their religious ideals into their environmental leadership and by broadening their environmentalism as they connect it to the social issues that demand their attention if they are to be responsive servant leaders. For example, Raul situates his leadership within the historical, social, cultural, and environmental history of Bahia, equating his work in environmental conservation to that of a mission. A practicing Evangelical, Raul also draws from the leadership of Jesus Christ in describing this mission—which is quite similar to the "new dominion of service" described by Daneel (chapter 10, this volume)—who viewed a mission as a promise to bring results. He indicates that simplicity, humility, cooperation, and actions that integrate and valorize nature and people are characteristics that we define as ours but are inspired by a divine presence. Another environmentalist, who adheres to a more humanistic approach rather than to one particular religion, discusses his social-environmental work in a way that mirrors the teachings of many world religions: "You start with the miserable—not the poor, but the *miserable*—you then work up from there. I start [my work] with the person who doesn't have a piece of bread to eat" (personal communication, February 28, 2007, Itacaré, Bahia).

Approaching environmentalism as a mission and connecting it to the broader social realities in Southern Bahia, like hunger, is also strengthened by the characteristic of tolerance, which many leaders here reflect in their daily work. Tolerance can dismantle differences of race, class, and even culture, differences that undeniably exist between the middle-class, educated environmentalists, and social movements that often comprise poor family farmers or marginalized quilombo residents. Raul explains, "The largest challenge of humanity is to love the stranger....And here you see Jesus. He was a large teacher of this. We need to love the one we don't understand, the one we consider different....Jesus is saying the stranger is good also.... Love your neighbor. To love your friend is easy." Boff (1995:87) echoes Raul's call to tolerate and to embrace "otherness": "We have to accept the otherness of all that exists in creation. Every form of being, animate or inanimate, has a value as such. It has its possibilities and limitations within the ecosystem itself. For human intelligence and affectivity, every being is a challenge to decipher the message of life, beauty, and rationality that it possesses in itself. All beings, especially living beings, deserve to be accepted and even respected in their otherness."

Adhering to these perspectives, leaders throughout the region use tolerance as a basis for acceptance, for embracing "the other" in their environmental work. As the founder of a regional environmental NGO, Raul acknowledges that "the foundation of Jesus' teachings is to love the other, like the good Samaritan." Such articulations also align with even broader calls for tolerance across different faiths in the name of environmental conservation. In WWF's publication *Beyond Belief*, it advocates for tolerance across religious beliefs in order to safeguard sacred spaces, many of which are located in priority areas for environmental conservation: "Tolerance of other spiritual practices is probably the rule rather than the exception, despite the dire warnings about the dangers of 'false beliefs' that appear in many of the world's religious writings. Most faiths, even those with apparently the strongest proselytizing approach, have proven adept at co-existing in practice" (Dudley, Higgins-Zogib, and Mansourian 2005:34).

Finally, environmental leadership appears to be fortified, in many cases, through a deep connection with the natural environment, which provides leaders with the spiritual sustenance that they then apply to their environmental activism. The leading environmentalists in Southern Bahia often talk of spending time in nature—fishing, hiking, watching the ocean, working on their land, and so on. Returning again to Raul, who serves as a fitting example of many of the environmental leaders I came into contact with, he observed how important it was to spend a weekend "camping on the land with [his] daughters, looking at the stars, taking them away from McDonalds and malls and reminding them of what is important in this world." More broadly, Maurilo, one of the country's most prominent environmental leaders, who has been involved in conservation initiatives throughout the Atlantic Forest for more than two decades, attributes his environmentalism to his direct experiences with nature when he traveled the country as a Boy Scout, which allowed him to connect with nature, and people, throughout Brazil.

While the connections between environmentalism and spiritual renewal through nature fuel many activists within the environmental movement on a deeply personal level, in the case of Bahia, these connections appear to be growing even beyond the individual to the very organizations and institutions that shape environmentalism throughout the region. One NGO regularly has group retreats to inspiring natural places to remind the staff of its organizational mission. Furthermore, new Evangelical religions that emphasize the deep connections with the natural environment are growing rapidly throughout the region. One of the fastest growing churches in Brazil is Bola de Neve, which means Snowball. In just ten years, Bola de Neve has grown to one hundred chapters internationally, mostly in Brazil (Barrionuevo 2009). Founded by an avid surfer, the church is commonly nicknamed the "The Church of the Surfboard" because, to express the intimate connection between the natural environment and religion, the founder uses a surfboard as an altar.

Bron Taylor (2010), who has long analyzed the growing connections among religion, nature, and environmentalism, asserts that such trends are producing what he calls a "dark green religion." This dark green religion does more than connect environmental conservation to a religious obligation by recognizing that nature itself "is sacred, has intrinsic value, and is therefore due reverent care" (2010:10). In one way, Taylor's recognition of a cross-religious ideology predicated on the sacredness of nature aligns with the ways in which the natural world spiritually fuels environmentalists in Southern Bahia. However, whereas Taylor is observing broader, even global trends, many Brazilian leaders still largely adhere to particular traditional Catholic, Evangelical, or newer Pentecostal communities like Bola de Neve. They show no signs of leaving their religious communities; rather, they are interested in keeping them to facilitate and inspire their leadership. Adriano, a young environmentalist who had moved to the region from São Paulo, observed about a prominent environmental leader in Southern Bahia who publicly follows an organized religion: "He is seen as part of the team of 'Good Christians,' implying that this identity lends to support for his [environmental] cause (personal communication, June 1, 2006).

However, at the same time, these leaders do appear to possess a cross-religious, spiritual characteristic that is rooted in nature and perhaps even hints at Taylor's "dark green religious ideology." Much of their servant leadership is fueled by connections to nature and serves as the foundation for defending an alternative vision of place and life that moves beyond the personal to the political. As nature writer Barry Lopez (1996:22) notes, connection to the land has transformative power: "In the face of a rational, scientific approach to the land, which is more widely sanctioned, esoteric insights and speculations are frequently overshadowed, and what is lost is profound. The land is like poetry; it is inexplicably coherent, it is transcendent in its meaning, and it has the power to elevate a consideration of human life."

Aligning with Lopez's ideas, Raul was moved to write about his personal experience with the broader natural environment, in critique of the the mining company's leading the proposed project. Because this company recently sponsored the Pan American surfing championships off the coast of Southern Bahia, which he considers totally ironic, given the environmental destruction of mining, Raul wrote a poetic account: "Over time, living so deeply with the nature of the coast of Bahia and Brazil, the surf and beauty of this coast are revealed today for me, I believe, and for so many surfers, like the two faces of the same coin.... Whales, turtles, dolphins, coral, and a myriad of fish are already feeling a strange presence on this coast, with the onslaught of [the mining company] over the oceans" (personal communication, October 2009).

In this way, drawing from his personal history and sense of place, as well as the other species living in this region, Raul takes poetic and activist stances against the mining project, drawing from the notion of a force larger than himself to make his point. Not incidentally, he describes a recent forum on the mining project between the public and the Brazilian Institute for the Administration of the Environment in the following way: "The [public] audience here was *um grito bravo* [a strong cry], by a group of people happy and enchanted with the beauty of Southern Bahia" (personal communication, February 28, 2010).

Although Raul could call upon the impressive scientific statistics of biodiversity that characterize the Atlantic Forest in Bahia (its global hotspot status, the vast number of endemic and threatened floral and faunal species), instead he employs an approach to place that translates beyond statistics and appeals to something even more primal—or a deeper "presence," as Raul calls it—thus aligning with Bron Taylor's aforementioned "dark green religion." In the context of Brazil, this perspective may hold more potential for transcending particular boundaries of class and culture. Sahr (2001:58) observes: "Under the Brazilian conditions, scientific modern thought represents a limited perception of the world, only based on empirical results from experiments, organized observations and intellectual reflections defined by rational rules and, typical for Brazil, controlled by a dominating class. In consequence, from an agency aspect, religious experience is far ahead of scientific practice as a social propulsion force in the Brazilian society."

ARTICULATING JUSTICE THROUGH ACTION

Building on this notion, if articulations of suffering and leadership create relationships of solidarity between environmentalism and religion, do these articulations have an end goal? Returning to the story that opened this chapter, as environmentalists and religious figures unified in opposition to the mining and infrastructure project that would certainly exert irreparable environmental damage throughout the region, the boundaries between religion and environmentalism thinned by moving beyond the discursive to the practical. As the group of activists, which included environmentalists and religious leaders, came together, the power of the union emanated not from narrow conceptions of environmental or religious issues but rather from an integration of the two. The action-oriented ways in which religion and environmentalism intersected in this experience can simply be described as an articulation of justice; environmental activists and religious leaders converged around a notion of environmentalism that included social justice issues and a notion of religion that incorporated concrete action in defense of people and place. Although the terms *environmental justice* and *ecojustice* (Carroll 2004) come close to communicating the reasons for this cohesion, perhaps the cross-movement notion of *justice*, which privileges neither environmentalism nor religion, is the most accurate term to describe this phenomenon. An articulation of justice may propel people to action more than environmentalism, which, despite its gains, can still at times be perceived as divorced from people's daily lives. An articulation of justice may also call people to actions that move beyond the narrow confines of particular religions that, at times, also are similarly disconnected from environmental realities that exist in the world today.

One of the most significant aspects of this potential for articulating justice through action is evident as environmental and religious ideologies merge. Caio Fabio, a well-known Brazilian Evangelical leader, visited Southern Bahia in 2008 to meet with environmentalists and community leaders. During this visit, he conducted a series of interviews about the importance of bringing a religious perspective into people's lives through their daily actions. He talked of things like reconceptualizing poverty—the more we have, the less the earth has. He spoke of reusing what is left over, citing how Jesus collected the leftover bread to distribute it to more people and how our actions in the local environment affect the global environment. Following this call for concrete actions, Raul is working with Caio Fabio to compile a series of interviews in a book on ecology and religion. More than this project and Raul's words, however, Raul's individual actions exemplify servant leadership. As one of his staff admiringly says, "Raul's actions toward others are reflective of a deeply rooted spirituality" (personal communication, June 1, 2006).

Padre Edinaldo, pastor of one of the large Catholic churches in Southern Bahia, also draws a strong connection between being a religious person and being active in environmental work: "I see the growth of religions [here] has helped to bring people into more consciousness. Those who are Catholic are more Catholic, more spiritual....There is a larger participation because of these groups, an assuming of more work within the churches. They are being awakened to assume their work." He continues by noting, "The church works a lot in the line of *conscientização* [consciousness raising; Freire 1972] so that people are inserted into this process, so that they are protagonists, not just waiting for the church to do it for them but that they get involved too" (personal comunication, Ilhéus, Bahia, July 25, 2009).

On one hand, calls to action have a distinct history in the Catholic Church, which advocates social justice through liberation theology. This concept, which began in the post–Vatican II Catholic Church, emphasizes the need to work for social justice of the poor and oppressed through political action that will make a difference in this life, as opposed to biding time suffering now with the hope of heaven in the afterlife. Liberation theology became prominent in Latin America more than thirty years ago (Gutiérrez 1988; Houtzager 1997) and has greatly influenced the Church in Brazil (Boff 1986; Burdick 2004). Sociologist Hewitt (2000:viii) observes, "Encouraged by official church programs designed to promote stronger links between the institution and secular society…clergy, nuns, and laypeople effectively committed themselves to the political defense of the weakest members of society—the 'poor and oppressed'—who in their view had been for far too long the primary sources of exploitation by a tiny elite of overzealous capitalists and uncaring politicians." This push toward action, however, also aligns the ideals of liberation theology with the contemporary growth of Evangelicism in Southern Bahia and, in particular, with the Evangelical emphasis on the power of individuals to change the world (Theije and Mariz 2008). When asked what message to send to other farmers struggling to align their farming practices with the regionwide call for environmental conservation, Maria, the president of a well-known organic farming community in Southern Bahia, said, "I just want to stand up and shout for all to hear that they can change their lives [through agrarian reform and organic farming]" (personal communication, March 22, 2007, Ilhéus, Bahia).

While social justice is being used by environmentalists and religious leaders to call for individual action, it is also being institutionalized in interesting ways within the environmental movement. For example, environmental leader Raul founded an NGO on the idea that better integration was needed to connect the secular science of environmental conservation with the social needs for long-term sustainable development that would bring economic benefits to the people of the region. Today, this NGO has become widely known for an approach to environmentalism that stresses social justice and more overtly religious connections to the broader goals of the environmental movement. Raul has been chosen by one of Brazil's oldest and widest-reaching domestic NGOs, based in São Paulo, to spearhead a national discussion on the emerging connections between religion and environmentalism. Not insignificantly, his NGO staff is largely composed of Evangelical Christians. One might expect such religious cohesion to be exclusionary and narrowly focused, but many staff members are exceptionally open to people who follow different religious traditions, as well as to other environmental and social movement groups in the region. They adopt the ideals of tolerance and eschew a dogmatic Evangelicism that stresses a single right path to salvation. Perhaps most important, however, this union of religion and environmental activism successfully capitalizes on a network of people who are cohesively united by a force that may well be even more profound than a common vision or mission of environmental conservation—they are directly applying their religion to their environmentalism.

PUSHING OUR ANALYSES AND "PERFORMING MAGIC"

Although faith-based communities will arguably persist until the end of human existence on earth, many claim that conservation science cannot survive without increased attention to the moral aspects of environmental conservation (Orr 2005; B. Taylor 2010; Van Houtan 2006). Even Stephen Jay Gould, one of the world's leading evolutionary biologists, deemed the convergence of events to form Earth as "something almost unspeakably holy" (Norgaard 2002:842). Both the growing dialogue between environmentalism and religion and the entrance of morality into the science that undergirds environmentalism have been gaining momentum over the past two decades (Gardner 2006; Gottlieb 2006a; M. Tucker 2009; Van Dyke 2005). This message is also clearly communicated in other chapters in this volume. In chapter 7, Hallum states E. O. Wilson's claim that "science and religion are the two most powerful forces of society; together they can save the Creation." She describes how science alone fails to provide a moral vision or inspire sufficient action toward ecological and social sustainability in Guatemala. Mathews (chapter 4) reveals how science is malleable and imperfect, while Daneel (chapter 10, this volume) tells the important story of how the most basic of human tendencies, such as greed and a search for power, can overshadow even the most promising alliances between the scientific, or the secular, and the spiritual, between environmentalism and religion.

Given these thoughts, I return to the concept of articulation, or what Ivakhiv (chapter 11, this volume) calls "constructive re-engagements" and "convergences." As leaders in the environmental movement continue to draw from religion and as religion increasingly engages with critical social-environmental issues, we still need a better understanding of how these relationships are realized beyond the discursive to the practical ways in which people live their lives. Furthermore, Choy (2005:6) notes that "scholars in numerous disciplines seem to agree that science, politics, and the relations between the two must be rethought." These growing connections will remain rich sites for interdisciplinary research on the connections among religion, nature, and culture (Ivakhiv 2007; chapter 11, this volume).

I have questioned how religion and environmental conservation articulate, engage, and converge in the context of contemporary political actions in Bahia. This type of probing was also central to our engagement at the School for Advanced Research seminar in Santa Fe in August 2009.

Drawing from these discussions, I offer points in conclusion as we continue to strive to understand important articulations in the world today.

First, *question and search for the deeper contexts within analyses*. In compiling this volume, we often vacillated in our efforts to arrive at a common understanding of terms that we were using to elucidate enormous concepts like nature, science, religion, and spirituality. In remarking on this chapter, for example, Andrea Ballestero observed that

> the question is not how Evangelicism or Catholicism views nature and human dominance over it—this is not the cosmovision perspective that we see in other papers—this type of debate is displaced by a localized appropriation of religion's power as a form of social convergence possible because of its moral authority. The work that religion does here is one of articulation... which poses an important question for the rest of our papers: what "religions" or dimensions of religion are we dealing with in our ethnographic encounters, and how do these encounters displace other dimensions of religion? [personal communication, Andrea Ballestero, August 2009]

As Ballestero (chapter 9, this volume) notes, we must question, both in reading the chapters in this volume and in future research on these convergences, what dimensions of science are we–you dealing with? What type of environmentalism, or natures, are we–you talking about? How are these dimensions delineated, defined, and dynamic in our–your work? Posing such questions uncovers the nuances of articulation and elucidates the ways in which various forces do, and do not, converge.

This notion leads to my second concluding point: *pay attention to the unexpected and often unlikely convergences across difference*. Schnell (chapter 8, this volume), for example, looks at how ritualistic practices set in nature create a cosmovision that transcends cultural and geographical boundaries because it is predicated on a view that emphasizes communion with nature through experiences in it, rather than dominion over the environment. Norget (chapter 5, this volume) reveals how the embeddedness of religion in people's everyday lives is an important force for mobilizing against ideas of development that counter the moral ecologies of a community. I have analyzed how religion can fuel an engaged environmentalism that is arguably stronger than an activism based on science alone. We discuss engagement with difference in specific chapters, as well as differences *among* the works that compose this volume, and we challenge one another to push the notion of difference. One afternoon, for example, in discussing how religion was instrumental for environmentalism, Robbins (chapter 3, this volume) provoked us with this question: "But how can being a good environmentalist actually make you a holier, or better, person? How can this bring out 'the good side of human nature'?" Such a question reminds us that articulations and convergences have many vantage points; as Ballestero pointed out in one of our countless discussions, "we need to not do away with difference but rather to embrace it as productive of the unexpected."

Finally, the type of deep thinking and committed engagement to elusive and difficult questions embraced in this volume demands a final point: *practice faith in the imperfect processes of discovery*. At times, faith is deeply personal. Much like the environmentalists in Bahia who defied strict delineations between their personal religious lives and the practical ways they engaged with the world, for some of us, the integration of our personal faith-lives provided a foundation for the intellectual questions driving our work. At other times, faith demands engaging with something that is difficult to understand and corner yet undeniably "present." Scott Schnell posed a poignant question in one of our discussions: "How is it that religion operates? How does it 'perform its magic'?" When future scholars take up where we have left off in this volume—questioning our arguments, raising new points, and pushing our analyses further in new contexts—perhaps a probing for how something "performs its magic" will be present in their quest.

Note

1. See website: http://www.santodaime.org, accessed July 12, 2011.

3

On Enchanting Science and Disenchanting Nature

*Spiritual Warfare in North America
and Papua New Guinea*

Joel Robbins

There is no shortage of grand theories aiming to link nature, religion, and science. Ever since White's classic 1967 article laid much of the blame for "our ecologic crisis" at the door of Christianity's claim that human beings possess dominion over the earth, for example, arguments have raged over the propensity of religion in general and Christianity in particular to push people toward a destructive or protective relationship with nature (for example, McGrath 2002). Similar contention surrounds discussion of the effects of modern science on people's approach to the environment, with some holding that its alienating effects and disregard for the uses that are made of its discoveries are primary causes of ecological destruction and others asserting that the understandings it provides must motivate and guide our efforts to reverse our environmental course (for example, Vogel 1996). Finally, well-known accounts connect Protestantism with the rise of science, thus rendering religion and science in some respects allied forces that have together profoundly shaped Western approaches to the natural world (for example, Harrison 1998). I am inclined to find some excitement in these kinds of broad pronouncements. But one of the most important points I took from the SAR seminar is the impossibility of making such grand theoretical claims stick in an area of study—the intersection of science, religion, and nature—in which the phenomena under study and the conceptual resources we have for studying them are both currently undergoing so much change. Giving voice to this key aspect of our discussions, Ivakhiv (chapter 11, this volume) says that the most conclusive finding of this volume is that the relationships that currently hold among nature, religion, and science are so fluid, so liable to take different forms in different places, that little can be said in a grand theoretical way about how they impinge upon one another. In line with that finding, a more cautious approach to our subject matter is called for—one that is primarily focused on ethnographic cases and open to unexpected and emergent developments.

In this spirit, this chapter sketches two settings in which two of our three terms—*nature, religion,* and *science*—come together in unexpected ways. In North America, where evangelical Christian scholars have developed ideas about the ways Christians can battle evil spirits by engaging in what they call spiritual warfare, we see religious people working to bring science (in most cases, scientifically understood versions of social science) to bear on the development of a spiritual understanding of earth's geography. In a second setting, among a recently converted group of Papua New Guinea (PNG) Christians who have taken up spiritual warfare and kindred ideas and used them to pursue their own ends, the relationship between religion and nature comes to the fore. The two cases are linked by rituals of spiritual warfare, yet the overall arc of the chapter brings out a compelling disjunction between the ways these rituals function in each case. In North America, they are part of an influential enchantment of science; in the Papua New Guinea case, they appear at the center of an effort to disenchant nature. I borrow the term "disenchantment" from Weber (1946:139), who used it to refer to the way magical explanations of the world that presume that spiritual beings help things take the courses they take are replaced by scientific explanations that presume only natural causality and hold out hope that human beings can "master all things by calculation." In these terms, North American spiritual warriors are working to apply the rational calculations of science to the very spiritual forces that the modern intellectuals who first developed them declared nonexistent or at least irrelevant. Yet the very rituals these spiritual warriors have developed to allow science to engage the spiritual world it once set aside are being used by Urapmin people to disenchant their environment in a classically Weberian way by ridding it of spiritual influence and thus rendering it amenable to calculation and easy material use. As spiritual warfare rituals travel from North America to PNG, they represent a key example of the great instability in relations between nature, science, and religion that this volume takes as an important theme.

This chapter joins others in the volume not only in documenting the instability of contemporary conjunctions of nature, science, and religion, but also in demonstrating how important ritual is in effecting such conjunctions. As Daneel (chapter 10, this volume) shows for the Earthkeeper movement in Zimbabwe, as Schnell (chapter 8, this volume) demonstrates for Japanese mountaineering, and as Tucker (chapter 6, this volume) shows for the way Hondurans relate to their forests, particular conjunctions of nature, religion, and science tend to gain their force in social life by being lodged in patterned ritual practices. Yet, as Schnell points out explicitly, the meanings of these rituals are not fixed in single societies over time or across different groups of participants. Thus, ritualization is no hedge against change in human–nature relations. The spiritual warfare rituals I examine here extend this point, showing that as such rituals travel, their seemingly tightly patterned conjunctions of nature, science, and religion can become remade in important ways. This argument, along with that of Schnell, can be taken as making from the side of religion a point that Mathews (chapter 4, this volume) makes from the side of science when he shows how the role of desiccation theory has changed historically as it has become the possession of rural Mexicans: even seemingly quite fixed bundlings of nature with other social forms are liable to be readily recast or repurposed in the contemporary world.

SCIENCE AND THE NORTH AMERICAN ORIGINS OF THE SPIRITUAL WARFARE MOVEMENT

Spiritual warfare constitutes an unusual conjunction of science and evangelical (including charismatic) Christianity. It arose in the 1980s and 1990s and briefly became a major feature of Protestant mission work. Designed to remove demonic barriers to Christian conversion in specific localities, spiritual warfare grew out of a broader "church growth" movement that has been highly influential in Protestant missionary circles since the 1960s. It inherits from the church growth movement an investment in bringing scientific forms of research to bear on missionization. What it adds to earlier forms of church growth thinking is a model of the earth that sees it as parceled out among demonic spirits who, as the "principalities" and "powers" of Ephesians 6:12, hold specific territories as their own possessions and work to maintain the allegiance of those who live within them. For spiritual warriors from the West, these demons are not identified with nature so much as with space; there is thus little in the spiritual warfare movement that bears directly on its advocates' views of nature. But as we shall see, their construal of earth in terms of territories held by evil spirits can in the mission field easily become the foundation of an ecotheology of disenchantment and environmental exploitation among converts.

The founder of the church growth movement was Donald McGavran. A third-generation missionary to India, the country of his birth, McGavran was educated at Yale Divinity School and Columbia University, where he earned a Ph.D. in 1936 (McIntosh 2004:10). As Marsden (1995:238–239) has noted, the combination of McGavran's missionary upbringing with his training at elite liberal theological schools made him a hybrid character who mixed "a thoroughgoing evangelical zeal for spreading the old-time gospel with a background that provided perspectives more common to the liberal theological position." Upon returning to India, McGavran's evangelical zeal led him to critique the liberal mission emphasis on good works and call for a return to putting the task of winning converts for Christ at the center of missionary efforts. But his liberal educational background did not simply disappear as his mission priorities changed (McIntosh 2004:12). Instead, it allowed him to put secular social-scientific knowledge and techniques of research and analysis, particularly those drawn from anthropology, to use in reaching his goal of most effectively making converts (Marsden 1995:239). Out of his work along these lines came the academic field of church growth studies, an area of research born of the "integration of theology and social sciences and the desire to create rational models to be used for the advancement of mission" (Holvast 2009:28).

The model of missionization McGavran promoted is based not on efforts to make individual converts, but rather on attempts to turn entire "people groups" or "homogeneous units" into Christian communities very quickly through "people movements"—religious movements that spread rapidly and transform whole societies. In communities that experience people movements, not all will be committed converts, but the process of abandoning an old religion for Christianity will take shape as a collective social project and, crucially, have its own local momentum, enabling it to grow even after the missionaries depart (Marsden 1995:241; Stoll 1990:75). One reason McGavran promoted this model of church growth was his conviction that people did not like to move outside their own groups—families, clans, or tribes—and would more readily convert if they could do so without having to breach community boundaries. The influence of anthropology, with its notions of shared culture and complex levels of social morphology, is not hard to detect here, and the church growth movement was committed to using anthropological research to identify the proper groups to target and the best ways of doing so. As the movement developed, it produced a sizable ethnographic-style literature detailing the course of conversion in various locales around the world, which missionaries new to an area would be expected to consult in choosing their approach and which all missionaries could study for the comparative insights they could glean regarding the most effective ways to accomplish their goals.

The influence of McGavran's church growth methods exploded after 1965 when he became the founding dean of the School of World Mission at Fuller Seminary in Pasadena, California (Marsden 1995:238; McIntosh 2004:15). Since the 1970s, Southern California has been a center of missionary thinking from which ideas diffuse rapidly. This is particularly true of Fuller Seminary. "By 1985," Stoll (1990:74) reports, "Fuller had trained more than 2,600 people in evangelical strategy, was enrolling around 500 students each year and...claimed to have produced half the missiological research in the world" (see also McIntosh 2004:27). McGavran had thus found a bully pulpit from which to promulgate his social-scientifically informed model of mission, and by the turn of the millennium, his influence had utterly transformed the way most North American evangelical Protestants think about missionization (McIntosh 2004:9, 22).

McGavran's commitment to bringing anthropology into mission work showed in his staffing of his new school (Marsden 1995:239). His first hire was Alan Tippett, a missionary and an anthropologist, most notably of the South Pacific, with a Ph.D. in anthropology from the University of Oregon. Another early hire was Charles Kraft, who had a Ph.D. in anthropological linguistics from the Hartford Seminary Foundation and had held professorial positions in African linguistics at Michigan State and UCLA (Holvast 2009:312–313). Both of these men, along with Peter Wagner, who possessed a Ph.D. in social ethics from the University of Southern California, would play important roles in the development of the notion of spiritual warfare. At this point, however, what I want to stress is the way McGavran brought together a staff of people with sophisticated training in the social sciences to produce a scientific approach to missions that would be judged by the numbers of converts it was able to make. The goals of the School of World Mission were thoroughly evangelical, as Marsden (1995:239) makes clear: "Church growth came first, and anthropology was to be used in its service." But the means, and the pragmatic approach to them, were recognizably drawn from the technoscientific framework that dominated secular culture at the time the school opened in the 1960s. Moreover, during these early years of the church growth movement, the professors' and their students' use of anthropology did not, itself, smack of enchantment. They took anthropological understandings of social structures and dynamics and used them to develop models of how social movements develop and cultural changes take place, fashioning a recognizable form of applied anthropology. This rather secular approach to science would change as the church growth movement added spiritual warfare to its kit of tools for fostering conversion.

Spiritual warfare does not appear to have had a place in McGavran's program, but one of its core features was introduced by Tippett, who argued that in many cultures a "power encounter" should be at the center of missionary efforts. In a power encounter, missionaries, or better yet, early converts from the targeted group, confront indigenous deities with God's power and vanquish them in the eyes of those who follow them. In the Tongan case that Tippett used to introduce the power encounter, the convert chief Taufa'ahau confronted the "old god" of his people, Haehaetahi, by beating a priestess while the "devil-god" possessed her (Tippett 1971:81). In light of Haehaetahi's assault, the old gods "found their authority greatly undermined" (Tippett 1971:81). Such dramatic encounters are necessary in places like Tonga, Tippett (1971: 81) said, because in such societies people judge one another and their gods in terms of relative strength. In full-fledged spiritual warfare thinking, the nature of evil spirits and of their effects on people and communities would be much more fully elaborated, but a confrontation between God's power and that of the devil and his minions remained fundamental.

The task of developing spiritual warfare into a focus of the church growth movement fell to a generation of scholars younger than McGavran and Tippett, led by Wagner, who had acted as McGavran's understudy (McGee and Pavia 2002). After Tippett died in 1988 and McGavran in 1990, Wagner "began to steer the movement toward spiritual factors, notably prayer and spiritual warfare" (McIntosh 2004:20). By the late 1990s, he had succeeded in making spiritual warfare its core technique.

The key link between spiritual warfare and church growth is the claim that communities are often both resistant to conversion and mired in all manner of personal sin (violence, sexual deviance, poverty, and so forth) because they inhabit territories controlled by demons. Demons gain control of territories because people let them, generally by worshipping them or otherwise making pacts with them. Until these demons are routed by God, members of the community will not convert in any numbers and their miseries will endure. Only through the work of committed Christians practicing intercessory prayer that asks God to help those in bondage to the spirits can the situation change. Intercessory prayer can take a number of ritualized forms, including prayer walks, where people walk through an area and pray at each place they suspect is inhabited by a demon, and all-night group prayer vigils. Prayers can also be accompanied by fasting. But however intercessory prayers are carried out, their most prominent feature is that they ask God to break the chains linking demons to specific persons or territories, and they do so toward the aim of growing the church. Charles Kraft (2000a:27) puts it this way: "We must take authority over the places and circumstances in which we witness. It is amazing how freely the gospel can be shared when the place has been 'cleaned out' of evil spirits beforehand by commanding them to leave in the name of Jesus Christ."

Practitioners of spiritual warfare see the battle they fight as unfolding on two levels. They refer to the first as ground-level spiritual warfare. At this level, they fight to release individuals from demons holding them in bondage to sin. Such engagements are crucial, but there is also a need to wage battles on a second level, which is "strategic" or "cosmic." The fight is with higher-level satanic spirits that "seem to be more powerful than ordinary angels and demons and to deal with groupings of people rather than individuals" (C. Kraft 2000a:27). The existence of these "territorial spirits" is attested to by the worldwide presence of communities resistant to the gospel and biblical references to such figures as the "Prince of Persia" and the "Prince of Greece" (Daniel 10:13, 20).

Spiritual warfare might appear to mark a retreat from the eagerness with which the founders of the church growth movement embraced a scientific approach. Missionary ignorance of social structure and the way social innovations spread are no longer the primary factors blocking church growth; rather, mission specialists now assert, it is supernatural forces that slow the pace of conversion, forces people must fight with supernatural means. Given this shift, is there anything left of the scientizing impulse that drove early church growth thinking, or has that moment of evangelical embrace of science passed? I suggest that it has not and that what we see in spiritual warfare is a more thorough synthesis of science and supernaturalism than early church growth work achieved.

The shape of such an argument becomes clear if one examines the development within the spiritual warfare movement of the specialized field of "spiritual mapping," a scientific "discipline" that lays the groundwork for successful spiritual warfare (Otis 1999:82). Its leading articulators were Peter Wagner and Charles Kraft, along with George Otis Jr., a man whose educational credentials are unclear but who has worked with many important evangelical organizations and describes himself as "the founder and president of The Sentinel Group, a Christian research and information

agency based in Seattle, Washington" (Otis 1999:back cover). All three
men saw spiritual mapping as a scientific endeavor, based on explicitly
formulated research techniques designed to generate data of value to missionaries seeking to use spiritual warfare in the field.

Mapping is most useful for strategic-level warfare because its research
techniques reveal where territorial spirits hold sway and how they influence
the human beings who live in their domains. One can approach this task
scientifically because interactions between spirits and humans unfold
along predictable lines. Charles Kraft (2000b:34) states this well: "The overall assumption from which the following [account of spiritual mapping]
flows is that *God has built regularities into the ways in which the spiritual and
human spheres interact.* Since science is the study of regularities, I conclude
that a science can be built that focuses on this area. In such a science, theories can be advanced, tested, and modified by those who have gone
beyond the 'ABCs' in their thinking and experiencing of spiritual warfare."
Because of these regularities in spirit–human interaction, one can expect
that territorial spirits hold sway in places where human sinfulness is con-
centrated: red-light districts; places in which political corruption is rife,
drug addiction is prevalent, or people worship or previously worshipped
gods other than the Christian one; and so forth. Mappers know how to
look in such areas for signs of territorial demonic presence in the visible
world, and their mapping efforts aim to discover places where those signs
are thick on the ground, trace the histories of those places, and ultimately
determine as fully as possible the demons involved so that prayer warriors
can "target" them with ritual attacks.

The scientific identity of spiritual mapping is revealed in its causal
worldview. It is also evident in the movement's commitment to rigorous
methods of conducting and reporting research. For Otis (1999:146), spiritual mappers should produce "datasets" that they and others can study to
discover patterns of spiritual activity. People produce these datasets by following sophisticated methods of social research, first reading historical and
ethnographic works about an area under study, then doing on-the-ground,
qualitative social research, which is key. Chapter 8 of Otis's (1999) book
Informed Intercession reads like a work on anthropological method, covering
such topics as identifying informants, building rapport, and developing
loosely structured sets of open-ended questions, plus offering sound advice
on practical matters such as how to choose a tape recorder. Like ethnog-
raphers, spiritual mappers expect to spend as long as two years mapping
even a small community, tracing its history and the present-day patterns of

sinful behavior that help reveal the demons that trouble it. Once they have completed their research, they produce a report that meets rigid formal guidelines and serves as the basis for a spiritual warfare campaign and as a document to submit to research centers like Otis's own Sentinel Group. These centers coordinate the dissemination of information and allow researchers to look for larger patterns of supralocal demonization.

The scientific commitments of spiritual mapping are evident in both its intellectual framework and its practical organization. References to science within the movement are not simply rhetorical flourishes. From its explicit assumptions about the uniformity of spiritual causality to its commitment to developing standardized research techniques that produce comparable results across cases, spiritual mapping could not exist as it does without its commitment to science. Otis (1999:88) allows that some Christians criticize spiritual mapping and spiritual warfare more generally as some kind of "new magic" or "Christian animism." In doing so, he asserts, they fundamentally misconstrue its scientific nature. As these "critics take a second look," he argues, "most are relieved to learn that the discipline is actually a close relative of both cultural geography and cultural anthropology" (1999:88). Its scientific qualities are fundamental to its identity.

The spiritual mappers' handling of science is different from the way it was handled by McGavran and other pioneers in the field of church growth. Spiritual warriors took a step beyond earlier church growth specialists by developing an enchanted form of science. Wagner, Kraft, and Otis fashioned a science that in its own self-understanding explores in rigorous ways the causal links between the supernatural and mundane worlds and naturalizes an enchanted world by producing copious data that point to its existence. This is a long way from McGavran's use of social science to teach missionaries how human groups are organized and can change. In his framework, science produced knowledge only about the mundane world, which the secular social sciences had already long ago naturalized. McGavran and the missionaries he trained may or may not have lived their everyday lives in enchanted terms, but if they did, they did not expect their science to illuminate the contours of their everyday lives. For the spiritual warriors, this is precisely what science does; they attempt to re-enchant daily life, and they make their science a key part of this effort.

Even as the founders of spiritual warfare have developed an elaborate and ritualized conjunction of science and religion, they do not say much about nature. True, they refer to strategic-level warfare as territorial, but "it is the people, not the land, within a territory that are their primary focus"

(C. Kraft 2000b:58). In order to bring nature into this account, I follow spiritual warfare to PNG. There, nature replaces science as religion's primary interlocutor in spiritual warfare.

SPIRITUAL WARFARE AND THE DISENCHANTMENT OF NATURE IN PAPUA NEW GUINEA

From roughly 1990 to 2000, spiritual warfare diffused around the world with remarkable speed. As Holvast (2009:283), who has written the most important scholarly work on spiritual mapping, notes, spiritual mapping alone, just a part of the broader spiritual warfare movement, "mobilized hundreds of thousands around the globe, presented dazzling global plans and prospects, published scores of books, brochures and websites.... It had praying Christians walking in every nation of the world, including areas like North Korea, the north and south polar regions, the paths of the Crusades and Mount Everest." The Urapmin community of PNG is one such group of Christians who took up spiritual warfare. In this section, I explore how they put it to use for their own ends, one of the most important of which was transforming their relationship with nature.

The Urapmin, a group of roughly three hundred ninety people, live in a community of villages also called Urapmin in PNG's West Sepik Province (figure 3.1). The most striking aspect of the Urapmin situation in the early 1990s—the time of my fieldwork—was the disjunction between their largely traditional subsistence techniques and social organization and the radically transformed state of their views of the world.

The traditional cast of Urapmin subsistence practice and social organization is not hard to account for. Remote even by PNG standards, the Urapmin live one-half day's arduous walk from the nearest government station, at Telefomin, one of the least developed district offices in the country. Without electricity, roads, or any routine connection to the global economy, the Urapmin are swidden farmers and hunters who build almost all their dwellings from bush materials. Although the period since contact and colonization in the 1940s has seen many changes in social interaction in Urapmin, patterns of marriage, residence, and co-operative work remain largely traditional, and their use of their environment has not changed in dramatic ways.

The stability of the Urapmin people's traditional way of using their environment and organizing themselves socially has not, however, prevented their understanding of the world around them from changing dramatically. An important contribution to this change has been the development since the 1970s of the Ok Tedi gold and copper mine about five

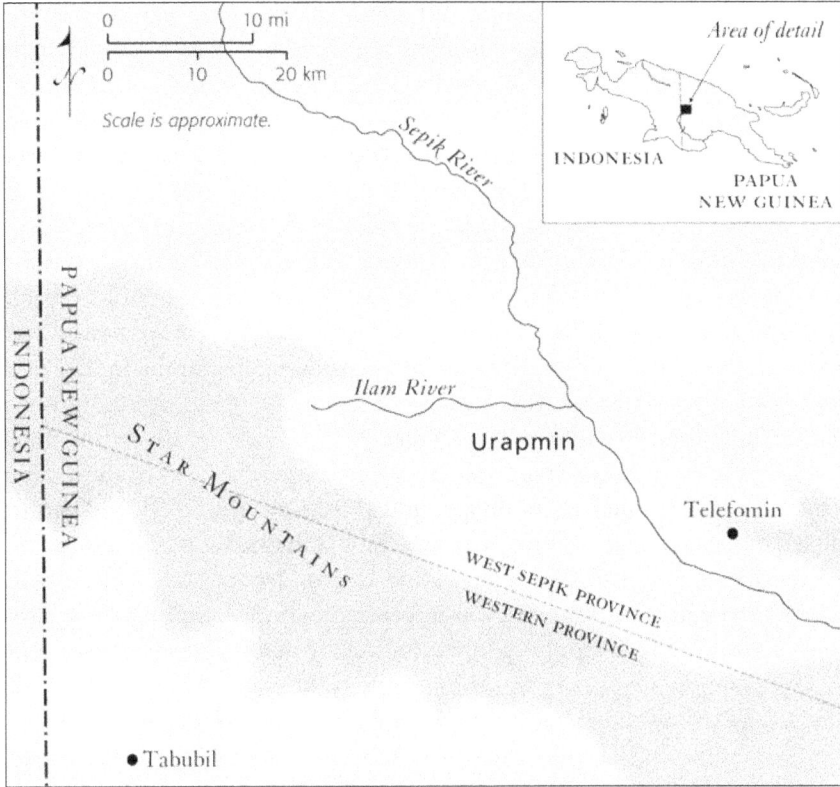

FIGURE 3.1

Partial map of Papua New Guinea's West Sepik and Western Provinces. In this remote area, the Urapmin live in a community of villages.

days' walk from Urapmin on the land of some of their traditional trading partners. Ok Tedi was once the largest producing gold mine in the world, and it is serviced by the town of Tabubil, a tiny but thoroughly "developed" place complete with twenty-four-hour power, a full-scale grocery store, sawn timber houses, a sewage treatment plant, and a hospital. Most adult Urapmin have visited Tabubil, and some have worked there for short stints in menial jobs. They thus have some familiarity with a town way of life quite different from their own.

Urapmin people intensely desire to live the way they see or hear about people living in Tabubil. They would like to do so as a community, not as individual migrants, so what they most want is to have a mine built on their land. Their hopes along these lines are fired by intermittent mineral prospecting on their territory by major multinational companies.

Prospecting visits, which have found some gold, cause great excitement and keep dreams of development vibrantly alive.

Another major factor driving changes in Urapmin views of the world has been their conversion to a charismatic form of Christianity. The Urapmin were never directly missionized by the Australian Baptists who set up mission stations among their neighbors. But in the 1960s, recognizing that the religious lives of those around them were changing while they sat on the sidelines, Urapmin parents sent young men to study with the Baptist missionaries, and these men brought back the gospel and began to teach it. Then, in the late 1970s, a charismatic Christian revival movement swept through the highlands of PNG. When it reached Urapmin in 1977, it ignited a period during which many members of the community were "kicked" by the Holy Spirit (*Spirit i kikim*[1]), becoming possessed as their bodies shook and they felt an overwhelming sense of their own sinfulness. Once the possessions began, people quickly started to convert, and within a year Urapmin had become a completely Christian community. In the early 1990s, living Christian lives in the hopes of being taken to heaven when Jesus returned was the most important collective and personal project of virtually all Urapmin people, and charismatic Christian ideas and practices dominated life in the community (J. Robbins 2004).

In discussing the changes Christianity brought about in the Urapmin understanding of nature, I start by describing some of the fundamental ideas about the spiritual world at the core of traditional Urapmin religion. Before converting, the Urapmin people saw themselves as having been created by Afek, a female ancestral spirit who also had created their neighbors, many of the customs that people followed, the crops they grew, and the game they hunted. Afek did not create the world itself, but she gave it its recognizable shape, creating many of its most important features (including human beings). She also made the world fit for human habitation. Before Afek created the Urapmin and other human groups, the world was populated with spirits (*motobil*) who occupied all parts of the landscape. When Afek was ready to give birth to human beings, she cleared the spirits out of the areas that would become human villages, and in return for their cooperation, she told them they could "own" everything else: all the land, trees, rivers, animals, and so forth. Then, in a multiple birth event, she gave birth first to the first dog (*kyam*) and then to the first human being (*unang-tanum*). Dogs are unusual in Urapmin, in that all dogs, even those running around today and living with people in their houses, are spirits (all other spirits were and still are invisible to all but a specialized group of Christian Holy Spirit mediums). The birth of humans thus made a sharp break in the order of the world, following as it did on the birth of an important but anomalous kind of spirit and introducing a new kind of being. After the birth of the first human, no new spirits or other beings were created.

Even keeping in mind the difficulty of translating complex terms across cultures, the break marked by the appearance of human beings in Urapmin can be understood as the advent of a distinction between nature and culture. As Soper (1995:40–41) puts it, crucial to the Western idea of nature is the sense of "human distinctiveness"—we define the natural by distinguishing the human from it (see also Agamben 2004; Milton 1999; J. Robbins 2003). The Urpamin make a similar distinction with their ideas about the motobil and their domain. Urapmin people live in villages (*abiip*), which they diligently clear of all grass and other growth, and their packed-dirt plazas make the villages stand out starkly from the rainforests that surround them. Motobil, by contrast, own the bush (*sep*), which includes in essence everyplace and everything else—the forests in which people hunt, the animals hunters catch, the land people clear to make gardens, the streams from which people drink, and all other important features of the natural world. Arriving on earth after the spirits already had their places, the Urapmin people are in important respects foreigners in the world beyond their villages, a world they can work with but which they do not control. It is this sense of a separation between people and the world around them that makes the nature–culture distinction an apt gloss for Urapmin distinction of abiip and sep.

The separation between people and the natural-spiritual world influenced daily life in the form of two wide-ranging sets of taboos (*awem*) that governed their interactions. Some places in the bush were taboo to hunters or gardeners because they were connected to Afek. She also put in place a complex system of food taboos forbidding individuals from eating many foods on the basis of age and sex lest their growth be stunted or they develop a common arthritic knee condition (*fum*).

Forest areas and foods not tabooed by Afek still belonged in the first instance to the motobil, and as owners of the land and its resources, these spirits enforced rules regarding their use. The rules required that people talk quietly in the bush when walking, hunting, or gardening, avoiding laughter or loud outbursts that could disturb the spirits. Particular spirits also interdicted the use of some land, food sources, and other resources that were especially important to them. Most sicknesses that did not result in the death of adults (which is always caused by sorcery) resulted from attacks by spirits disturbed by people's disregard of these taboos. Once upset, spirits would clutch people with their hands and feet, refusing to let go and thereby causing illness. When someone was sick, family members searched their memories for instances in which a rule might have been broken. Sometimes, if a sickness lingered, they would consult male diviners, who would identify the responsible spirit by examining the patterns formed by leaves floating in water. After the spirit involved had been identified, people sometimes sacrificed a pig (*kang anfukeleng*) to it, asking the spirit to take the smell (*tang*) of the pig and release its victim. Through the spirits' connection to illness, they were a very active presence in everyday life in the traditional Urapmin world.

As the forgoing makes clear, Urapmin people's interactions with nature were deeply shaped by their relationships with Afek and the spirits, just as spiritual beings profoundly shaped human–nature interaction in the Honduran and Mexican cases discussed by Mathews and Tucker (chapters 4 and 6, respectively, this volume). But it is important to note that Christianity transformed Urapmin relationships with Afek and the spirits in different ways. In Urapmin people's understanding, conversion to Christianity required them to leave behind their old religion (*alowol imi kukup*, literally "the way of the ancestors"). During the height of the revival, as more and more people converted, they "threw out" (rausim) most of their traditional religious life that was connected with Afek and other early ancestors. People disposed of magical objects, and leaders removed the bones of the ancestors from village cult houses. People also ceased practicing all traditional rituals centered on Afek and aimed at soliciting ancestral support for agricultural work and for the growth of boys into strong warriors.

The Christian erasure of Afek and other ancestors has been almost complete. People now disregard almost all of her taboos—because it has allowed them to enjoy the present as what they call "free time" (fri taim) and because doing so is a way of proving their faith that God has the power to prevent Afek from punishing them. Afek, people now say, was just a mortal person who "lied" about creating human beings and who lived after the time of Adam and Eve. She and other ancestors rarely come up spontaneously in daily life anymore.

The same cannot be said for the motobil, who are at least as prominent in Urapmin life today as they were in the past. Although the ancestors have been discredited in their claims to have created the Urapmin people, Urapmin Christianity has not developed an argument that the motobil are not real or not dangerous. People still attribute all illnesses short of death to them. One thing that has changed, however, is the legitimacy of the spirits' attacks on human beings. People no longer see motobil as legitimately defending their prerogatives as original owners of the land and its resources. Instead, they assert that God created and is the true owner of everything on earth and wants people to be able to use what he has made. When spirits attack now, they are simply confirming the Urapmin sense that they are evil beings committed to selfishly protecting their illegitimate prerogatives.

Along with this new Christian understanding of the motobil as one-sidedly evil, the Urapmin people have developed new ways of handling the trouble they bring. Important to these innovations has been the rise of a new kind of ritual specialist known as the Spirit woman (Spirit meri). This Christian role developed during the revival in Urapmin and neighboring communities. Usually middle aged or older, Spirit women can become possessed by the Holy Spirit at will. A sick person visits a Spirit woman, who prays over him–her and begins to shake and speak in tongues as the Spirit reveals the identity of the motobil clutching the person and the reason for the attack. The Spirit woman then prays with the Holy Spirit's power to ask God to tear the motobil off the victim and bind it in hell. This healing is the most important kind in Urapmin today and is practiced on almost a daily basis.

With the Spirit women's offerings of intercessory prayers, we have arrived on ritual and conceptual ground Urapmin Christians share with the Western spiritual warriors. The Spirit women's practice of prayer for single, afflicted individuals corresponds to ground-level spiritual warfare—an attempt to treat individuals suffering from demonic affliction. Yet despite the similarities between the two practices, I am wary of making an argument for direct influence in this case. This is not because Urapmin religious thought and practice are not tightly connected to developing trends in global charismatic Christianity. The opposite is very much the case (J. Robbins 1998). Rather, I fight shy of asserting a direct link between the way Spirit women heal individuals and ground-level spiritual warfare because people in Urapmin report that Spirit women and their healing techniques arose during the revival in 1977, long before spiritual warfare ideas began to circulate in global evangelical circles.

But the Urapmin people also occasionally enact rites similar to strategic- or cosmic-level spiritual warfare—aiming to cleanse whole areas of spiritual inhabitation—and these rites appeared to be a recent phenomenon during the time of my fieldwork, with people more tentative in resorting to them, talking about them far more often than practicing them. For these reasons, the case for a link with Western spiritual warfare is stronger here. And regardless of whether the links are direct, the practices that make up these rites and the ideas on which they are based are so concordant with those of spiritual warfare that they bear comparative consideration.[2] This point is important because when we turn to cosmic-level spiritual warfare in Urapmin, we begin to address changing notions of the environment quite directly.

In exploring cosmic-level spiritual warfare in Urapmin, I note that the emergence of free time changed people's relationship with the environment around them in profound ways. It allowed men and women of various ages to eat foods, especially animals, they could not eat before. Equally dramatically, it opened the whole of the bush to hunting and gardening. At least, this is the ideal that free time holds out. But the motobil remain powerful, which leads people to be apprehensive when they exploit previously taboo areas or eat formerly taboo foods, as they generally do despite their worries. Yet there is at least one very attractive hunting spot over which Afek's presence still hovers too closely to make it truly "open" (op)—Wim Tem cave, the most important ritual site in Urapmin, where some of Afek's bones lie. The Urapmin community's possession of these bones made them in the past some of the most important ritual specialists in their region, responsible for prospering sweet potatoes not only for themselves but also for all of their neighbors. Along with Afek's bones, Wim Tem is home to many *kuyam* marsupials, a species traditionally taboo to almost everyone. During the enthusiastic early days of revival, some men organized a hunt in Wim Tem and brought kuyam meat back to the church, where everyone—men, women, and children—ate some. It was to have been a locally staged power encounter of the most impressive kind, proving the reality and extent of free time. Instead, it was a spectacular failure. Many people got sick, and Wim Tem was again declared off limits. People still disregard almost all of Afek's other taboos, just as they pay the motobil little heed until they become sick. But people's sense that the environment is freely given by God remains haunted by presences that remind them of the limitations that once marked their use of it. In Urapmin, cosmic-level spiritual warfare aims to remove these last haunting vestiges of spiritual control over the land and its resources.

Cosmic-level spiritual warfare takes three forms in Urapmin. First, when a string of illnesses occurs in a village, a Spirit woman will sometimes try to rid the area around the village of motobil. She does this by praying to God to bind all the motobil in the area and take them to hell and by "planting" a series of small crosses made from tree branches around the perimeter of the village as a "fence" designed to keep the motobil from entering the village should they come back. I saw this done only once, and my sense is that it is a legitimate but relatively rare ritual.

The second form of spiritual warfare is one carried out when prospecting teams show up to look for gold. For Urapmin people, the motobil see themselves as the rightful owners of the gold, and the difficulties prospectors have finding enough traces of gold to initiate work on a mine are due to the motobil's holding and not releasing it. With the aim of making them let go, a group of Spirit women work together, all becoming possessed at once, and ask God to chase all the motobil away from the land from which the company will take samples. They can remain possessed for more than an hour during this rite, speaking in tongues and entreating God to tie the motobil's clutching hands and feet and carry them away.

To this point, this ritual looks like standard-issue spiritual warfare. The possibility that it is directly influenced by North American models is enhanced because it is sometimes led by an Urapmin woman who is married into the much more cosmopolitan milieu of Telefomin and who spends a good deal of time in Tabubil and is thus in touch with the latest fashions in charismatic practice. But rituals aimed at mineral prospecting success also have a second act, which has a more local cast. In this part of the rite, people sacrifice to the motobil a number of pigs the prospectors have purchased. These sacrifices are surrounded with Christian prayer, but in important respects they echo traditional sacrifices people made, and sometimes still make, to ask the motobil to let go of people they were making ill (J. Robbins 2009). In this case, however, people do not ask the spirits to let go of a sick person, but to release the gold and relinquish their claims on it. In performing these sacrifices, the Urapmin people hope the spirits will take the smell of the pigs and go away for good.

A third kind of spiritual warfare in Urapmin involves people's discussion of the possibility that Spirit women could work together to clear powerful ancestral spirits from even the most sacred places, such as Wim Tem, or that they could clear broad areas of all motobil. I often heard such discussions after the Spirit woman from Telefomin had visited, and her prestige and perceived power helped make the possibility of these large-scale efforts at spiritual cleansing seem credible. This kind of spiritual warfare played an important role in people's fantasy lives, at least for the few weeks each upsurge in talk about such measures lasted. Yet the community has never tried such large-scale spiritual warfare. For now, it remains only a potent idea, and one that reinforces people's sense of the power of the Christian God.

In determining what these three kinds of cosmic-level spiritual warfare mean for Urapmin understandings of the environment, it is important to note that the aim of each is to clear particular areas of spiritual influence so that people can use these areas in new ways: to live in villages free of illness, to hunt and garden on land that was formerly too dangerous to work with, or to mine on land from which gold is not now easily available. Although the first kind of cosmic-level spiritual warfare—clearing areas around villages—is undertaken in response to a string of illnesses, its goal is not to heal a particular illness, but to keep spirits out of the village so that its inhabitants will not get sick in the future. The other two do not respond to illness at all, or at least not in any proximate way. They simply aim to render motobil and ancestors irrelevant to future Urapmin use of their environment. If successful, these will further expand and entrench the already potent idea that people now live in free time, able to use the environment as they please. In performing or thinking about performing these rituals, people's goal is to finish the job of disenchanting nature that was begun by their original Christian conversion.

The fact that disenchantment is the goal of spiritual warfare in Urapmin becomes more evident when we compare the sacrifices deployed for mineral prospecting to the sacrifices for curing individuals of spiritual affliction. Sacrifices to heal individual illnesses are done after a person has breached the rules that in traditional terms (under which the motobil still operate) should govern their relationships with the motobil. They aim to repair this breach by giving a pig and in this way to restore the relationship to its normal functioning. Sacrifices done in the course of spiritual warfare, by contrast, are done before a breach occurs, and rather than repair a relationship, their purpose is to end it. Motobil should take these sacrifices and leave the gold free for the Urapmin people to give to the mining companies. In the more Christian first part of these warfare rites, people aim to accomplish the same ends by having God clear out the spirits, binding them in hell, where they no longer have any relationship with the Urapmin people and their resources. The two parts of the rite are thus consistent with each other—both seek to leave the territory to be prospected free of the influence of the motobil. These forms of sacrifice are thus innovative rather than wholly traditional, and people have developed them in disenchanting directions that spiritual warfare, along with mineral prospecting itself, has taught them to regard as desirable (J. Robbins 1995).

One index of the Urapmin people's sense that complete disenchantment of their territory is possible comes in their attitude toward the potential building of a mine on their land. In 1991, representatives of Kennecott came to Urapmin to hold a meeting they were required to organize in order to renew their mineral prospecting lease. The Urapmin community prepared an elaborate performance that climaxed with a local leader announcing that the Urapmin people very much wanted the lease to be renewed. "If you have the power," he went on to add, "take our land and destroy it [by building a mine] and move us to a town somewhere else." This is a chilling image: a group of swidden horticulturalists and hunters, who live on intimate terms with the bush around them and know it well in both physical and spiritual terms, asking to have their land destroyed by the development of a mine. It is also an indication of what one can do when various forms of Christian thought and practice have rendered the times free and gone a long way toward disenchanting the earth.

CONCLUSION

As I foreshadow in the introduction to this chapter, my presentation of the two ethnographic cases on which I have focused has not led to any firm, general conclusions about the ways in which Christianity relates either to science or to nature. Even in cases in which such relationships have been cemented through ritualization, they do not remain stable across cultural contexts. But perhaps my accounts, even as they have not led to the formulation of a general statement about relationships that hold among nature, science, and religion, have accomplished something equally valuable by showing how fluid these relationships can be. Both of my cases share a certain in medias res quality—neither exhibits a firmly settled way in which Christianity interacts with science or nature. The extent to which this is true is evident in the fact that despite their successes, the efforts of spiritual warriors to create an enchanted science and of the Urapmin people to create a disenchanted nature have stopped short of fully realizing their most ambitious goals. In the North American case, this failure is brought out clearly by the way in which, after the turn of the millennium, spiritual warfare and spiritual mapping lost their spot at the center of evangelical mission thinking (Holvast 2009). The techniques of spiritual warfare are still practiced, and Otis and a few others still make spiritual mapping their life's work, but the movement as a whole has faded into the routine background of evangelical concern. And the Urapmin community appears to choose to bring about the failure of its efforts to disenchant nature. Despite all the attractions of an earth free of motobil and ancestral influence, the community never does give the Spirit women license to bring it into existence.

The open-ended quality of the two cases I have examined—an open-endedness that has prevented people from turning their considerable ritual accomplishments into the stable realization of their most ambitious goals—suggests that there is something inherently unsettled about the

63

hybrid formations of enchanted science and disenchanted nature. Determining the reasons for such instability would require another kind of argument. In the present context, I hope that simply documenting its existence has been enough to point to the value of the careful examination of emergent, hybrid situations in the pursuit of answers to questions about how nature, science, and religion are related to one another.

Notes

1. Terms in Tok Pisin, Papua New Guinea's most widely spoken lingua franca and a language important to Urapmin Christianity, are underlined. Terms in the Urap language are *italicized*.

2. Near the beginning of 2002, Western spiritual mappers went to Telefomin in person to help destroy the most important Afek cult house in the region. Jorgensen (2005) reports on this event in an important article that represents the first major publication on spiritual warfare in PNG. His work has been a great influence on my understanding of spiritual warfare.

4

Technologies of the Real

Science, Religion, and State Making in Mexican Forests

Andrew S. Mathews

In Mexico, as in many places around the world, many environmentalists see logging of forests as immoral and destructive. Over the past thirty years, industrial logging has been called into question by environmentalists of all stripes, inspiring actions such as road blocks, marches, and protests (figure 4.1). For both urban and rural Mexicans, forests have come to stand for what is most natural, most threatened, most sacred, and most in need of protection. Protesters argue that logging causes deforestation and that deforestation causes rainfall decline, reduced water flows, and floods.

How have rural and urban people come to share this common conception of environmental degradation, this language of drought, rainfall decline, and deforestation? The idea that deforestation causes declines in rainfall and streamflow, the drying up of springs, and disastrous flooding is known to scholars as desiccation theory. In one form or another, desiccation theory is more than two thousand years old, but it became a globally traveling scientific theory during the nineteenth century and the first half of the twentieth century (Andréassian 2004; Grove 1995; Saberwal 1998). Desiccation theory was used by the Mexican state to justify control of forests until the mid-twentieth century and most recently has been incorporated into popular knowledge about Mexican forests. Urban Mexicans and most environmentalists often see rural people as destructive fire

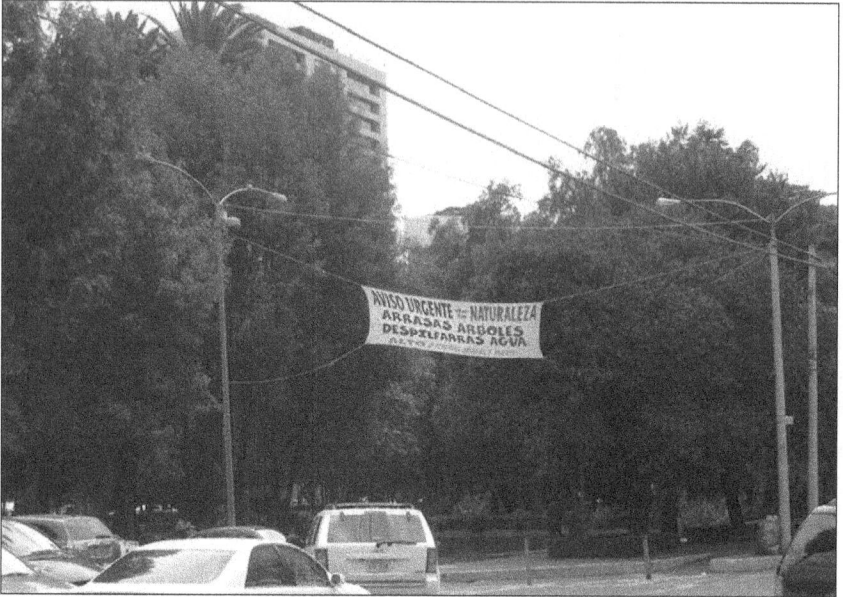

Figure 4.1

Protest banners in Mexico City, 2009. Banners say, "If you cut down trees you steal water: high risk of drought and death." Road blocks, marches, and other protests against logging have been staged by environmentalists across Mexico.

setters who threaten the environment through ignorance or desperation (Mathews 2008). How, then, has the belief that deforestation causes climate change come to be so different?

In this chapter, I outline the intricate braiding of scientific knowledge, political authority, and religious practice that has cemented desiccation theory in popular understanding. I also show how the present-day separation between science and politics has relatively marginalized the epistemic authority of religious rainmaking practices among some indigenous forest communities in Oaxaca, even as these practices engage the idealisms and political imaginations of people in nearby communities (Norget, chapter 5, this volume). I trace the threefold division among science, politics, and religion over the past hundred years of Mexican history and argue that constitutive divisions are made between these different domains. Formerly official scientific knowledge has become braided with formerly indigenous ritual practice and knowledge of landscape. Religious practices of producing knowledge through public practice and canon law were displaced into the sphere of belief by an aggressively secular, nineteenth-century Mexican state, even as the political came to be constituted not against the religious, but against the scientific and the technical. Rather than disappear, however, the domain of religious practice continued to flourish, continually separated from and bounded against the domains of the political and the technical. Politics, science, and religion remain resources for building lively and sometimes dangerous political and epistemic alliances among rural indigenous people, urban environmental activists, and intermediary environmental-political entrepreneurs.

Protests against logging and official concern about the impact of deforestation on climate or watersheds are not confined to Mexico (Forsyth 2005; Kaimowitz 2004), nor is the arrival of desiccation theory and its application to forestry unique; in varying ways, desiccation theory was promoted by forestry bureaucracies around the world in the late-nineteenth and early-twentieth centuries. However, Mexico is unique in that the majority of its forests are owned by rural, mainly indigenous communities, which means that urban-based environmentalists, protests against logging inevitably require some kind of alliance with indigenous landowners. A famous example of this alliance building is the work of indigenous environmental activist Rodolfo Montiel, who used desiccation language to forge a tenuous alliance with sympathetic urban and elite environmental supporters:

> When there is enough forest the winds lift up the clouds in their due time, and it rains, but when one ridge has trees and one has been converted to desert, the clouds pass by, you see the water come but it doesn't rain there, and when it rains it rains very little and the soils are eroded, human lives, homes and goods are lost; also, it rains when it shouldn't. The reason the rains fail is excessive logging....We have to understand that cutting trees doesn't just hurt a state or a country, but the whole world. [Camacho Torres 2004:52]

In 1995, Montiel helped found the Organization of the Campesino Ecologists of the Sierra de Petatlán (OCESP), a group of indigenous farmers who opposed logging, and who mounted protests and set up roadblocks against logging trucks. OCESP became embroiled in a violent conflict with small ranchers and farmers, and a number of people on both sides were killed over the next few years. In 1998, Montiel and an associate were arrested and tortured by the army; their case came to the attention of Greenpeace Mexico and became a national and international scandal.

They received the Goldman Environmental Prize in 2000 and were finally released by the Mexican government in 2001 (Camacho Torres 2004). People like Montiel were prepared to risk their lives to protect forests from logging, and they explained what they did in terms of the effects of deforestation upon climate. This logic was attractive to Greenpeace and urban audiences, making it possible for Montiel to become an environmental hero. Desiccation theory linked rural people and distant forests to urban audiences who were acutely aware of water scarcity and environmental degradation, resulting in a shifting and risky alliance. It is certainly conceivable that urban environmentalists might attack the rural poor as degraders of the environment or that new climate-change mitigation policies might seek to make rural people protect forests in order to produce carbon offsets for national budgets.

Rural indigenous people in the state of Oaxaca have come to understand and explain their forests in ways that are sympathetic to urban and international audiences, and desiccation theory enables them to be cosmopolitical actors who can undermine official knowledge, claim technical knowledge of their own, and find distant allies. They are engaged in making new forms of nature, culture, and knowledge, weaving potentially dangerous collaborations with environmentalist allies in Oaxaca and Mexico City. This is a complex story of encounter and mixing, in which the boundaries between the technical, the political, and the religious continually change, with the making of the boundaries itself a critical part of environmental politics. This boundary making is constitutive: separating the political from the religious and the technical is precisely part of what gives politics its particular character and energy, and science its particular authority to speak "for the facts."

When I came to the SAR seminar, I had already written about the separation of science from politics, drawing upon some of the material that I present in this chapter (Mathews 2009). What I had not realized was that the longer-term history of politics, secularism, religion, and science would so complicate and enrich my thinking; Kristin Norget, in particular, pushed me to think more deeply about the longer-term history of state making and religion in Mexico. As I dug deeper into the history of the wars of reform and arguments over the curriculum in the Escuela Normal Superior in nineteenth-century Mexico, I came to realize that bringing religion into play against both the political *and* the technical forced me to change my thinking about the relationship between science and politics. From thinking with a binary separation between science and politics, I had to think in three categories, a small shift that made a great difference. In the field of science and technology studies (STS), scholars such as Latour (1993) have long pointed out that the separation between the technical and the political is constructed; in a kind of flattening move, STS scholars have showed how technical and political facts are made in the same kinds of ways, using the same kinds of material resources, political rhetorics, documents, and laboratory instruments. In the seminar, Joel Robbins suggested that there was some kind of energy in making separations, that separating the secular from the religious was a powerful move, and that I could resist explaining away the differences between politics, religion, and science even as I tried to hold them against one another. I came to see that I could think of three categories and of continually shifting practices of boundary making among science, politics, and religion—powerful categories that allow official and indigenous people to contest what the world is, what ought to be done, and how human beings should live a good life. These practices are, I argue, contests over *technologies of the real*, ways of performing, witnessing, and assenting to technical knowledge, religious authority, or the nature of the state.

Desiccation theory traveled to Mexico in the nineteenth century through the hands of Mexican environmental scientists, and it encountered indigenous people in Oaxaca in the 1930s. Traditional rainmaking rituals in forested and mountainous places made desiccation theory attractive, and indigenous people rapidly adopted it. More recently, rainmaking and associated rituals have declined, whereas desiccation theory is used by indigenous people opposed to logging. Indigenous people in Oaxaca now protect their forests in the name of technical and scientific knowledge of nature, but government officials argue that this overly conservationist attitude is due to indigenous religious beliefs and rituals.

BACKGROUND

Contests over the control of Mexican forests are embedded in a long history of state relationships with indigenous communities. At present, as over the past century, the vast majority of Mexico's industrial timber comes from pine species that grow in the temperate climates along the principal mountain ranges (figure 4.2). Most of these forests passed into the hands of rural, mainly indigenous communities in several waves of land reforms during the 1930s and 1970s (Klooster 2003), resulting in a level of community title to forests that is unique in the world (Bray et al. 2003). Over the past sixty years, after many struggles with the state and outside logging companies, forest communities have achieved a considerable degree of autonomy and exercise varying degrees of control over forest management

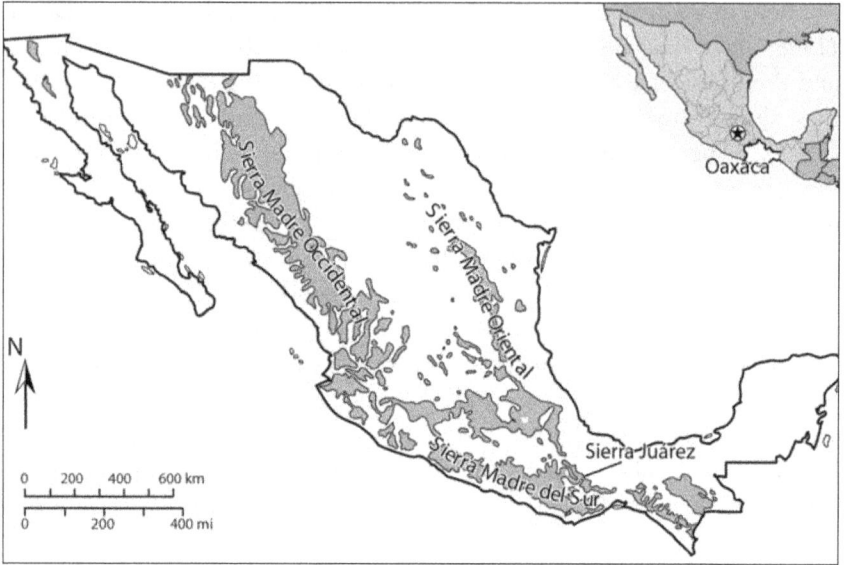

FIGURE 4.2

Original distribution of pine and pine–oak forest types in the principal mountain ranges of Mexico. Map courtesy Metaglyfix and © Andrew Mathews.

(Bray et al. 2003), articulating their livelihood practices and communal government systems with forestry science and the Mexican state.

SCIENTIFIC, OFFICIAL, AND POPULAR UNDERSTANDINGS OF FORESTS AND CLIMATE

Desiccation theory is a vague association of forests with water supplies and, in its simpler forms, has largely been rejected by mainstream environmental scientists, although some recent literature (Bruijnzeel 2004; Wang et al. 2009) supports a relationship between deforestation, reduced cloud cover, and reduced rainfall (see Forsyth 2005 and Mathews 2009 for nontechnical summaries). Classically, desiccation theory predicted that deforestation caused declining rainfall, streamflow decline, and floods in deforested watersheds when it did rain. Desiccation theory circulated globally and was hotly debated during the nineteenth century and much of the twentieth century (Andréassian 2004; Grove 1995), formed much of the scientific rationale for modern forest management (Rajan 2006), and became an article of faith among forestry officials around the world, only to fall into general disrepute with environmental scientists from the 1940s onward. In Mexico, while foresters and environmental scientists have largely abandoned desiccation theory and openly doubt its main tenets, politicians, environmentalists, and the general public strongly affirm a connection between deforestation, drought, and declining water supplies from springs.

This tension between official and popular views was vividly present at a government-sponsored community forestry conference I attended in Oaxaca in 2000. At this event, forestry officials presided over an audience of forest community representatives. Several community members spoke of the importance of protecting forests because of their significance in maintaining rainfall and water supplies. Echoing the kind of language used by Montiel, the representative of San Martín Cuxpalapan from the Cañada region northeast of the city of Oaxaca asked for support in preventing careless logging and agricultural clearances. He said, "[Deforestation] is leading us to defeat. After a while, there will be no more rain. There will be dangerous diseases because trees clean the air. Comrades, if the environment is shaved bare [deforested], the rain that comes in the rainy season will cause mudslides. There will be disasters" (translated from a tape recording, Oaxaca, November 8, 2000).

Other community representatives echoed his warning that clear-cutting could threaten climate and water supplies. Forestry officials and foresters present at the meeting did not openly disagree with these statements, but in private conversations, they strongly disagreed that forests were linked to rainfall, expressing frustration with what they saw as the overly conservationist impulses of community leaders. The senior forester Francisco Maldonado told me, with some exasperation, that fragments of forest in many communities have been left on the highest parts of the mountains "because they believe that this will protect their springs [*veneros*], their famous springs [*manantiales*] of water" (personal interview, Oaxaca, November 15, 2000). Maldonado went on to claim that this belief was cemented by traditional religious rituals related to a *culebra de agua* (water snake) and that these beliefs often caused communities to refuse to log their forests, even when they allowed agricultural burning and grazing.

Across Mexico, forest policies are affected by the strength of popular desiccation theory as forestry officials are forced to modify policies and classifications in order to win the support of their urban political supporters and rural clients. A recent program that paid forest landowners for the environmental services produced by their forests was forced to use hydrological services as one of its primary justifications, due to the strong belief among policy makers, environmentalists, and rural people that forests were linked with water (Muñoz Piña et al. 2008). From the perspective of some policy makers and foresters, this was problematic because there was considerable scientific uncertainty about the relationship between forests and water supplies, but they felt that they had to accede to popular understandings of the relationship if they were to succeed in implementing the environmental services program.

SCIENCE, STATE, AND RELIGION

Modern states make great claims to deploy scientific knowledge to manage and protect nature. Ideologies of reason, science, and nature protection are therefore central to the idea of the modern state, and performances of science and reason are central to the production of political order. A number of STS scholars have argued that the authority of scientific knowledge is linked to the authority of the state through performances of public reason and expertise and through the role of witnesses in assenting to these performances (Jasanoff 2005; Shapin and Schaffer 1985) and that the boundary between science and non-science is contested, shifting, and culturally produced (Gieryn 1995). These boundary-making practices are critical to asserting the contours of the state itself: the ways that government officials claim rationality and scientific authority are important practices of state making (Mathews 2008). For anthropologists and historians, recent studies of the state have hinged on the insight that it is fragmented and often conflicted and that its unity is an ideological construct deployed by powerful elites. This critique has shifted the analytical focus to the ways in which real institutions and powerful people assert the idea of the state in micropolitical encounters, the "everyday forms of state formation" described by Joseph and Nugent (1994) in their account of state making in Mexico.

Like science, religion is a key category in practices of state making, and performing a separation between science, religion, and politics is central to the authority of modern states. It is therefore important to consider the cultural models of politics, science, and religion that are deployed by first-world scientists (see Hayden 2003 for Mexico and M. Fischer 2007 for examples from the anthropology of science). In these countries, scientists and their publics tend to assume that religion is different in kind from science and, especially, that science and scientists are concerned with essentially public contests about knowledge whereas religion is concerned with private beliefs, moral questions, or values. Although this epistemic settlement is often taken for granted in modern knowledge cultures, the apparently neat separation of science, politics, and religion is the result of a specific political history, a constitutive separation that is continually called into question. A canonical text for scholarly accounts of the emergence of the religion–politics and politics–science divides in early modern Europe is Hobbes's (1651) *Leviathan*, but curiously, these two divides are seldom considered in conversation with each other. Political theorists have understood *Leviathan* as being concerned with the ways in which political order is established in secular societies, which demarcate religion from the political, whereas STS scholars and historians of science have been concerned with understanding how politics is separated from science and the technical.

Writing in the aftermath of the English Civil War, Hobbes argued that theological conflicts had been one of the primary causes for the breakdown of the authority of the state. Hobbes's solution to the problem of political order was to push religion into the realm of private belief and make the absolute sovereign responsible for policing orthodox public worship. Never again would religious belief come to be a publicly shared fact upon which sectaries could base political action and upset the state. However, Hobbes was concerned not just with religious disputes, but with the relationship between political order and authoritative knowledge in general. For this reason, he attacked the emerging experimental science of Robert Boyle (1627–1691), fearing that the separate spaces of laboratory experiment too closely resembled the separate spaces of religious sects and that science might exert the kind of influence upon politics that had been exerted by religion (Shapin and Schaffer 1985).

Working in this tradition, STS scholars have highlighted that defining the technical always involves defining the political and that the technical and the political are always coproduced (Jasanoff 2004a; Latour 1993). Each redefinition of the technical redefines expertise, the role of audiences, and forms of witnessing; building on this insight, we can see that defining the technical also defines how and by whom public knowledge is produced. Public performances of science as the sole guarantor of public knowledge implicitly relied on a separation of science and politics and effectively displaced religion to internal psychological states and private beliefs. This STS tradition can fruitfully be turned to look at the continuing and unfinished business of performing separations of religion as private belief, science as publicly shared knowledge, and politics as authority. Lilla (2008a) calls it "The Great Separation," when early modern secular societies successfully expelled religion from public politics to private belief. Similarly, Asad (1993:46) has argued that the historical emergence of the unified category of religion, in itself, made religion marginal and quasi-ideological and that the modern dispensation in which religion refers to private belief is at odds with medieval Christian conceptions, in which belief emerged from publicly available knowledge of church courts, canon law, and sacred shrines.

In Mexico, the separation of science, politics, and religion has followed its own complex trajectory, but the cognitive authority of the state has increasingly rested not on religious sanctions, church courts, and institutions, but on the shared public facts produced by natural scientists. During the first half of the nineteenth century, disagreements over the political and economic status of the Catholic Church contributed to almost sixty years of civil wars (1811–1857). Bitter controversy about whether the Church could own property, have corporate privileges, and be allowed to suppress rival forms of religious expression caused Church leaders to take an active role in political conflicts between liberals and conservatives. With the victory of anti-clerical liberals in 1857, ecclesiastical courts and Church property were suppressed, and severe restrictions were imposed upon public religious practices. By the late nineteenth century, de facto toleration largely prevailed, allowing public ceremonies such as processions, the tolling of church bells, and the wearing of religious clothing by priests (Schmitt 1962). This economic and political displacement of Church power was accompanied by a cognitive and epistemic displacement in which the technical fields of science and law came to produce publicly accepted facts and the Catholic Church came to be associated with privatized belief and moral instruction. From the mid-nineteenth century onward, the positivism of Comte (1798–1857) was the official doctrine of state education. By the 1880s, positivist teaching curricula at the prestigious National Preparatory School taught students the natural sciences in a hierarchy that moved from the simple to the complex, from mathematics to physics and natural history, and finally to a study of the scientific method that would help students understand the world of phenomena. Parents and other critics objected to what they saw as materialist scientific skepticism that was contrary to religion and morality, and an uneasy settlement affirmed a de facto separation between state-sponsored teaching of positive science and religious and moral instruction, which was to take place elsewhere (Hale 1985). Public facts about the world were claimed by positive science, and religion had become "metaphysical" and "spiritualistic."

At the same time that this boundary between science and religion was being contested in the public education system, a cadre of technically trained scientists became the administrative elite of the Mexican state, under the command of the eternally re-elected Porfírio Diaz (president from 1872 to 1910). For late Porfirian natural scientists, the goal of scientific training was to carry out a technical administration that would be explicitly apolitical (Wakild 2007). State-sponsored projects of railroad building, environmental restoration, and public health were completed by technicians who thought of their work as explicitly separate from politics. Over the course of the late nineteenth century, then, the Mexican state sought to perform itself as a certain kind of actor, as a more or less unitary, knowledgeable institution that acted on the basis of scientific knowledge in order to improve the economy and human health. The epistemic authority of the state rested not on religion and morality, but on science, order, and progress.

BRINGING DESICCATION THEORY TO MEXICO AND PERFORMING STATE SCIENCE

By the late nineteenth century, a group of engineers, meteorologists, and scientists based in Mexico City were concerned about the impact of deforestation on climate, water supplies, and flooding. The leading light of this circle was the wealthy engineer Miguel Angel de Quevedo. Over forty years of publication and advocacy, Quevedo and his associates produced a coherent scientific discourse of public reason and of environmental degradation, deploying visual representations of ruined landscapes and poor farmers to represent the Valley of Mexico as devastated and in need of restoration and protection (de la Vega 1933). Quevedo (1930) argued that this restoration should be carried out by the state and guided by scientists and technicians and that the causes of degradation were largely the inappropriate conversion of forests to agriculture by indigent and ignorant rural people. At this time, indigeneity was a much less important political category than "peasantness," so these ignorant, rural agriculturalists were not usually described as indigenous, but as traditional and backward, with the occasional suggestion that peasants were degrading the environment because of incorrect religious beliefs. Like other Porfirian elites, Quevedo occasionally celebrated the former achievements of Aztec rulers who had protected forests, and he even claimed that indigenous religious beliefs had safeguarded forests that protected streams and springs. Nevertheless, for Quevedo, indigenous ecological knowledge was firmly located in the past, and the traditional beliefs and practices of the rural poor were the polar opposite of modern technical knowledge.

In one particularly revealing article, Quevedo (1935[1910]) proceeded to justify environmental protection in a classical positivist fashion, moving from the scientific laws of human biological needs for light and water and adding, with the authority of Jean-Jacques Rousseau, that excessive concentrations of humans corrupted the soul. It is highly significant that even as he worried about the soul, Quevedo made no mention of any biblical or religious authority. For a Porfirian scientist like Quevedo, religion was a matter of attending church and perhaps of good works, and his religiosity remained strictly separated from his science, although in later life he attended mass regularly and pressed for the reopening of closed churches (Quevedo 1943).

Quevedo and his circle succeeded in codifying their concerns in successive forest laws, beginning in 1926, and he was head of the Department of Forestry between 1935 and 1940. Although Quevedo was ultimately dismissed from power for obstructing land reform, he and his circle of entrepreneurial scientist-administrators had succeeded in linking secular state making, technical authority, and desiccation theory, initiating desiccation theory's century-long journey from state-sponsored scientific theory to tenaciously held, popular environmental knowledge, even as desiccation theory was largely rejected by the Mexican state from the 1940s onward.

STATE SCIENCE MEETS INDIGENOUS KNOWLEDGE: FORESTRY AND DESICCATION THEORY COME TO OAXACA, 1922–1956

Desiccation theory traveled to Oaxaca with federal forestry officials, who began to apply forestry regulations over firewood sales in markets immediately around the city of Oaxaca in the early 1920s. Through contact with forestry officials and state rituals of tree planting, forest communities learned official ideologies of natural resource control: cutting trees could dry up springs and threaten the climate, selective logging would protect forests, and forest fires were officially forbidden. Rival communities increasingly used accusations of clear-cutting and illegal burning in order to embroil the state in long-standing land disputes, arguing that their neighbors were cutting down forests and threatening water supplies. In 1956, the vast majority of the pine forests in the state of Oaxaca were concessioned to the private logging companies Fabricas Papeleras de Tuxtepec and Compañia Forestal de Oaxaca (Presidencia de la República 1958a, 1958b). Members of the forest communities in the Sierra Juárez and Sierra Sur (mountain ranges northeast and southeast of Oaxaca City, respectively; figure 4.3) became part-time employees of these logging companies, working as loggers and truck drivers. New structures of community forest management formed around the state-created Community Commons Commission (Comisariado de Bienes Comunales) in each community, a specifically secular institution that took control of logging and forest management fromthe sthe logging companies in 1983, after a protracted struggle (Bray 1991; Mathews 2003).

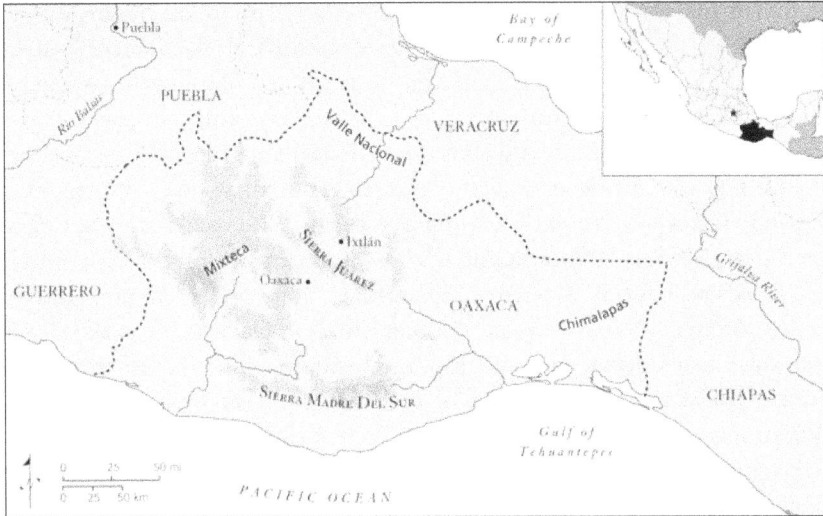

FIGURE 4.3

Map of Sierra Juárez and the state of Oaxaca.

ZAPOTEC KNOWLEDGE OF FORESTS AND WATERS

Local environmental theories at present are the product of the centuries-long encounter between indigenous and Spanish theories about environment and health, so the mid-twentieth-century encounter with desiccation theory is only the latest moment in a much longer history of traveling theories. Because the introduction of industrial forestry has had such an overwhelming effect on local people's understandings of the forests, it is impossible to reconstruct from present-day interviews the beliefs about forests and agriculture held before the arrival of state-sponsored forestry in the 1930s. However, De la Fuente's (1949) classic ethnography *Yalalag, una villa Zapoteca serrana* contains detailed accounts of Zapotec peoples' understandings of agriculture, forests, and climate immediately before the arrival of industrial logging in the Sierra Juárez, which strongly suggests that contemporary beliefs in desiccation and environmental degradation are the product of encounters with logging and state desiccation theory between the 1920s and 1940s.

De la Fuente (1949:256–266, 303–308) tells us that ceremonies asking for rain were already a dim memory when he carried out his fieldwork in 1937–1941. He found that people had a vague belief that witches could ask for rain by carrying out ceremonies near springs high in the mountains and near carved stones associated with pre-Christian "idols," that is, with remnants of pre-Colombian settlements, which are scattered throughout the Sierra Juárez. High and forested places were inhabited by the supernatural *dueños de los cerros* (lords of the mountains), who could be associated with good crops, rain, witchcraft, or good luck. Mountains, springs, and waterfalls were appropriate places to ask for rain through prayers and offerings of food, because they connected with supernatural forces that inhabited places inside or above the earth. Human society was separate from but materially connected to nature spirits. The association between water and the spirits of mountains, springs, and caves continues to be widespread across central Mexico (Goloubinoff, Katz, and Lammel 1997). Writing about contemporary rainmaking rituals in Oaxaca, Barabas (2008) argues for a reinvigorated concept of animism, in which the environment is made social through practices of reciprocity, rather than through the separation between nature and society described by De la Fuente. I find interesting echoes of this argument in Ivakhiv's highlighting of the return of animism in the cosmopolitical thinking of Stengers and Latour (chapter 11, this volume). Critically, such rituals created enduring associations between Zapotec people and powerful places, associations that, in the case of Ixtlán, have largely outlasted actual ritual practices.

The meticulous detail of De la Fuente's (1949) ethnography allows a comparison of the kinds of reasons people gave for droughts in the 1930s with the kinds of reasons they give now. Although people told De la Fuente that the rains were not as regular as formerly, they did not attribute this to the effects of logging. By comparison, at present, *serranos* (inhabitants of the Sierra Juárez) more or less universally believe that deforestation can cause climate change by reducing rainfall, although they are less sure that this change has taken place in the Sierra Juárez, and they are deeply concerned that *manantiales* (springs) may dry up if nearby forests are logged. It is highly significant that people complained to De la Fuente that the rainy season was later and more irregular than it used to be but they did not tell him that declines in rainfall were due to deforestation. Possibly, they thought that nature spirits and their management were more important than events such as logging.

CULTURAL POLITICS OF FORESTS AND WATERS IN IXTLÁN

The forest communities in the Sierra Juárez are currently a global flagship of sustainable community forestry, supported by a World Bank project and widely considered to be one of the best examples of community forest management in the world. Presently, perhaps sixty or so forest communities in the state of Oaxaca have direct control of forest management activities, and another eighty or so sell timber to outside logging companies. During my fieldwork in 2000–2001, the community logging business of Ixtlán employed approximately 170 people out of a total population of approximately two thousand and drew from about eleven thousand hectares of pine forest out of the twenty thousand hectares of community forests (TIASA 1993). People I talked with regarded the forestry business as broadly legitimate, but they also repeatedly told me that logging was strictly controlled and that the community forester would be heavily criticized if he allowed logging near streams or the source of the town's water. People in Ixtlán were so concerned about the effects of logging on streams that when the first community management plan was inaugurated in the 1990s, the assembly decided to completely protect more than one thousand hectares of forest near the town's water supply. During the summer of 2007, concern over the watershed protection forest erupted once again, when a mistletoe outbreak caused the community forester to propose preventive or "sanitation" logging to remove diseased trees. He argued for the orthodox scientific position that rather than preserve water supplies, trees suck water out of the ground. His proposal for an aggressive sanitation cut encountered bitter opposition, and although the logging was ultimately carried out, his authority was gravely undermined and he was fired not long after.

What were the reasons for this conservatism? By the time I arrived in Ixtlán in 2000, it was common sense among the young indigenous forestry technicians with whom I spent most of my time that the *ancianos* (elders) would not allow this area of forest to be logged because it was "the place where the water is born." They did not question or remark on this ideology, and they did not discuss nature spirits or indigenous knowledge; rather, they saw it as a technical decision that had been made by their seniors. The spring providing the town's water was northwest of town, several hundred meters higher, and was indeed in a wetter area due to the pronounced increase in rainfall with elevation. None of these younger forestry technicians mentioned any religious connotations to the place where water came from. Nevertheless, the physical places that are protected for technical reasons in the present are the same kinds of places where nature spirits and rainmaking rituals were located in the past. I suggest that it is through these springs and water supplies that folk and state environmental theories have been stabilized and layered with each other; forested watersheds continue to be connected with water, forest, and springs even as most young people no longer talk of nature spirits.

Presently, for most people in Ixtlán, rainmaking rituals are a distant memory; however, in interviews with four ancianos in 2008, I heard consistent accounts of former rainmaking practices. They told me that until the late 1940s, when rains failed, believers from the community would lead a pilgrimage from the town church of Santo Tomás Ixtlán (figure 4.4) to an area of springs called Los Pozuelos (Little Wells), near a small lagoon on a mountainside far above the town. Doña Pérez told me, "They would go out from the church singing, praying [to Los Pozuelos, to the lagoon]. They would do their ritual. That is where they asked for water. I don't know with what prayers the ritual was done, but they would come back singing, and halfway down the drizzle would start. By the time they were back in town the [rain] had arrived" (Doña Pérez, Ixtlán de Juárez, personal communication, August 6, 2008, translated from notes).

Doña Pérez also suggested that contemporary climate change was due to the religious and moral failings of the younger generation. She described nature as powerful and dependent on moral behavior and proper relations of reciprocity, rather than vulnerable and possibly being degraded by logging, which is how it was described by working-age people. Although rainmaking rituals are no longer practiced in Ixtlán, they are widespread in other communities in Oaxaca and across Mexico (Barabas 2008).

CONTEMPORARY POLITICS OF FORESTS AND WATERS IN THE SIERRA JUÁREZ

By 2000–2001, the theory that forests protected water supplies and could affect rainfall was widely shared in the Sierra Juárez and in the city of Oaxaca, allowing forest communities to build discursive alliances with urban audiences and institutional alliances with environmentalists. A good example of this theory sharing is the case of the forest community of Yavesia, about an hour's drive from Ixtlán, which made use of desiccation theory to build an anti-logging alliance with environmental NGOs in Oaxaca. During my time in Oaxaca, I became friendly with members of the environmental NGO Sierra Norte, which comprised a small group of idealistic young biologists who were opposed to logging. These young peoples' families came from the Sierra Juárez, but two of them had been trained at the Institute of Biology of the National Autonomous University and, like most Mexican biologists, regarded logging as environmentally degrading and morally corrupt. I spent much time with the forestry logging faction in Ixtlán, as well as discussing forest protection and logging with a young man named Gustavo. For Gustavo, all logging was suspect, and he believed that deforestation had profoundly desiccated the climate

FIGURE 4.4

The main square, town hall, and church of Santo Tomás Ixtlán in Ixtlán de Juárez, Oaxaca, 2001. Until the late 1940s, believers from the community would lead a pilgrimage from the church to springs on a mountainside far above the town when the rains failed. There they would perform a ritual and pray for rain.

of Mexico, including the Valley of Oaxaca. Gustavo and his friends advised the community of Yavesia in a series of petitions against the logging of its forests by its associated communities Lachatao and Amatlán, helping Yavesia's leaders frame their opposition to logging in terms of biodiversity protection and prevention of climate change (Yavesia 1999). In a series of documents prepared with the assistance of Sierra Norte AC, Yavesia accused proposed logging of threatening water supplies, rainfall, and streams and emphasized that it would directly threaten the water supplies of the city of Oaxaca (Yavesia 1999). Desiccation theory was shared by

Yavesia, Sierra Norte AC, and Oaxaca-based environmental organizations, which were more than happy to provide symbolic and scientific support to the anti-logging faction in Yavesia.

In this conflict between community loggers (in Lachatao and Amatlán) and community conservationists (in Yavesia), environmental NGOs offered the forest protection faction within Yavesia an alternative alliance that could be used to escape from the institutional connections of the logging business. Gustavo and the environmental NGO members who sought to help prevent logging in Yavesia were trying to build new political alliances, drawing on a discourse about the relation between local forests and global climate. In doing so, they articulated community members' concerns about the impact of logging on springs and streams, general concerns about global climate change and the impact of deforestation on rainfall, and the Oaxacan urban public's concern about water supplies. This reframing of local interests sought to produce a new set of discursive and institutional relationships that connected a heterogeneous array of actors and scales, from logging practices in the forests of the Sierra Juárez, state-level political discourse about urban water supplies and state biodiversity protection institutions, to fears of global climate change, drought, and floods.

CONCLUSIONS

In this chapter, I draw from the classic ethnography of De la Fuente to argue that in the Sierra Juárez of Oaxaca, the encounter between state and indigenous environmental theories produced a dramatic transformation in popular understanding of the relationship among forests, springs, and nature spirits. The popular belief that deforestation causes declining streamflow and rainfall anchors former state environmental theories on the community watershed-protection forests, the material places that were formerly linked to indigenous theories about mountains, forests, nature spirits, and waters. In Ixtlán, indigenous peoples' understandings of place and nature have become layered with the place- and nature-making projects of state-mandated forest management plans and the logging practices of community members. Although nature spirits are no longer discussed by most people in Ixtlán, the former association of nature spirits with forested mountains has allowed these same areas of forest to firmly support popular desiccation theory. Increasingly since the early 1990s, desiccation theory has provided a means of critiquing state forestry, of building alliances with other places, people, and scales, and of undermining the moral authority of the state.

A key reason for the stability of popular desiccation theory lies in its ability to build connections, to link local knowledge of forests and water supplies with faraway places and audiences. Just as desiccation theory facilitated former state efforts to control remote forests, it now helps rural people opposed to logging resist the state and find urban allies who are concerned about water supplies. The public performance of desiccation theory formerly asserted the state as the source of scientific knowledge and political authority and demarcated it from the ignorance and religious beliefs of indigenous people. Although officials continue to complain about indigenous beliefs and rituals, which they claim make people overly opposed to logging, popular understandings of forests are based on what was formerly state science. For both officials and publics, authoritative knowledge is scientific knowledge, and religion is relegated to the category of belief. Current protests by activists and environmentalists express a popular desiccation knowledge that asserts global significance and can reach urban audiences. In this regard, water, science, and religion seem to be particularly potent in mobilizing protests. I find it suggestive that the protests against dam building in the nearby Valle Nacional, mentioned by Norget (chapter 5, this volume), similarly concerned water and forest clearance and that here, too, the charisma of science was recycled into the domain of religious practice in the person of the Ingeniero el Gran Dios. Perhaps we can explain this kind of movement if we trace substantive relationships between humans and socialized nonhuman natures, whether in former nature rituals or in current logging practices that seek to protect watershed forests. In each case, desiccation theory allows indigenous people to make connections between their knowledge of their particular local environments and, sometimes, to link these lived experiences with distant urban publics.

The questions of whether and how religious belief affects conservation typically assume that science and religion are already separate and clearly recognizable categories. In this chapter, I instead outline the coemergence of the categories of politics, science, and religion in Mexico. This constitutive separation, a division of powers and of degrees of reality, has taken the form in Mexico of political authority, technical knowledge, and religious belief. In modern Mexico, practices of state making and knowledge making coproduce the boundary between science and politics, implicitly also reinscribing the proper location for religious practice as being specifically *not* concerned with matters of public fact. Rather than accept such boundaries as given, I suggest that it is helpful to think of both science and religion as "technologies of the real," examples of people's efforts to make sense of what it is to be humans who act in the world. The separations among science, politics, and religion emerge from human engagements with our social and natural worlds, but these worlds can be reimagined and reconfigured in other ways. In questioning the boundary between the political and the technical, I do not suggest that we need to erase all differences between these categories, but rather to look at how the continual remaking of boundaries has political and environmental consequences. We can ask who was able to imagine the natural and the political, whose practices are relegated to the slot of belief. We can ask who participated in transforming and using Mexican forests, who was allowed to criticize or invoke the Mexican state, and what material and cognitive resources they brought to these efforts. Seen from this point of view, humans have the capacity to be cosmopolitical actors who remake multiple nature–cultures (Ivakhiv, chapter 11, this volume) to forge extralocal alliances, to make knowledge, and to express moral concerns.

The concept of cosmopolitics suggests that we should ask why some concepts, theories, and practices travel and flourish while others fail; it directs our attention to the ways in which local and global practices become entangled and coproduce each other, sometimes hopefully, sometimes less so. In Robbins's chapter 3 (this volume), the missionary science of spiritual warfare has been transformed in unexpected ways by Urapmin people in New Guinea, who seek to eliminate nature spirits and make their land suitable for mining and development. Like popular knowledge of forests and waters in Mexico, this adoption is a claim to technical expertise, to remake the local environment and to make connections with distant places. These connections are inherently ambiguous; certainly many of us would not see Urapmin efforts to make forests safe for transnational mining companies as a positive development. In Mexico, desiccation theory is a similarly risky collaboration in motion: I can easily imagine that economically critical community forestry businesses could be shut down in the name of water supplies; the environmental activist Rodolfo Montiel suffered greatly because of his alliance with desiccation theory and his opposition to logging. The travels of desiccation theory from state science to popular knowledge suggest that one reason for the flourishing of a theory is the degree to which it engages with local understandings. Another reason may be that the imprecision and vagueness of desiccation theory made it a valuable resource for cosmopolitical alliance building among rural indigenous people, environmental activists, and urban audiences. It is this looseness that makes desiccation sufficiently strong to allow the weaving of political and epistemic alliances, the creation of new areas of protected forests, and the imagining of new worlds.

5

Surviving Conservation

La Madre Tierra and Indigenous Moral Ecologies in Oaxaca, Mexico

Kristin Norget

In 1973, a messianic movement arose among Chinantec communities in the southern Mexican state of Oaxaca (refer to figure 4.3 in Mathews, chapter 4, this volume) in response to federal plans to construct a hydroelectric dam, El Cerro de Oro, which would submerge their lands and displace their communities. The Chinantec addressed their situation by taking their complaint to the state and federal government bureaucracies to collect critical allies. But they also called on their local shamans to send their *nahuales* (companion spirits) to assassinate then president of Mexico Luis Echeverría, considered the author of the plans for the dam (Barabas 1977; Barabas and Bartolomé 1973; Barabas cited in Varese 1996:61). As the movement heated up, a millenarian vision appeared to the son of a local *curandera* (female healer) in the form of a "Great Engineer God," with the Virgin of Guadalupe perched on his back. He demanded that rituals be performed "in which certain environmental or ecocultural units (such as the rivers, mountains, trees, springs, caves, trails) were ideologically or physically reinforced through a liturgy of cultural interpretation" (Varese 1996:61). An envoy of Jesus, this hybrid sacred personage embodied attributes of both the Hombre del Cerro, a powerful being who controlled natural landmarks of the local Chinantec territory (Barabas 1994:9), and a messianic savior who, as an engineer himself, could stand up to the slew of foreign technical experts who threatened to expel the Chinantecs from their ancestral lands.

If the obvious desperation of Chinantecs to defend their territory before such an aggressive proposal of development is easily understandable, why exactly their anti-dam campaign took such an apparently irrational form is perhaps less transparent. Yet their mobilization, in which *curanderos* (male healers) and the Virgin of Guadalupe were sent to do direct battle with the head of a *secular* state, emerged from a perspective that saw such beings as sacred projections or embodiments of morally opposed positions. Varese (1996:60, 63) argues that such a "sacred non-Christian hermeneutics" is integral to what he names an "ecological cosmology," or a cosmovision with strong, material, ethical underpinnings, based on the logic of reciprocity and on the right to subsistence. In this ecocosmology, the Chinantecs' understanding of their usufruct rights to a collective territory was fundamentally opposed to what they saw as a foreign order directed by the very different economic (and ethical) rationale of exchange value (Varese 1996:62).

As it turned out, the Chinantecs' efforts were futile: the dam project, completed in the 1980s, displaced thirty communities of twenty-six thousand inhabitants, some to as far away as the state of Veracruz, hundreds of miles from their home (Barabas and Bartolomé 1992). Yet the movement spoke to a reality uneasily handled by a wide variety of nonindigenous planners, environmentalists, or even anthropologists: the embeddedness of religion in people's everyday perceptions of the world and its capacity to rapidly mobilize a community to defend itself against perceived aggressors to the very conditions of their way of life.

I return to the Chinantec case later. Yet I begin with it to flag the concept of moral ecology in the context of Oaxaca with the aim of underlining the scope and salience of what is at stake in current grassroots efforts toward environmental conservation in both rural and urban regions here and elsewhere. Specifically, my discussion addresses the plastic and locally embedded nature of popular and indigenous religiosity in Oaxaca, of which the Chinantecs' messianic movement is a reflection, to emphasize the sacred dimensions of a lived, embodied moral ecology—a "moral management of the cosmos" (Varese 1996:62)—in which individual and collective ties are deeply rooted, interdependent, and intertwined with a "placedness" (Casey 1996) within the landscape.

Although such a cosmovision has been described for indigenous communities in Latin America and beyond (Escobar 2008; Lorentzen and Leavitt-Alcantara 2006; Monaghan 1995; J. Nash 2001), I want to suggest the need to recognize the potential of the indigenous moral ecology, an economy of sacred precepts, values, and practices constituting an ethics of sustainability, as a necessary beginning point for reevaluating the environmental political field, including dominant universalist understandings of conservation and development. Global environmentalism is impoverished because local indigenous sacred understandings and practices are integrated within a model of *belief* distinct from scientific knowledge—that is, as a somehow less true and illogical mode of apprehending reality. This division sidelines ethical and political considerations relevant to local contexts. Thus, in the encounter of universal, scientific, and particular, sacred understandings of the environment, senses, and definitions of place and landscape are in conflict, as are, indirectly, dominant and alternative ways of perceiving the world and dwelling within it.

I consider the implications of initiatives now underway in Oaxaca, which began with moral ecology as a multifaceted platform for raising awareness of the urgency for environmental protection and conservation, as part of an integral holistic plan for social and cultural survival. Although I underline the limitations of such initiatives, owing to their immediate location in an unstable political context, my intention is to introduce questions regarding the possibilities for a revised paradigm for working toward a new platform and framework of sustainability. I present such initiatives as spaces of ethicopolitical coproduction that are as yet inchoate and uncertain, emergent in the conjuncture of events and a diversity of local and nonlocal actors, perspectives, and knowledge forms. Such hybrid spaces integrate both scientific ecological knowledge and other epistemologies. As such, they provide the seedbed for cultivating forms of counterknowledge (Choy 2005), articulating an array of local (sacred) and nonlocal, universal (scientific-secular) discourses so that both are remade in the process. Contrary to pervasive views of religion as constraining or duping, the source and reflection of ignorance, I want to consider sacred-cosmological knowledge and faith as productive and potentially liberating platforms for moving beyond and even dissolving the supercharged binarisms that have encumbered so much Western thinking about environmental change, chief among them nature–culture, traditional–modern, particular–universal, and sustainability–conservation. I must add religion–science, so pervasively regarded as bounded, opposed, internally coherent spheres of thought and practice.

As we participants in the SAR seminar quickly learned, getting a clear idea of the relation among religion, science, and the environment is greatly compromised by the language available to us. For example, rather than a universally applicable category, religion is a product of modern secularist thought that relegated it to the private sphere based on an ideology of moral individualism that arose in Western Europe with the formation of the modern state (Asad 1993; Latour 2009b). Similarly, the notion of the sacred as a quality or social sphere wholly distinct from a nonsacred (profane) quality or space—like the distinction between natural and supernatural—is arguably a creation of European religious thought rather than a universal criterion (Goody 1962). Yet many Euro-Western commentators use these terms and others (for example, spirituality) interchangeably to make sense of non-Western or indigenous views and understandings of the world, frequently leading to grave *mis*understanding. The terms impute a certain quality, in Eliade's words (drawing on Rudolph Otto), of "wholly other"-ness to a view that local people may see as simply commonsensical, as part of the taken-for-granted *nature* of things (Latour 2009b). In this chapter, I consider the term *religion* as a subject of discourse, though not to indicate a rejection of the validity of the term's referent altogether. Religion's unique capacities are vital in connection to the sacred. Numerous classical anthropological considerations of sacred experience (Douglas 1966; Durkheim 1976) fasten on sacred norms linked to certain transformative forces and powers and considered to be dangerous or beneficent, or both. But apart from religion's role in defining moral proscriptions, it is the source of extraordinary moments of emotional and psychic intensity of consciousness or being-in-the-world—what Otto (1958) called the numinous.

This chapter is based on several years of research in the state of Oaxaca on popular religiosity and the engagement of the Catholic Church with indigenous populations in rural and urban settings (Norget 2006). In particular, extensive fieldwork study of the progressive liberation theological wing of the Church in Oaxaca has allowed me to observe settings in which certain clergy and nuns work to tailor their pastoral agendas and practices to the pressing material needs of indigenous communities in rural regions (Norget 1997, 2004). Whereas these efforts became more explicitly politically oppositional through the 1990s, over the past few years, a worsening political crisis in Oaxaca has meant that this anti-state stance has grown more robust as initiatives take part in national, transnational, and global mobilizations (Norget 2010). Within local "conscientizing" (consciousness-raising) efforts, a particular practice of environmentalism has emerged that sees focused concerns with environmental conservation link with more overtly ethical and political ones. A concurrent, broader development of global environmentalist ideas has permitted particular articulations to happen. Produced from this "global encounter across difference" (Tsing 2005), I argue, is a new language of universals and particularisms that has gained traction in this contemporary setting where ideas and images are coalescing in messy, uncertain, but productive, ways. It is at these peripheries that environmentalism is being remade.

ENVIRONMENTALISM AND TRADITIONAL ECOLOGICAL KNOWLEDGE IN MEXICO AND OAXACA

Oaxaca is the most biologically diverse state in Mexico and the most ethnically diverse, with sixteen indigenous groups, distinguished by language, composing a population of some 1.6 million out of a state population of 3.4 million. The vast majority of Oaxacans reside in small villages and have customarily lived by subsistence farming, with a very small amount of production for the market. Significantly, around 77 percent of Oaxaca's land area is under some form of common-property rights (Anta Fonseca and Merino 2003:3).

The so-called neoliberalist social and economic adjustment programs of state and federal governments over the past three decades have spurred overall rural impoverishment, massive outmigration, and environmental erosion and have severely compromised the sustainability of many Oaxacan communities. In 1992, then president Carlos Salinas's rescission of Article 27 of the 1917 Constitution, the critical legislation concerning land tenure, erased the social pact that had undergirded the Mexican nation-state since the Revolution, permitting the private sale of *ejidos* (community land grants). The privatization of national banks and utilities, the deregulation of the market, the removal of trade barriers with the North American Free Trade Agreement (NAFTA) in 1994, and Salinas's slashing of government subsidies deepened disparities.

Such changes, especially NAFTA, led to a number of profound social and ecological consequences for rural communities (González 2001: 248–249; N. Harvey 1996; J. Nash 2001:80–90). As self-subsisting smallholders and *ejidatarios* (cooperative members)were pushed deeper into poverty, their reliance on nonagrarian production intensified as the cost of petroleum, chemical fertilizers, and pesticides spiked. Environmental degradation—soil erosion, deforestation, depleted or polluted soil and aquifers, and diminishing biodiversity—has driven many rural dwellers to seek jobs in the cities or in the USA (Blackman et al. 2005).

As villages and towns have emptied of young adult men and women over the past thirty years, rural indigenous communities have formed coffee cooperatives, fishery cooperatives, and locally based forest companies (Mathews 2009 and chapter 4, this volume) or have taken other community-based measures to protect their communal territories and natural resources. Some of these diverse, new natural-resource management schemes and strategies have emerged through collaborations between local actors or communities and external organizations from within Mexico or elsewhere. For example, prominent foundations sponsoring environmental protection programs and projects in Oaxaca include the Rockefeller Foundation, the World Wide Fund for Nature (Tavera and Heredía 2002; Umlas 1996:248), and the Rainforest Alliance.

In the midst of social mobilization that grew in the 1980s, a range of local and national environmentalist organizations emerged in Mexico, including the Mexican Ecology Movement, the Ecologists' Pact, the Ecological Alliance, the Pact of Ecological Groups, and the "Group of One Hundred," comprising well-known intellectuals, artists, and celebrities (Carruthers 1996:1008). As Carruthers (1996:1010) points out, one result of the 1980s mobilization was the emergence of an environmental critique of development itself. Sustainable development became the new theme of international meetings such as the 1992 Earth Summit (formally, the United Nations Conference on Environment and Development) in Rio de Janeiro. The imperative of promoting bottom-up, local grassroots participation in design, decision making, and management—participatory development—was part of a democratizing of the whole model for projects for positive social change that would sustain future populations and the ecosystems they inhabit.

For nonlocal–nonindigenous environmentalist activists and collaborators in Oaxaca and Mexico, environmental sustainability initiatives stem from an interest in including indigenous people's traditional local knowledge as a means for enriching and democratizing environmentalist projects. In the academic and development literature, such local reservoirs of knowledge are neatly packaged within the concept of traditional ecological knowledge (TEK), also known as traditional environmental knowledge, indigenous knowledge, ethnoecology, ethnobiology, folk biology (Krech 2005:79), or even "local natural history" (Hunn 2006). TEK was a conspicuous theme at the 1992 Earth Summit, where indigenous delegates took part in several forums for examining the role of indigenous people's TEK in the search for the sustainable management of complex ecosystems. As the concept has been translated and discussed, TEK is seen to subsume indigenous cosmological beliefs and spiritual values in the concern to enfold local cultural understandings related to the management of natural resources into creative collaborations, sometimes co-management regimes, aimed at conservation and sustainable development.

In Oaxaca, the range of such nongovernmental, collaborative environmentalist efforts is very broad: some are projects supported by non-Mexican, transnational organizations, some by Mexican NGOs, and some by members of the Catholic Church. Although no consensual common pool of knowledge defines *exactly* what TEK is, nonlocal and local people agree on the imperative of incorporating local cultural understandings and practices within initiatives of environmental protection and the saving of Madre Tierra (Mother Earth). These may be conceived quite specifically (for example, organic agriculture and reforestation efforts) or holistically (for example, in the Church's efforts at cultural and social rescue, described later).

Regardless, as such intercultural projects permit the possibility for distinct, situated knowledge forms—indigenous, bioscientific, global-popular; particular, universal—to meet and interact continuously, definitions and understandings may be swapped, internalized, rejected, or even syncretized with other beliefs in unexpected ways. The emergent, ambiguous, unpredictable nature of such connections was evident in the cases many of us discussed at the SAR seminar, which stirred my own thinking about the broader resonances of Catholic Church environmentalist efforts I had recently witnessed in my research. They are settings involving, for example, the "complex story of encounter and mixing" that Mathews (chapter 4, this volume) describes as the case for the circulation of knowledges about the forest in Oaxaca, "where the boundaries between the technical...and the religious continually change." As Mathews underlines too, shaping these interactions are the politics of such contexts: certain types of knowledge may be distinguished by external experts as more important or useful than others, either by externally imposed categories (for example, spirituality–sacred versus nonsacred knowledge) or in terms of their presumed ontology as closed knowledge systems (environmental knowledge, traditional knowledge, and the like). Regardless, such categorical translations are part of a reformulation of local and universal knowledges whenever they are brought into dialogue (Tsing 2005). Nevertheless, expert outsiders rarely engage with local religious expressions except by the yardstick of their relative value as objective knowledge about the world.

Considering the preoccupation with ensuring that indigenous–nonindigenous alliances work toward the common interest in the integration of local knowledge, it seems important to ask not only how aspects of belief systems are being defined, discerned, and understood, but also who is translating such understandings, and to what end. In particular, I am interested in how external conceptions of religion, and views of its relation to nature, inform the interaction of local indigenous knowledges and knowledges from outside the community.

Thus, I want to shift conceptualizations by rejecting the basis of the religion–science dichotomy from the outset, in part because it excludes questions of ethics and social justice from religion or spirituality in considerations of transformative social change. This exclusion prevents traditional ways of life from being taken seriously as potentially viable alternatives to European modernity and the global capitalist system. I propose that a phenomenological understanding of morality, pointing to a "moral imagination" (M. Johnson 1993) based on a locally rooted, particular, sacred identity that is now globally intelligible, enables us to approach collaborative sustainability from a different direction. If neoliberalism (D. Harvey 2007:22) can be understood as directed by a particular moral logic of "creative destruction," one that prioritizes (at great social and ecological costs) untethered individual liberty and market forces, I want to explore the indigenous moral ecology as a possible way forward. In the indigenous moral ecology, social justice and sustainability come together in a sacred perspective on ecology. Local ethnographic contexts allow for the analysis of the close dynamics of intercultural exchange. I move on, therefore, to explore in more detail the setting of Oaxaca.

SACRED LANDSCAPES AND INDIGENOUS MORAL ECOLOGIES

The indigenous moral ecology in Oaxaca entails a fundamentally material, sacred vision and performance that ground local identities in multifaceted ways, in everyday life. Understanding the contours of this sacred geography requires going beyond the concrete objects, signs, and avowed beliefs of religion and sensitizing ourselves to the myriad ways in which sacred conceptions inscribe themselves on both personal and collective consciousnesses in the realm of the everyday (Norget 2006).

Below, I briefly sketch the framework of the scheme of indigenous religiosity in the area of Oaxaca and the formation of its moral ecology. Far from reflecting a passive, static cosmovision, indigenous sacred expressions shaped themselves over time in line with fluctuating political and cultural circumstances, retaining fundamental ethical-metaphorical contours despite changes to their frames for interpretation and forms of expression.

Barabas (2006:22) contends, with certain caveats, that it is possible to apply pre-Hispanic notions to indigenous peoples' current modes of conceptualizing space and the forms of constructing territoriality. The pre-Hispanic texts of the cosmologies of peoples' dwelling in the area of present-day Oaxaca depict an earth in which humans are inextricably inter-connected with sacred landscapes, animals, and spirits—a natural world that is the source of health, fertility, protection, and general well-being. Myths designate caves, hills, or sources of water as places of origin of distinct peoples (López Austin 1988; Terraciano 2001). Toponymic markers throughout the landscape were sources of power and augurs and coincided with ancient cardinal points used during purification rituals aimed at the restoration of collective equilibrium (order, strength, health) (Barabas 2006:21; López Austin 1988). An isomorphism between the human body and the landscape informed understandings and practices surrounding personal and cosmic health and well-being and the mapping of different ethnic groups across space. Still today, the native names to distinguish different ethnic or sociolinguistic groups often derive from aspects of the lands they inhabit: Mixteca means People of the Cloud Place (Terraciano 2001:319), the Cajonos Zapotec are Dry People from the dry, scrubby land where they reside (González 2001:62), and so forth.

As part of such cosmovisions, the ancestors were dual deities, *padre-madre* (father-mother), that served as protector gods who resided in such sites or who anchored a community in a particular territory—a conceptualization later transferred to the characteristics and functions attributed to the patron saints (Barabas 2006). Indigenous peoples conceived all space as belonging to the gods, who ceded parts of it to humans in exchange for ritual acts of devotion. Thus, various ritual practices, undertaken individually or collectively, were preoccupied with the preservation of links with the ancestors and the maintenance of cosmic balance, order, and harmony (Barabas 2006:21–22; Gruzinski 1993; Marroquín 1989; Daneel, chapter 10, this volume, describes this conceptualization as integral to all "primal" religions in Zimbabwe).

During the colonial period, although initially imposed by the Spanish, the traditions of the *cofradía* (religious brotherhood) and the civil-religious hierarchy it eventually evolved into allowed a complete reworking of the Spanish Catholic festival calendar as indigenous communities organized elaborate fiestas associated with pre-Hispanic agrarian rituals or in honor of patron deity-saints (Farriss 1984; Greenberg 1989). Building and buttressing community identity through a system that was at once material and spiritual, the cofradía acted as an important safeguard against external influences, whether non-Indians sharing the same territory or members of other indigenous groups. The cofradía system thus continued to emphasize reciprocities among man, animals, and gods, reciprocities that operated to maintain ecological and cosmological balance.

Such forms constitute the dimensions of what Barabas and other scholars of Oaxaca have termed an "ethnic landscape" (González 2001) or "ethno-territory" (Barabas 2006; Carmagnani 1988). The colonial period saw Indian republics that had been established in the early decades after the Conquest converted into Indian pueblos, with limited power to control key natural resources—water, woods, and lands—within their boundaries (J. Nash 2001). Carmagnani (1988) states that the ethnic landscape formed from the beginning of the 1600s through the next one hundred years and was key to indigenous recovery following the losses of the Conquest. Natural resources were seen as conceded by the gods, who required constant interaction with the ethnic group that, through the religious-political structure, defined, defended, and organized the space the divinities had given it (Carmagnani 1988:15).

Still today, throughout Oaxaca, the cult of the saints, who often embody nature deities, is vital in anchoring and revitalizing people's sense of identity as tied to territory. The performance of the series of rituals associated with the cult of the saints, in which Catholic sacred personages merge with earthly deities, renders the community as fundamentally a *sacred* community, not merely a political entity. The landscape is permeated with sacred sites—mountain peaks, streams, forests, lagoons—that are enfolded into ritual processes aimed at the retrieval of a condition of harmony, balance, continuity, purity, and therefore a sense of order. For example, on the edge of Oaxaca's northern (Zapotec) Sierra, the feast day dedicated to San Isidro, the patron saint of campesinos, coincides roughly with the timing of pre-Hispanic rituals done in the planting season; thus, food (maize, beans, panela) is offered to this saint, whose image carries an armadillo-shell seed basket and a planting stick and wears huaraches (González 2001:109).

These examples are just some of the rites that have coexisted with beliefs and practices of diverse sources (Barabas 2006). Such devotions need not even be cloaked in Catholic guise. For example, in 2008 Miguel Pérez, parish priest of the Zapotec community of San Pedro Cajonos, elsewhere in the Sierra Norte, told me of local customs such as placing crosses at important crossroads and entrances to towns "as a means of receiving help," bathing in water springs as a mode of sacred purification before *mayordomías* (annual saint's day festivals), healing rites for *espanto* (shock, often of supernatural origin) that take place on a nearby hill, and rites that initiate planting involving the "feeding of the earth" by placing shrimp, mezcal, cigarettes, and bread in a hole in the ground (personal interview, Padre Miguel Pérez, San Francisco Cajonos, April 7, 2008). In addition, in the Mixe region around the community of Tlahuiltoltepec, for example, the annual pilgrimage at the beginning of each year to the sacred mountain Zempoaltépetl involves sacrifices to the Rey Condoy (King of the Mixes) in a crucial act of community revitalization. The rite is a significant point of blessing for those community members who are beginning their annual service to the pueblo in their roles as president, municipal alcalde (treasurer), and the like (Barabas and Bartolomé 1984; Libert 2003).

What can we glean from such ritual practices? Above all, a strong sense of interdependence between the human community (outside) and the animate, sacred earth (inside), whose landscape issued forth humans and communities, an identity reflected in toponyms and people's very names. The rituals discussed above are not merely symbolic but are seen as efficacious; they are performed with particular goals in mind but also for the securing of sacred blessing or protection. Through these rites and other practices, such as pilgrimages to shrines and other sites of sacred beings embedded throughout the landscape, popular-indigenous sacred performance traces the lines of individual and collective histories and identities while reiterating principles of sacrifice, balance, and reciprocity—the core of the indigenous moral ecology—that are deeply embodied.

The affirmation of an embodied identity between people and place woven through this fabric of beliefs and practices deserves emphasis. "Place" here connotes a phenomenological framing of the lived body in culturally shaped "existential space" (Casey 1996:14) or a structure of feeling nurtured over generations of living-in-place. The placedness of the indigenous cosmovision, bound up as it is with the imperative of sustainability of the cosmos, the intimate relatedness of all beings, including the earth and elements, is the basis of the indigenous moral ecology and many traditional indigenous economies in Mexico and elsewhere.

Thus, as the history of indigenous resistance in Oaxaca and Latin America testifies, apparitions such as the Chinantecs' Great Engineer God and phenomena such as the messianic movement it unleashed tend to arise whenever the balance of this moral ecology is upset or challenged (Barabas 2006:200; Varese 1996:60). The Chinantec case shows how, in the face of a threat to the integrity of their sacred, ethnic territory, people were impelled by a call to return the cosmos to an original state of sacredness and wholeness—"to purify," as Varese (1996:60) suggests, "a nature contaminated by foreign oppressors." Varese's comment returns us to the material and vital dimensions of the moral ecology: resistance manifested in an obviously sacred idiom corresponds to a perception of earth as a living being capable of seeking vengeance against people who might exploit it unduly. The hazard to sustainability, to life itself, demands the most appropriate, powerful, and drastic response possible, one that can answer to a universe thrown harshly out of balance.

What is part of the sacred vision and what belongs to the world of the "really real" are inseparable in this perspective: sacred-metaphysical personages (for example, the Virgin of Guadalupe) and arguably the most earthly beings possible (development planners, engineers, politicians!) mix with each other and even combine; they play out a sacred drama that is a cosmic display of a mortal—and moral—struggle taking place on earth. Whether this particular expression of the cosmovision is directly contiguous with the outlines and content of pre-Hispanic cosmologies is irrelevant. An insistence on authenticity misses the point. The continued vitality of such popular sacred schemes resides in their inherent flexibility and capacity for absorption as they wrap themselves around particular situations and needs. However, we must remind ourselves that such millenarian visions, while distilling desires and compelling people to action, do not always achieve their immediate aims (Burridge 1969). And where they confront the secular strength of authoritative agroecological science and developmentalism in efforts at collaboration, they may be belittled as spirituality or ignored as ignorance and irrationality (Berkes 2001).

Nevertheless, current arenas of transnational, environmental, political interactions in Mexico are more complex than ever because environmentalist concerns have leaked into wider political mobilizations. It is worth asking how diverse knowledge forms—of different ontologies, of different origins—are linked and mobilized (Choy 2005; Tsing 2005).

In this light, I want to move on to address initiatives currently underway in Oaxaca, in both indigenous and nonindigenous communities, where people are embracing environmental conservation as part of an integral sacred plan for community survival. The initiatives represent a new purposeful mixing of indigenous sacred-ecological conceptions and liberationist Catholic social justice and integral development. In the case I discuss, religion-as-moral-ecology—or an ecocosmology—is the central inspiration of activist efforts aimed at "conscientizing" and motivating local populations to defend themselves against forces of neoliberal globalization that have thrown askew local social systems and relationships with the land. The independent character of these mobilizations, free of ties to the state, NGOs, and even the Catholic Church, is key to their creative, productive potential. A language of environmental degradation is produced from these efforts and allows a cementing of alliances and a "scale-making project" (Tsing 2005), by which the indigenous moral ecology is encompassed within a movement of wider political import, in which religion has a central rather than peripheral role.

THE CATHOLIC CHURCH AND THE INDIGENOUS RESURGENCE: CONSERVATION AS SURVIVAL

Since the 1970s, like-minded leftist clergy and nuns in Oaxaca have been deeply immersed in the indigenous grassroots struggle for local autonomy, spearheading mobilizations, including the organization of cooperatives and human rights groups (Norget 1997, 2004). Clergy and nuns motivated by Vatican II and Medellín-inspired exhortations of human rights and the model of the Church as the people of God (rather than the institution) have been active in the defense of indigenous peoples, especially in southeastern Mexican states. A program of *el pastoral indígena* (indigenous pastoral care) represented the realization of the ideals of a liberationist union of politics and religion. The Church has undertaken projects of cultural recovery or rescue as part of its mission, including the rescue of the customs of collaboration and mutual aid mentioned above, which are regarded as essential aspects of rural indigenous life and the basis for communal mobilization (Norget 1997).

These clergy and nuns are guided by the liberation theological concept of *inculturation*, a program for incarnating the Christian gospel in the community and democratizing relations between Church agents and indigenous peoples. In the philosophy of indigenous theology, the Church calls for the incorporation and reinvigoration of local traditions and culture within a revised Catholic doctrine, the liturgy, and pastoral activities in indigenous communities. With the aim of identifying the causes that kept indigenous people poor, following the liberation theological credo of *ver, pensar, actuar* (observe, think, act) so critical to the process of "conscientization," in collaboration with lay Catholic groups such as Christian Base Communities (CEBs), representatives encourage people to critically assess, in the light of the gospel, the social situation in which they are immersed. Such a process is assumed to lead people to identify the causes of poverty and marginalization; in Oaxaca, the entailing discourse gradually solidified during the 1980s and 1990s into a position that was overtly critical of the government. With the onset of the 1990s, the progressivist tone in the region of Oaxaca began to erode as liberationist bishops, one by one, were replaced by conservatives with ideas more in step with the Vatican line and as priests were removed from the communities where they worked (Norget

2004). Nevertheless, many remain in their parishes, continuing to promote processes of political consciousness raising and mobilization.

Over the past decade especially, similar to Scanlan Lyons's (chapter 2, this volume) account of the progressivist Catholic Church in Brazil's Atlantic Forest, these Church-mobilizing efforts have increasingly taken on a conspicuously environmentalist turn. This new direction probably was a result of the dovetailing of ecotheological influences of liberationist theologians (Boff 1995; Lorentzen and Leavitt-Alcantara 2006:516–520) and Mexican environmentalist campaigns that have gained momentum and visibility in the country, partly in response to obvious signs of environmental degradation, some due to government negligence. The Church initiatives I refer to are part of an endeavor to use locally rooted, indigenous perceptions or configurations of the sacred for the purposes of promoting indigenous knowledge, sensibilities, and practices seen to be relevant to sustainability (understood in social, cultural, and environmental senses), self-determination, and cultural survival. These efforts have intensified especially since evidence of worsening environmental erosion and state-sponsored neoliberalist transformations have put the squeeze on small-scale, subsistence producers. From these contexts, new kinds of political alliances are created between rural indigenous communities and urban mestizos.

Priests are critical cosmopolitan interlocutors in such settings. While they may originate from small communities within the state, they are well educated and well traveled compared with most Oaxacans. In addition, in the context of projects within the community in which they may work, they frame knowledges, translate and articulate them, rendering them intelligible through, for instance, identifying local realities and problems with Christ's suffering or social and political struggles elsewhere in Mexico or beyond. Such work of translation is important since it is key to the process of articulation among different knowledges within a given setting and beyond it (Choy 2005:11). Choy (2005:15) found that "local appropriateness" is a powerful factor in assessments of the perceived legitimacy and authority of environmentalist leaders in such settings, evaluated by how well people mix a scientific critique of universalism and a normative theory of simultaneous universality and particularity. A powerful blend of global universalisms and local particularisms in diverse knowledge forms also characterized progressivist Church-sponsored meetings I attended in Oaxaca.

For example, a workshop event outside the city of Oaxaca at the beginning of February 2008, attended by CEB members, clergy, and nuns—a mix of mostly urban mestizo Oaxacans and a minority from indigenous communities—explored themes ranging from "The Relationship between

Social Movements of Liberation and Christian Faith" to "Indigenous Theology" and "Caring for Mother Earth." As suggested by these workshop titles, the event's objective (handwritten on a poster board at the front of the room) was to "articulate and strengthen [their] pastoral path to create a church with an indigenous face and heart." The construction of a more just and dignified society is seen as possible only by means of the rescue of values of our ancestors (communalism, living in harmony with the earth) and related cultural practices, including the cherished systems of *tequio* (shared labor), *asamblea* (collective assembly), traditional medicine, and agricultural cooperatives—all part of an integral and multifaceted opposi-tional culture of markedly defiant, indigenous character. One might say, then, that the indigenous moral ecology referred to earlier inspires the directive ethos of the Church's efforts, although it is now situated in a revised framework of social justice and human rights emphasized to be of global relevance and reach.

These circumstances also set the tone for a gathering in March 2008 in the region of the Mixteca Alta, where I saw these concerns cohered by a theme that made me aware of what people saw as hanging in the balance in their struggle. The Mixteca, covering much of the western half of the state, embraces some of Oaxaca's poorest communities. The soil is parched semi-desert, making many of the dirt roads sometimes impassible by car. The region suffers from a severe scarcity of water and one of the highest erosion rates in the world. Deforestation and soil erosion have ravaged the countryside and have been main reasons for outmigration, especially to the USA. Indeed, many adult males in the town where the meeting was held were either absent or newly back in town after a period in California, Texas, or Arizona. They, as most men and many women in the region, are subsis-tence farmers, growing corn, beans, and squash for household consump-tion and selling small excesses for profit. Some households also raise goats, cattle, or sheep for extra cash.

I had been invited to the weekend event by the parish priest, whom I will call Padre S., a self-identified indigenous Mixtec from one of the larger towns of the parish. Led by Padre S., the aim of the gathering was "to know and practice forms of making organic fertilizer to return vitality to our Mother Earth, the base of our sustenance" (a poster translated by author). The event, attended by roughly thirty men, women, and children repre-senting the parish's fourteen municipalities, took place in a half-completed stone chapel covered by a large blue tarp. Even in late March, it was bitterly cold, and fog enveloped us for much of the weekend. We slept in blankets and on *petates* (bedrolls) in various structures on the property of one CEB member. Despite the simplicity of the setting, the meals we shared boasted the richness of local foodstuffs: large handmade tortillas, an array of beans, local grains, even a goat *barbacoa* (underground barbecue) on the last day.

As at other liberationist Church events I had been to over the years, this Mixteca gathering was a typical intense mix of serious, practical, and spiritual business. At the meeting, ceremonies with indigenous content (incense-laced prayers to the four cardinal directions, invocations of Papa and Mama Dios), Catholic prayers, and a general Catholic format began and ended most days. A large part of the weekend was spent making a giant *abonera* (compost heap) of cow and goat dung, earth, ash, foliage, and water just down the hill from our meeting place. This central activity was interspersed with other workshops, where representatives learned about the chemical composition of the soil and reflected on problems of malnutrition in their communities, the effects of chemical fertilizer on Madre Tierra, and how *los abuelos* (the ancestors) used to fertilize their fields. At these sessions, a narrative framework of self-determination and moral rootedness and authenticity underlay comparisons continually made between the state of Madre Tierra and the quality of life from generations past and today. For example, at an orientation for one workshop, participants were asked to divide into groups and address a list of specific questions: What was the harvest like before, and how was people's quality of life? How did los abuelos fertilize their lands, and what did they recommend to take care of it? Why are people suffering from malnutrition, and how is it manifesting itself in your community?

People's responses, written on poster boards visible to all, spoke clearly of an interlinkage in the well-being of land, bodies, and community:

> [Before], there was practice that harmonized with Mother Nature. How it costs us now to try to get back everything that our abuelos had. There must be willingness, but also [political-moral] consciousness.

> The soil began to lose its vitality, its nutrients. The water began to erode the soil, taking with it the fertile layer. And we who are her children, we began to grow poorer, malnourished. It's a chain that stems from the impoverishment of Madre Tierra, who nurtured us for so long.

> We are going to go back to what the abuelos taught us. To not keep enriching those who are already wealthy—those who have always enriched themselves by taking from us. [Translated by author]

Such references to past remembrances of fertile fields and better, healthier living should not be regarded as sentimental yearnings for some authentic, lost lifeway, spoken from a place of mourning and resignation. Expressed in the context of workshops, such statements are clearly spatialized, defiant declarations of people's cognizance of the value and salience of what is theirs, of what has been (and continues to be) done to them, and of what must be done to survive—as individuals, as community, *in their place.*

As part of this highly localized, self-defensive language, government programs for reforestation and health programs were repeatedly maligned as covert attempts at destroying local ecosystems, promoting biopiracy, and thus undermining the long-term viability of local communities. The claims are true to some extent, for it is well known in Oaxaca that government reforestation plans have sometimes involved the planting of species foreign to the region and inimical to the delicate balance of local ecosystems. The Mexican National Forestry Commission (CONAFOR) coordinated reforestation programs that have planted more than 250,000 hectares. The Mixteca region, which covers parts of Oaxaca and Puebla, was a favored site of CONAFOR for combating degradation. However, many of the non-native trees, such as eucalyptus, demand a great deal of water from the soil and are dangerous to biodiversity because they kill competitors. Hence, environmental organizations criticized CONAFOR for using "dangerous biology" (personal communication, Andrew Mathews, August 21, 2009). The discourse of Padre S. framed the implications of their practices thus: "On this hill, there was a great diversity, maguey, canuela, so many things.... With government reforestation projects, they planted only ocote [pine] trees. This makes the earth bitter [acidic]. It is part of a plan to drive the rightful owners off the land so that the land can be plundered for resources."

This context seemed wholly and authentically indigenous, but it was far from the case. The languages and knowledges of natural science, religion, and what may be seen as a popular global environmentalism were tightly intertwined, complementing one another rather than being discordant. The abonera (figure 5.1), for example, reflected a kind of generic, very alternative *paquete tecnológico* (technological package: hybrid seeds, chemical fertilizers, machinery), indicating the interests of participants to strengthen themselves with resources from the outside. One community member who served as the abonera expert, Tio Adam, had acquired his know-how at a workshop he had attended elsewhere in Mexico; such practical workshops and meetings on aspects of self-organization and self-sustainability are now commonplace throughout the country, often organized by the more progressivist wing of the Catholic Church.

FIGURE 5.1

Making the abonera, La Mixteca, March 2008. The abonera is a compost heap made locally from materials at hand and is used in hillside farming.

The abonera—a means of generating organic fertilizer locally from materials at hand—stands in stark contrast to the paquetes tecnológicos traditionally doled out to Mexican farmers by the government. Similarly, references to Madre Tierra that I heard regularly at this and other events were enunciations of a generalized indigenous–ecofeminist–new-age environmentalist language, which has come to inflect discussions of environmentalism at international venues such as the United Nations (Gill 1991; Pulido 1998; Roach 2003). Evocations of Madre Tierra and ecofeminist extollings of nature might be seen to further patriarchal, capitalist interests based on a nature–culture binary divide that situates nature as a passive resource (Alaimo 1994). But, as deployed in this Oaxacan context, Madre Tierra resonated with local perspectives of a personified, powerful, sacred Earth-cosmos-landscape suffering as a result of immoral acts of exploitation at the hands of the anonymous giant of capitalist greed.

It was not just a corrupt government that was seen as the source of the community's ills. For Padre S., for example, the evil ones were both wealthy Mexicans and transnationals, whose growth and expansion had been spurred by NAFTA and neoliberal globalization more generally. Reflected in his discourse during the Mixteca gathering was the moral narrative underlying liberationist theology that is key to its conscientizing pull, namely, a particular biblical hermeneutics that privileges the poor and oppressed of the world, whose suffering is exemplified by Jesus' suffering and death on the cross. Sin is embedded in social structure, and suffering and pain become motivating forces for knowing God.

Padre S. clearly articulated a concern with identifying the enemy as a collusion of unwelcome forces and things coming from *outside* (genetically modified corn, junk food, government programs, neoliberalism, environmental degradation, multinational corporate capitalism, even Protestantism) that targeted the community at its *inside* core (the social fabric, community identity, language, traditional ways of life, foods, agricultural practices). At times, his discourse rang of xenophobia, leading to a deep suspicion of outsiders and an insistence on outward signs of purity (for example, the priest's preference for people to wear traditional clothing to the gathering I attended, as they must do for sacramental rites he presides over) and hence a closure to the outside world. This attitude points to one of the vulnerable areas of liberationist praxis: priests (even indigenous ones) and other representatives of the Church can sometimes patronize, cloister, and essentialize indigenous culture in a way that is limiting (Norget 2004). But they can also act as critical bridges between rural and urban spaces, cultures, political communities, and even knowledges.

Thus, the space of this liberationist Catholic workshop was exclusive but, as noted earlier, had its unmistakably cosmopolitan elements. In a parallel manner, the event was also characterized by a unique consciousness: workshop participants lamented their marginality, their treatment by the government and people or organizations who colluded with the state, yet they also had a sense of being part of a larger, even global, struggle. Some participants, for example, had taken part in similar Church-sponsored meetings in Veracruz and Mexico City. Documentaries were shown about the global shortage of water and the Other Campaign (Otra Campaña) of the Zapatista Army of National Liberation—a revolutionary leftist movement that came to public view when NAFTA began in 1994. In this and other contexts, connections among local, national, and global—between particular and universal—were continuously underlined. Participants also displayed awareness that what they had—their land, their resources, even their knowledge—was coveted by the government and the transnationals. Like Ballesteros's (chapter 9, this volume) discussion of faith as involving an open-ended stance, a predisposition that can tolerate the unknown, these workshops and meetings were distinguished by a deferral of closure, resignation, and hopelessness. Indeed, it was the people's clear identification with the poorest of the poor, the exploited, and sacrifice that imbued their suffering with a moral and even transcendent quality that compelled them to not give up, despite all odds. Certainty was elusive, evasive; the future could not be known. One middle-aged female participant stated, "The seeds we scatter will come up in ways we can't predict." Palpable at the meetings was participants' sense that they were up to something important, a deeply moral project that fed the conviction that their activism, while not necessarily supported by others in their communities, was essential to their own survival and perhaps even to others far beyond.

Thus, like the Chinantec messianic movement discussed at the beginning of this chapter, the Mixtec hybrid liberationist environmental workshop was precipitated by a climate of desperation and acute threat to the community's survival. Conservation then becomes a *rescate*—a retrieval of the idealized ways of the ancestors, a renewal, a redemption of sorts.

CONCLUSION

The Mixteca event and others I witnessed reflect a bleeding of a condensed, highly romanticized version of the indigenous moral ecology into other arenas of anti-state protest. Connections among land, traditional knowledge, and self-determination promote a distilled sacred perspective and ethic and link the indigenous moral ecology with the imperative to defend local rights to territory and natural resources. I suggest that in Oaxaca, the indigenous sacred idiom has offered the possibility for such conceptions to act as an ecopolitical (new, politically ideological) "middle ground" (White cited in Conklin and Graham 1996:695), a "shared idiom of solidarity" in which even mestizo members of Oaxacan and national Mexican society are willing to stake their allegiances and activist efforts. The focus on the moral ecology, representing reciprocity, communality, and "eco-kinship" (Grim 2006) with the sacred, vital Madre Tierra, is also a mode of *localizing* and emplacing struggle, a way of underlining the authenticity, importance, and essentially moral nature of the perceived battle against the encroachment of ravenous, unmistakably deterritorializing global capitalism.

Problems related to its inherently contradictory and institutional position mean that such Church mobilizing efforts can be seen as "risky collaborations" in the terms Mathews (chapter 4, this volume) uses. Nevertheless, the progressivist Catholic Church has opened important mediating spaces in this critical political organizing. The new kind of environmentalism promoted by Oaxacan clergy, nuns, and others suggests the promise of efforts wherein, as Scanlan Lyons (chapter 2, this volume) describes in her account of environmentalism in Brazil's Atlantic Forest, sacred understanding and faith are not assessed against rational, objective knowledge forms. Instead, local sacred conceptions and experience stand on their own as means of revealing the importance of the struggle to transform people's conditions. Now inflected with universal images, knowledges, and discourses, they are harnessed into efforts aimed at progressive social change.

The local, place-based, indigenous moral ecology, in which landscape, body, and community are firmly interdependent, is a version of faith that deconstructs the knowledge–belief opposition and experiential domains often held separate. The acceptance of the sacred as a presence animating and permeating all dimensions of human life leads us to the potentially transformative cosmopolitics discussed by Ivakhiv (chapter 11, this volume) and other authors in this volume, in which different kinds of knowledge interact in a tentative, exploring way that can lead to new epiphanies, new understandings. In this way, the ability to recognize the promise of a religious consciousness in energizing political commitment may be the work of building a global environmentalism in and for the future.

Acknowledgments

Research on which this article is based was generously funded by a Standard Research Grant from the Social Sciences and Humanities Standard Research Council of Canada. James Brooks and Leslie Shipman were amazing hosts at our seminar at the School for Advanced Research in 2009 and conjured an idyllic setting for a special synergy among us at both intellectual and personal levels. The SAR Press staff, led by Lynn Baca, were eminently professional: sensitive, efficient, and thorough. Many thanks also to seminar leader Catherine Tucker, who infected us with her enthusiasm and whose patience and grace know no bounds. I am deeply grateful to all other seminar participants for their intellectual and personal generosity and for making our week in Santa Fe such a deeply stimulating, fun, and memorable one. I owe a huge debt to Padre S. and members of his community in the Mixteca for their understanding and welcome at what I know was for them a difficult time. Thanks also to Adaeze for being such a sport "in the field."

6

Syncretism and Conservation

Examining Indigenous Beliefs and Natural Resource Management in Honduras

Catherine M. Tucker

Early on a January morning in the mountains of western Honduras, I join my friend José and his son Elmer to help harvest their maize. Working with José's two brothers, we pull the dried ears of corn from the bent stalks in the field, toss them into net bags, and talk as we work along adjacent rows. "Why are you harvesting now?" I ask, because they are several months behind their neighbors. José's response does not quite answer my question, but it echoes principles that other farmers described. "You have to wait until the new moon is past," he explains. "This is a good day to pick, because it's the fifth day after the new moon. The sixth and tenth days are good too, or you can wait until the waning of the full moon, because maize picked at these times will resist pests and rotting." Elmer looks up with a quizzical gaze, "This is the fourth day after the new moon." "No, it's the fifth," responds his father. Elmer holds up one hand and counts off the days. "See, it's the fourth." José pauses with consternation plain on his face, then shrugs in resignation. We resume picking in silence.

Time after time across nearly twenty years of longitudinal fieldwork among Lenca people in rural Honduras, I have encountered practices based on traditional understandings and spiritual beliefs. Although many farmers attend agricultural seminars, use fertilizers, and experiment with the latest scientific recommendations, they also draw on indigenous knowledge and beliefs to make decisions. My experience with José and Elmer marks one of the conundrums that I have encountered in trying to understand how beliefs, practices, and different kinds of knowledge interact to shape land use, natural resource management, and livelihoods. José's beliefs did not stop him from harvesting maize once he had begun, but he was not happy to discover his mistake. The incident is among the many that caused me to wonder how beliefs matter in my study site—a rural municipality that has retained certain cultural traditions and practices while experiencing rapid social and economic transformations (C. Tucker 2008, 2010).

When I went to the SAR seminar, I hoped that discussions about our case studies might reveal patterns in which religious beliefs and scientific knowledge interact to encourage conservation. If such patterns could be discerned, perhaps they could be systematically studied and encouraged. Our research revealed great fluidity and variability in the ways people engage religious beliefs and scientific understandings as they deal with environmental-social-political-economic challenges. Distinctions between religion and science, never as clear as popularly supposed, became more blurred as we talked. We questioned whether certain ways of living, thinking, and perceiving lead to sustainable social-ecological systems, and if so, why?

A body of research among indigenous and traditional societies has found an association between sustainable practices and spiritual beliefs expressing respect for the natural environment (for example, Berkes 2008b; Dorm-Adzobu and Veit 1991; González 2001; Salmon 2000). Similarly, mapping projects have discovered that indigenous territories correlate strongly with forest cover and biodiversity hot spots (Ayres 2003; Souza 2006; Stepp, Castaneda, and Cervone 2005). In this volume, Hallum (chapter 7) discusses how Mayan beliefs have contributed to successful reforestation projects in Guatemala, while Norget (chapter 5) examines the power of indigenous moral ecologies to support environmental consciousness and cultural resilience. It is difficult, however, to assess the degree to which spiritual beliefs influence natural resource management. After all, a related body of work has found indigenous societies that have overexploited natural resources (for example, Brightman 1987; Krech 1999; Redman 1999), which undermines any supposition that indigenous beliefs and practices inherently achieve social-ecological sustainability. It follows that beliefs that espouse respect for nature—however constructed—may contribute to but do not assure sustainability.

Rather than claim direct relationships between belief systems and conservation, nuanced studies show that numerous factors interact to influence local processes of conservation or degradation (Brosius, Tsing, and Zerner

2005; Gezon 1999; Haenn 2005; Jacka 2010; P. West 2006). Interactions with nation-states, processes of market integration and globalization, and inequitable political-economic relationships can inhibit or undermine local social and institutional arrangements, resulting in environmental degradation, loss of traditional ecological knowledge (TEK), and erosion of beliefs (Godoy et al. 2005; Gross et al. 1979; Henrich 1997; Humphries 1993; K. Moran 1999). Market integration and imposition of Western models of agriculture and conservation are among the frequently noted factors in destabilizing traditional social-ecological systems, although people's experiences vary greatly (E. Fischer and Benson 2005; Godoy, Wilkie, and Franks 1997; Netting, Stone, and Stone 1989; Rudel 2002; Tsing 2005). In some situations, indigenous societies may be able to engage their belief systems and traditional knowledge to manage change processes without degrading their natural resource base (for example, Gomez-Pompa and Kaus 1999; Stephenson 1999; Tiedje 2008).

In this chapter, I explore how different systems of belief, knowledge, and practice are interacting and influencing people's relationships with their natural resource base in contexts of market integration and social transformation. What are the implications for environmental conservation at the nexus of TEK, spiritual beliefs, and Western science? My research focuses on the Lenca people of La Campa, a *municipio* (similar to a county) in western Honduras. I first visited the site in 1992 and since then have returned nearly every year to continue research on natural resource management. The data in this chapter are drawn from interviews, surveys, archival research, and participant observation. Along with the rest of Honduras's indigenous populations, the Lenca have endured economic and political marginalization and ongoing threats to land rights and cultural autonomy (Rivas 1993). In the past few decades, western Honduras has undergone rapid changes in infrastructure, accessibility to basic services, market integration, and access to modern technology and information. The changes occurring in La Campa have presented challenges for Lenca beliefs, TEK, and practices as people interact more frequently with Western religious and scientific perspectives. To explore these changes, I frame my discussion with respect to transformational processes occurring in La Campa and to scholarship on belief systems, TEK, and institutions for natural resource management. I then focus on three dimensions of Lenca experience that reveal the confluence of Western and Lenca ideas and the syncretic transformations that carry impli-cations for environmental conservation: traditional beliefs and rituals, methods of coffee production to protect forests, and forest and watershed management.

BELIEF SYSTEMS AND TRADITIONAL ECOLOGICAL KNOWLEDGE

The world's cultures vary in how they conceptualize humanity's place in the world, understand local ecology, and interact with natural resources (Nazarea et al. 1998). All cultures have a cosmology (cosmovision or world-view), a belief system that encompasses fundamental conceptualizations about the way the world works, what is real, and what is true; it provides an axiomatic set of convictions and understandings that inform knowledge and practice. Many indigenous peoples envision a cosmos infused with sacred meanings, in which all things are connected and interdependent (Toledo 2001). Cosmologies can be expressed through ideology, religion, doctrines, rituals, and norms, as well as through the mundane practices of daily life. As a people's experiences and contexts change, cosmologies evolve.

Systems of knowledge such as TEK interrelate with cosmologies to communicate useful information and guide practice for interacting with the material, spiritual, and social-ecological worlds (Gurung 1997). Among many traditional and indigenous societies, TEK links cosmologies to practices of natural resource use. Berkes (2008b:252–253) notes, "Almost all traditional ecological knowledge systems may be characterized as a complex of knowledge, practice and belief."

Indigenous knowledge can constitute a form of adaptive management (Berkes, Colding, and Folke 2000). Although Western science typically disdains indigenous knowledge and practices, indigenous peoples accumulate knowledge through procedures similar to ones espoused by Western science. They develop and test hypotheses, examine outcomes, integrate useful results into their practices, and adapt their practices as continued experimentation and experience provide new information (González 2001; Malinowski 1992). Their knowledge draws on observations accumulated across generations and differs from Western scientific facts because it has acquired sacred, social, and practical meanings imbedded in a specific ecological and sociocultural context (Berkes 2008b; Nazarea 2003). Thus, beliefs, knowledge, and practice intertwine in people's lives and play out in distinct ways of perceiving the world and interacting with it. Therefore, people with contrasting systems of belief and knowledge can be said to live in different worlds (Callicott 1994), which come into contact as groups of people interact with one another and all living and nonliving things. The potential for syncretic expressions exists wherever different cosmologies and knowledge systems overlap or collide. As used here, syncretism includes the blending or mixing of religions (S. Kraft 2002), especially

Catholic and Lenca beliefs, but goes further to encompass conjunctions or merging of contrasting cosmologies or systems of knowledge such as TEK and Western science. Institutions may also be understood as the result of syncretic processes, broadly conceived (Berk and Galvan 2009). In the Lenca context, market integration and improving infrastructure have increased exposure to Western knowledge and practices. Certain beliefs and practices have been changing, as have the institutional arrangements for relating to the land and natural resources.

INSTITUTIONS, BELIEFS, AND ENVIRONMENTAL CONSERVATION

Barrera-Bassols and Toledo (2005:10–11) note that "human use of landscapes is not a mere materialist, techno-productive phenomenon, but a complex process always mediated by intellectual functions, such as knowledge and cosmology, and organized by social institutions." Institutions are the formal and informal rules in use that guide human behavior (Ostrom et al. 2002). They include norms, regulations, and laws that people generally obey. Conditions associated with the development and maintenance of institutions for sustainable natural resource management include frequent face-to-face contact and trust among members of a group, ability to monitor natural resources and interpret observations, gradual rates of change (as opposed to rapid change) in ecological and social conditions, feasibility of monitoring the resource, and ability to exclude outsiders (Dietz, Ostrom, and Stern 2003). These factors facilitate but do not guarantee effective institutions for sustainable resource management. It has been argued that a resource must be perceived not only as important but also as scarce (or otherwise threatened) before people will develop rules to protect it (Gibson 2001). Among some indigenous groups, however, institutions exist to protect natural resources that people do not perceive as scarce. Such protection may be unintentional, because cultural beliefs and practices may reflect purposes or convictions unrelated to goals of conservation. For example, people may believe that certain animals and plants are toxic or morally or spiritually dangerous for humans to touch or use. Taboos can serve to protect a species and perhaps the environments in which it lives (Ntiamoa-Baidu 2008). A study of species-specific taboos found that 30 percent of documented taboos involved mammals or reptiles that are threatened or endangered, but the study did not find that people consciously aimed to protect the species (Colding and Folke 1997). Robbins (chapter 3, this volume) discusses how newly Christian Urapmin decided to hunt marsupials traditionally held as taboo but fell ill when they consumed the marsupials' meat. Thus, scarcity is only one of the possible explanations for the existence of taboos and other beliefs that conserve natural resources (Balée 1985; Ross et al. 1978; Turner and Berkes 2006).

Evaluating whether beliefs and practices constitute conservation proves difficult for many reasons. Conservation has numerous contested definitions and meanings (Hunn et al. 2003). Among Western environmentalists, conservation can be sustainable or limited use of specified places and resources or preservation in which human interventions are prohibited. For the purposes of this chapter, I understand conservation to mean that a natural resource retains its viability and inherent characteristics and, if used by humans, does not suffer irreversible degradation. Furthermore, a belief or practice should not be interpreted as conservationist unless it is consciously intended to conserve a resource (Baland and Platteau 1996; Hames 1987; E. Smith and Wishnie 2000). The rationale is that people who are not aware that beliefs and practices facilitate conservation or who do not consciously aim for sustainable use of resources may not recognize the risks of abandoning the conservative dimensions of their beliefs and practices. Indigenous peoples' apparent conservation of natural resources can also be the tangential result of low population density, subsistence-oriented production, or technical constraints. If maintenance of natural resources results as an accidental consequence of local contexts, then natural resources will lack protection when those contexts change. Nonetheless, beliefs and practices may implicitly support conservation and sustainable management of natural resources.

Ecological anthropologists have found examples in which rituals and spiritually based practices act as powerful mechanisms for sustainable management of natural resources. In Bali, traditional water temples, a trained priesthood, and associated rituals served to govern the distribution of water in a sophisticated wet rice system (Lansing 1991). Although individual farmers did not grasp the system's complexities, their religious beliefs and rituals reinforced and gave meaning to the mundane activities upon which the entire system depended. Rappaport's (1984) study of the Tsembaga Maring people in New Guinea revealed that the *kaiko* ritual cycle maintained an ecosystemic balance among pigs, humans, and natural resources. Subsequent modeling supported Rappaport's analysis that the kaiko cycle mitigates sources of local instability and environmental variability (Anderies 1998). These studies, among others, indicate that religious beliefs can be a way for humans to encode knowledge of ecosystemic relationships that reflects experiences and observations gained over generations-long residence in a specific environment. Religion provides a means for humans to pass on knowledge of risks or relationships that may be too complex, subtle, or infrequent (such as rare weather events or centuries-long cycles) to communicate and maintain efficiently by other means. By invoking spiritual causes and consequences, religious beliefs can induce behaviors with practical benefits of which believers may not be aware. Thus, conservation or sustainable management of natural resources may be an implicit but disguised motivation for some spiritually based beliefs and practices, but it cannot be proved that such beliefs evolved for that purpose in the absence of conscious understanding. Certain modern environmental problems may result from failures to realize the advantages of traditional practices. In Bali, the Green Revolution dismantled the ritual system of water management with the consequence that rice production fell, water was poorly distributed, and damage from pests increased dramatically. Belatedly, farmers realized the functional benefits of their traditional beliefs and practices and returned to the ritual system (Lansing 1991). This example supports the argument that where environmentally conservative behaviors occur unconsciously or as an invisible counterpart of a belief system, they do not provide a strong basis for maintaining sustainable practices. The Balinese example is unusual in that the farmers managed to restore the traditional system when they realized its advantages. Bateson (2000) argued, however, that beliefs and rituals work because they affect people at an unconscious level; making their purposes transparent may rob them of power and efficacy.

LA CAMPA, HONDURAS

La Campa is located in the Department of Lempira (figure 6.1), which is one of the three departments (similar to states) where Lenca-dominated communities survive. These departments (Lempira, La Paz, and Intibucá) coincide with the region dominated by Lenca cultural groups at the time of the Spanish Conquest (Newson 1986).

La Campa was founded in the mid-1500s during Spanish efforts to relocate indigenous peoples into nucleated settlements. Over the past five hundred years, the people of La Campa have faced pressure by the Catholic Church and colonial and national governments to abandon traditional beliefs and practices. The people have responded by merging symbols, practices, and beliefs with Catholicism to create a richly syncretic faith (Chapman 1986). In the past three decades, local priests have been prohibiting syncretic rituals and imposing conservative Catholic doctrine; disillusioned parishioners have turned to recently founded Evangelical churches.

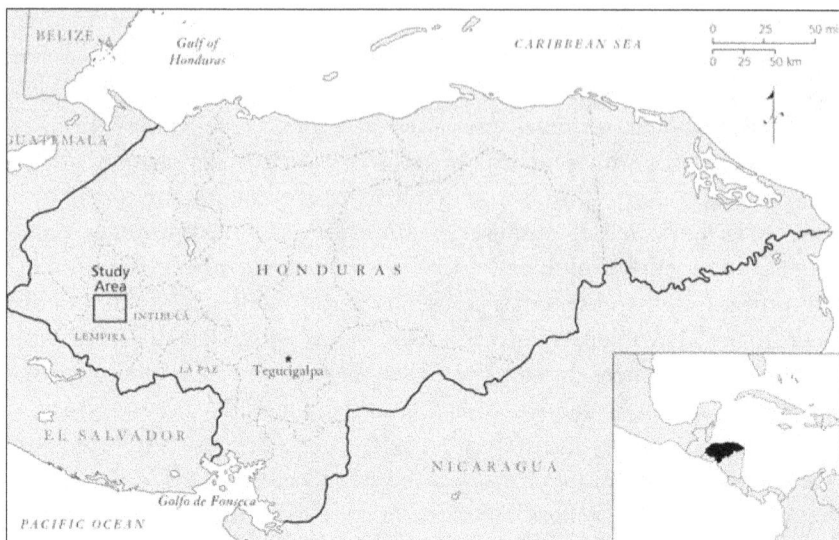

FIGURE 6.1

Map of Honduras with the study site location.

The Lenca language disappeared during the early twentieth century, before linguists could complete an analysis (Hamp 1976). Due to the loss of their language and other transformations, Lenca people may best be considered as inheritors of a syncretic cultural tradition. Many of the people consider themselves to be *indios* (Indians) and recognize their Lenca heritage, but La Campa residents call themselves Campeños (people of La Campa). Several characteristics distinguish the Lenca from mestizos, including artisanal pottery making, a preference for brightly colored clothing among the women, and unique linguistic expressions (Chapman 1992).

La Campa's population is approximately 4,460 (UNDP 2003). It has a municipal center (Centro Urbano de La Campa; hereafter, the Centro) and seven villages. Most households have a diversified economy that includes subsistence agriculture, small-scale coffee production, temporary wage labor, and production of artisanal pottery and crafts. La Campa has gained national fame for its artisanal Lenca pottery, which is sold regionally for practical use and nationally to tourists (Ardón Mejía 1989; C. Tucker 2010).

Nearly every household has enough land for a *milpa* (maize field), a *frijolar* (bean field), and a *huerta* (orchard) or coffee plantation. Many households raise sugarcane to sell as *panela* (unrefined cane sugar). Historically, Campeños held the land communally, and any native-born resident could claim a parcel of communal land for slash-and-burn agriculture (C. Tucker

1999). Beginning in the 1970s, increasing population density and changing national policies gradually compelled farmers to give up slash-and-burn agriculture and adopt extended cultivation. During the 1990s, a national land-titling program formalized private property rights, and rights to occupy communal land ended (C. Tucker 2008).

The past forty years have also brought major changes in services and infrastructure. Telegraph service reached La Campa in the 1970s, and bus service started in the 1980s. In 1990, La Campa began to produce enough coffee to qualify for a national road-building subsidy, and the municipal government completed a road into the coffee-producing highlands in 1994. Coffee production expanded dramatically as farmers realized its potential to provide income. Road improvements facilitated transportation to and from regional markets. Electricity reached the Centro in 2003, followed by television and cell phones. These changes have engaged many Campeños directly in markets, exposed them to national culture and rhetoric, and reduced dependence on subsistence production.

The spread of coffee and market integration is frequently associated with deforestation and degradation of natural resources. In La Campa, the story is not that simple; there has been forest regrowth, as well as deforestation. Despite market incentives to clear forests for coffee plantations, La Campa experienced forest regrowth during the 1990s (Southworth and Tucker 2001). Today, forest covers more than 60 percent of La Campa (C. Tucker 2008). While most communal lands have been privatized, each village set aside at least one communal woodlot to supply firewood and timber. A majority of farmers maintain a patch of forest on their land and explain that it serves for firewood, timber, and future agricultural expansion; several say that they enjoy the beauty of forests.

TRADITIONAL BELIEFS AND AGRARIAN RITUALS

Traditionally, Lenca people perceive that every place and water source is owned by a specific spirit, or *angel de la tierra* (angel of the earth). Spirits and their resources, including wildlife and plants, need to be treated with respect. Agricultural fields and forests have generous but easily annoyed spirits, usually perceived as male. They punish disrespectful farmers with failed harvests and protect wildlife from avaricious hunters. *Sirenas* (sirens) own water sources and have high expectations of human devotion; they can tempt foolish men into dangerous rapids to drown them. Sand and clay deposits, which provide the raw materials for La Campa's potters, are controlled by female spirits. Benigna, the spirit of La Campa's finest claybed, replenishes the clay for potters who use it with care but causes pots to break when potters fail to honor her. Spirits can cause someone to fall ill if he or she wastes resources. When I asked people how they knew that an angry spirit was causing an illness, they answered that Western medicine cannot cure diseases caused by spirits. With this reasoning, people have accommodated Western medicine while affirming the higher power of spirits over humans. Spirits can become angry at minor infractions, such as using more water than necessary while washing clothes or processing coffee. They can also reward people who use resources carefully. Thus, the simplest actions of daily life carry spiritual implications. This type of understanding typifies indigenous cosmologies, which recognize intrinsic connections among all living and nonliving things (Toledo 2001).

To stay in the spirits' good graces, faithful Lenca offer *pagos a la tierra* (payments to the earth). One woman (personal communication, March 21, 1994) explained the rationale behind pagos in these terms: "We should pay the earth because if someone gives you a gift, shouldn't you repay that gift? Wouldn't you return it? Of course. It's the same with the earth. It gives us food. And it seems to me, we should return the gift." Formerly, Campeño households conducted several pagos each year to honor the spirit of each location on which they depended for sustenance, including each agricultural field, water source, and house garden and the claybed. A pago involves a series of prayers and ritual stages, centering on the sacrifice of an animal, usually a fowl. The ritual presents a syncretic combination of Mesoamerican and Hispanic elements. Mesoamerican elements include copal (a fragrant resin burned as incense), a turkey, wax from native black bees, and *chicha* (a fermented corn beverage). Hispanic elements used in pagos include a wooden cross, a picture of a Catholic saint, white votive candles, and a chicken or rooster. The type of animal sacrificed depends on the spirit and resource used; in previous years, a cow or calf might be sacrificed to honor the spirit of a pasture. The pago is conducted by an *encargado* (literally, responsible one), whose role has parallels with a priest leading Mass, with the participants forming a congregation (Chapman 1992). The part of the pago called *compostura* (act to put things into balance) occurs as the encargado and several helpers sacrifice the animal, mix the blood with chicha, and sprinkle it on the ground before a cross and burning candles (C. Tucker 2008) (figure 6.2). In Intibucá, the entire ritual is known as the compostura (Chapman 1992). The ritual culminates in a feast at which participants consume the sacrificed fowl and other festive foods to honor the spirit. Through participating in pagos, I discovered them to be very moving experiences. The pago affirms a sacred interrelationship among spirits, the earth, and human beings. As Schnell (chapter 8, this volume) notes, rituals

FIGURE 6.2

Preparing for a pago, 2006.

convey symbolic meanings in ways that renew and affirm transcendent values; they may impact individual understanding in ways that influence personal relationships with nature, however conceived.

Historically, many pagos were public celebrations and served to reinforce shared beliefs and social ties. Today, the criticism of traditional beliefs by the Catholic Church and urban-educated school teachers has compelled people to abandon pagos or perform them in secret. Even so, allusions to spirits occur among nonbelievers. I have heard spirits blamed when hunters inexplicably miss shots, when people get lost in forests, when strange accidents happen, and once when hail destroyed a single maize field on a cloudless day. Two encargados confided that several Campeños who had stopped performing pagos changed their minds when Western medicine did not cure their illnesses.

From a conservation perspective, the most intriguing aspect of the pago is the explicit intention to make amends to the spirit for any waste or disrespectful use of the resource in question. Encargados pray repeatedly for the spirit to forgive any transgressions or wastefulness committed by human acts and request that it accept the sacrifice. The prayers thank the spirit for the resource that has been consumed or used, especially water, clay, sand, land, or a crop. Comparable rituals exist in other agrarian cultures, including parts of Asia and Latin America (Barrera-Bassols and Toledo 2005; Michaelson, Jacobson, and Goldschmidt 1976; Samaddar 2006), suggesting that rural, agricultural populations experience contexts that evoke similar responses.

Agrarian rituals, including pagos, constitute a set of institutions that dictate how to restore a spiritual and natural balance upset by human exploitation of the environment. The interesting question is whether these rituals have an impact on daily behavior. Do pagos convince people to act conservatively? Or do pagos release them from further responsibility, a sort of get-out-of-jail-free card that gives them license to do whatever they wish as long as they periodically request forgiveness? Hypothetically, the question could be answered if a sufficient sample of believers and nonbelievers could be followed for a period to determine whether there were any consistent differences between the two groups. A formal study to randomly enlist believers and nonbelievers cannot be carried out because of the ridicule participants would risk, given Catholic priests' and schoolteachers' disapproval of Lenca rituals. Instead, I rely on observations of people's daily lives and agricultural practices. My observations include ten families who maintain traditional beliefs and practices and with whom I share confidence. I have not discovered systematic differences between the daily behaviors of believers and the rest of the population. What appears to differ is the underlying rationale for certain practices. For example, most Campeños leave a portion of ripe fruit and bananas in their plantations and orchards for wild animals and birds to eat. Traditional Lenca believers explain that the spirit of the place will grant abundant harvests if the bounty is shared with wildlife, the spirit's "children." The nonbelievers explain that leaving fruit is a form of caring for wildlife or they feel it is the right thing to do. My observations of mestizo farmers in other parts of Honduras have been that they do not leave fruit behind unless it is rotten or they lack resources to harvest it. The maintenance of this practice in La Campa suggests an enduring sense of connection with wildlife and responsibility for nature, even among people who deny the existence of earthly spirits.

Some beliefs survive untouched by Western critiques, including respect for the power of lunar cycles to influence agricultural outcomes. Many Campeño farmers, like José, affirm that the moon's movements draw or suppress the living essence of plants and determine which days are most propitious to plant and harvest crops. Beliefs related to lunar cycles have been found in other agrarian societies; their presence in La Campa may represent a syncretic belief. A well-educated farmer explained that the moon affects plants just as it affects the tides, presenting a syncretism of TEK and science.

THE FLUID INTERSECTION OF SCIENCE AND TRADITIONAL BELIEFS IN COFFEE PRODUCTION

Campeños have been producing coffee since the nineteenth century for household consumption. Under traditional coffee production, coffee was raised in the shade of fruit trees, often in house gardens, and usually produced in small quantities. When coffee production began to expand with national road subsidies and improved market linkages, technicians from the Honduran Coffee Institute (IHCAFE) advised farmers to plant high-yielding hybrids in full sun and to use fertilizers, fungicides, and pesticides. Farmers discovered that coffee grew poorly without shade in La Campa's long dry season. They resumed planting trees in coffee plantations, and shade reduced the need for chemical inputs. They used banana (*Musa spp.*), guamo (*Inga spp.*, native nitrogen-fixing trees), and fruit trees and left pine trees bordering their plantations.

In comparative research of coffee farmers that I have been conducting in La Campa and the mestizo municipio of Concepción del Sur in the Department of Santa Bárbara, a significant difference (0.001 level) exists in the diversity of trees planted in coffee plantations. The biophysical, topographic, and climatic characteristics of the two sites are similar, as is the prevalence of shade in plantations. Household surveys and observations between 2006 and 2009 revealed that Campeño coffee producers had, on average, 5.95 species of trees in their plantations; one farmer reported 21 kinds of trees. The predominately mestizo producers of Concepción del Sur planted an average of 4.19 species in their plantations; 10 species was the highest number reported. These figures underestimate the diversity because the survey counted banana and citrus only once each, although farmers plant several species of each (citrus trees include oranges, limes, and lemons). Moreover, 95.5 percent of Campeño farmers (as contrasted with 71 percent of the farmers in Concepción del Sur) reported planting trees in the preceding five years. Campeños explained that planting trees was a custom and fruit trees added variety to the diet. Tree planting apparently constitutes a norm, an informal institution that guides people's actions, which in this case contributes to biodiversity. Campeños gladly

TABLE 6.1

Comparisons of diversity of shade trees and coffee plant varieties between Lenca and Mestizo producers (independent samples t-test)

	Lenca Producers (La Campa) (s.d.) N = 66	Mestizo Producers (Concepción del Sur) mean (s.d.) N = 95	T (df)	Significance
Mean number of shade and fruit tree species planted with coffee	5.95 (3.656)	4.19 (2.223)	98.2021	0.001
Mean number of coffee varieties planted	2.97 (1.347)	3.00 (1.161)	159	0.879

1. Equal variances not assumed. Levene's Test for Equality of Variances: F 8.534, Sig. 0.004.

adopt introduced trees and experiment with new crops; therefore, they have exotic and native species. Their openness may increase local vulnerability to ecologically invasive species and changes in native vegetation composition, but they achieve the goal of augmenting food sources.

The number of coffee varieties planted does not vary significantly between mestizo and Lenca farmers (table 6.1). IHCAFE has advised farmers to plant one variety in each plantation because similarly shaped beans will more likely come from plantations with a single variety and consistency earns higher prices. Campeño farmers formerly planted different coffee varieties together to increase plantation resilience against variable weather and infestation. Evidently, this ecologically wise practice has been compromised by IHCAFE's advice and market incentives.

Compared with annual crops or pasture, shade coffee plantations mimic forest cover, provide shelter for birds, insects, and wildlife, sequester carbon over time, and protect biodiversity (Moguel and Toledo 1999; Perfecto et al. 1996). In addition, La Campa farmers raise a variety of crops, native fruits, herbs, and medicinal plants in their gardens and fields. They use few chemical inputs, with the exception of fertilizer, but increasing costs have compelled farmers to experiment with organic fertilizers such as chicken dung. These practices indicate syncretic combinations of traditional and Western agricultural knowledge and reveal sustainable and conservationist dimensions. At the same time, the Lenca willingly transformed highland mountain forests to coffee plantations, thus reducing habitat for native flora and fauna. From a Western environmentalist perspective, cutting pine-oak forests threatens native vegetation composition, endangers wildlife, and contributes to climate change. From another perspective, western Honduras has no original forests. Pine-oak forests are a human-maintained vegetation; indigenous peoples have burned and cleared the forests uncounted times since coming to the region about ten thousand years ago (M. Williams 2003).

The advantages of La Campa's diversified agricultural practices became apparent in the early twenty-first century. A global coffee glut caused prices to plummet, and coffee producers' income dropped dramatically (CEPAL 2002; IDB-USAID-World Bank 2002). Many coffee farmers in Central America experienced severe economic hardship, but in La Campa, farmers appeared to adapt more readily to the market conditions. A cross-national household survey (Mexico, Guatemala, and Honduras) of coffee producers in 2003 found that 86.7 percent and 67.9 percent of Mexican and Guatemalan respondents, respectively, experienced a decline in household income during the coffee crisis. By contrast, only 37.8 percent of the Honduran respondents (in La Campa) reported a decline in household income (Eakin, Tucker, and Castellanos 2006). Most Campeño households diversified their economic activities, and 29.7 percent increased their income during the crisis. Compared with their counterparts in Mexico and Guatemala, La Campa's coffee growers produced more crops, reported greater biodiversity in their plantations, and had options other than coffee to meet their needs (C. Tucker, Eakin, and Castellanos 2010).

As a result of the coffee crisis, IHCAFE began to promote planting diverse fruit and shade trees with coffee and using organic fertilizers to reduce chemical fertilizer expenditures. Although IHCAFE presents these methods as the cutting edge in modern coffee production, they have many similarities to what Lenca farmers have done for generations. Moreover, certification programs now offer better prices for shade-grown and organic coffees, in recognition of their richer flavor and ecological benefits. In this instance, Western science has discovered justifications for traditional methods of coffee production. The convergence reinforces traditional practices and may open avenues for the Lenca farmers to position themselves on the forefront of high-quality, sustainable coffee production.

Although coffee has created new opportunities and increased many farmers' incomes, it has also exacerbated social inequality. Outsiders have been buying land for coffee plantations from poorer families, creating La Campa's first landless farmers. Better-off Campeños have leveraged coffee income to increase their local political influence. The municipal government has become dominated by a few wealthier families, which has undermined principles of democratic governance and weakened arrangements that support social equity (C. Tucker 2008).

A SHIFT TOWARD CONSCIOUS ENVIRONMENTAL CONSERVATION IN FOREST AND WATERSHED MANAGEMENT

La Campa's population reveals signs of a nascent conservationist ethic toward forests and water resources. Forest conservation efforts appear to be more related to recent experiences and change processes than to traditional beliefs. Historically, people had little concern for forest resources because these were abundant and farmers knew that pine regenerated readily in the agricultural cycle of slash-and-burn clearing and long fallows. Concern for forest conservation emerged from exposure to industrial logging in the 1970s and 1980s. In 1974, the Honduran government nationalized all of the country's trees and created the Honduran Forest Development Corporation (COHDEFOR) to manage forest resources. COHDEFOR approved a series of contracts for sawmills to log La Campa's lowland forests. The loss of autonomy over their communal forests and the deforestation from clear-cutting angered residents. Large-scale forest clearing and the severe erosion caused by irresponsible logging practices jarred Campeño perceptions of forests as endlessly renewing and regenerating. They realized that forests could be damaged beyond recovery, and they formed a grassroots organization to end the logging. In 1987, the group's efforts culminated in violent opposition, and loggers and COHDEFOR agreed to leave (C. Tucker 2008). La Campa's municipal government regained the right to govern the forests, passed new, popular ordinances to prohibit logging and the use of chain saws, and began to require permits for cutting trees for construction. Subsistence use of forest resources was still allowed. After the loggers departed, forest began to regenerate in some of the logged areas. In 1995, La Campa won a national forest conservation award.

Despite interest in conserving forests, farmers have had a concomitant desire to expand coffee plantations and agricultural fields. Beliefs in protective earth spirits and concern to maintain forest cover have taken lower priority than the opportunity to improve household incomes. Through the 1990s, Campeños improved management of the lowland forests that had been devastated by loggers, but areas near roads became house lots and agricultural fields (C. Tucker 2008). Meanwhile, farmers proceeded to clear forest at higher elevations conducive to export-quality coffee production. Coffee plantations spread in small patches, interspersed with communal woodlots and private forests. Farmers who believed in earth spirits conducted pagos after planting coffee, in order to placate spirits for the destruction of the forest and assure good harvests. Prior to the spread of coffee production for the market, the Lenca people did not have specific pagos for coffee plantations. Today, these have become almost as important for believers as the pago for the milpa, which is the most important agricultural ritual. Although believers use pagos to compensate spirits for deforestation, the traditional beliefs did not impede forest clearing or encourage conservation.

During the 1990s, the spread of coffee began to threaten the cloud forest on Montaña Camapara, the highest point in La Campa, whose springs provide water for most of La Campa. Residents feared that deforestation would reduce water supplies, as they had begun to observe declines in village reservoirs. They realized by experience what ecologists discovered through empirical measurement: deforestation of cloud forests can reduce water flow. Desiccation theory, the idea that deforestation reduces water availability, has not been supported in studies of most forest types (Mathews, chapter 4, this volume) but does apply, to some degree, in cloud forests. The scientific explanation is that the forest canopy intercepts cloud water and increases net precipitation; therefore, cutting down cloud forests eliminates the additional water captured by the canopy (Ataroff and Rada 2000; Hamilton 1995). As coffee plantations and agricultural fields expanded on Montaña Camapara, people also worried that runoff from fertilizers and soil erosion would contaminate the water and damage the water projects they had painstakingly built with their own labor.

Village water committees began a grassroots effort to set aside the watershed as a community protected area, the Montaña Camapara Reserve. The process required nearly ten years of negotiation with farmers on the mountain, but municipal authorities and nearly all Campeños supported the effort. Eventually, the farmers, nineteen in all, agreed to relocate. Every household that benefitted from Camapara's water contributed a fee to compensate them and provided volunteer labor to fence the cloud forest reserve. Today, natural regeneration is occurring in former plantations and fields. A municipal forest guard patrols the reserve regularly, and neighboring farmers monitor it informally. Interestingly, the effort to protect the cloud forest grew out of the experiences of building potable water systems from its springs. People working on the water system, many of whom had never visited the cloud forest, discovered that it was a special place with plants and animals they did not see elsewhere. Campeños interviewed about this work reveal a sense of connection with and concern for the forest. When the Centro's water system suffered a series of burst pipes, believers performed pagos to calm the siren suspected of causing the damage. As households acquired potable water, believers began to offer pagos at cisterns and faucets, adapting the ritual to new contexts.

The creation of the Montaña Camapara Reserve heralded a new stage in local conservation because no one is allowed to enter the reserve except to maintain water projects. Previously, Campeños opposed strict forest protection, but exposure to national conservation rhetoric, NGOs, and school-teachers espousing Western conservation evidently influenced the decision. It also related to Campeños' reasoning: if farming could harm the water, then any human intervention might pose a threat. The strict institutions that protect the reserve represent a syncretic merging of Western conservation ideals with Lenca understanding of a connected world in which people are interdependent with nature. But it was the need for water that motivated people to work together to protect the cloud forest. Every village water committee requires beneficiary households to take turns cleaning the cistern, maintaining pipelines, and doing repairs. Households that attempt to avoid their duties risk social ostracism and fines; shirking is rare. People must also help to maintain reserve fences. These new institutions serve to maintain the reserve, its springs, and the infrastructure for water provision. Moreover, they make clear to Campeños that their access to water depends on a joint commitment to protect the reserve.

ARE CAMPEÑOS CONSERVATIONISTS?

Compared with North Americans, the people of La Campa use far less water, consume less energy, require fewer trees (for paper or timber), and demand fewer manufactured goods. With their modest consumption levels, Campeños require less resource exploitation than the average dedicated environmentalist in the USA. Even so, their acquisitiveness is increasing as exposure to goods continues to grow. Catholic and Evangelical churches encourage Campeños to follow a faith that acknowledges a patriarchal deity, associates material well-being with divine favor, and envisions a world devoid of earthly spirits. The Honduran educational system promotes mestizo identity as integral to full citizenship, with mixed messages that support consumerism (exemplified in the list of required school materials), as well as conservation of natural resources. Meanwhile, Lenca practices and beliefs do not reveal intentional commitment to conservation as understood in Western terms. Instead, beliefs and practices emphasize maintaining reciprocal relations and recognizing connections among spirits, humans, and natural resources, as evidenced in pagos, continuing allusions to spirits, and attention to the lunar cycle. Prayers offered to spirits during pagos apologize for waste and damage to resources, even if unavoidable. One of the pagos I attended was for a potter suffering pain in one arm. The encargado identified the spirit of the family's water source (a nearby spring) as the cause of her suffering. As the encargado sacrificed a rooster to the siren, he prayed and offered thanks for all the water the woman had used over the years, and he apologized for every drop that had been wasted, splashed unused to the ground, or contaminated with other substances. Insofar as traditional beliefs regret waste, they may provide a subconscious basis for a conservation ethic, even though health and spiritual protection are the conscious goals.

As the Catholic Church and the educational system continue to disparage beliefs in earthly spirits and pagos, Lenca traditions appear to be waning. Chapman (1992) noted as much in the 1980s in Intibucá, and yet those Lenca communities continue the public practice of pagos despite opposition by the Catholic Church. The possibility of renewal, resistance to Western beliefs, or maintenance of certain traditions cannot be discarded. In La Campa, a recent mayor allowed school children to make and sell chicha to earn money as part of the national Lempira Day celebration, which honors a Lenca leader who died fighting the Spanish conquistadors. Although the priest disliked the sale of chicha, its public use during a national holiday honoring Honduras' indigenous heritage hints at a resurgence of Lenca traditions. Similarly, the integration of pagos for coffee plantations and potable water systems shows the flexibility of remaining believers to adapt to changing circumstances. Campeños' creation of the Montaña Camapara Reserve indicates that their conscious interest in conservation has grown and that Western approaches to conservation are viewed as compatible with certain goals.

Campeños have neither protected nor destroyed their environment as much as they have reshaped it. They have used the land and forests in cycles of clearing and regrowth since before the Spanish Conquest. They willingly razed forests to plant coffee, but to support their livelihoods, they incorporated shade and fruit trees. In the process, they reproduced forest-like environments. They opposed forest destruction by outside loggers and created rules for lowland forest management that fostered forest regrowth, but they allowed agricultural fields in parts of the logged forests. When coffee expansion threatened the mountain springs that provided their water, they created a protected area, even as forest clearing for coffee plantations continued on private land. They profess multidimensional and varied goals; their fields, forests, and coffee plantations serve many purposes. Like many other rural populations, they see their land as their home and source of sustenance, a place to use and live in, not a place to set aside and observe from afar (Berkes 2008b). The prevalence of this attitude in nearly all land use decisions makes the creation of the Montaña Camapara Reserve all the more remarkable.

In general, the ways in which Campeños have created syncretic blends of TEK and modern principles for agricultural practice and resource management affirm a pragmatic sense of connection with the environment that they have shaped and rely upon. Their perceptions of an interconnected world, which apparently persist even as traditional beliefs in spirits have diminished, seem to facilitate their ability to develop syncretic practices and institutions to fit changing circumstances. In contrast to the dynamic interrelationships that Campeños have with their natural resource base, Western conservation aims to diminish or prohibit human interactions. By Western standards, Campeños' record of natural resource management and conservation is mixed. By local standards, they are endeavoring to build better lives for themselves and their children, and part of this endeavor means maintaining the viability of their profoundly transformed resource base to meet their livelihood needs. When Campeños clear forests for coffee or agriculture, they are not destroying nature but working with it to create their futures, informed by perceived interdependence with nature. When they set aside forest, they aim for the same goal. The transformations that they continue to make to their natural resource base have not destroyed it, and the rapidity with which forests regrow on fallowed land suggests that they have maintained its fertility. With this perspective, Campeños are conservationists in a way that fits their evolving realities.

REFLECTIONS ON LENCA EXPERIENCE AT THE INTERSECTIONS OF NATURE, SCIENCE, AND RELIGION

Berkes (2008b:252–253) notes that "almost universally, one encounters an ethic of nondominant, respectful human–nature relationship, a sacred ecology, as part of the belief component of traditional ecological knowledge." Although the Lenca people reveal evidence for this sacred ecology, their recent experiences show that beliefs are open to interpretation and adaptation as new ideas and opportunities emerge. Some mourn the decline of traditional syncretic rituals. Others believe that modern beliefs and practices signify spiritual and moral progress, in accord with doctrines of Catholic and Evangelical churches and Western science taught in schools, which critique Lenca beliefs. To a large degree, Campeños concur that things have improved over the past decade. They enjoy reliable public transportation, electricity, television, and cell phones. Coffee provides the best source of income the farmers have ever had, even if prices fluctuate.

The instances of collective action to conserve natural resources imply that many Campeños share similar values and trust one another. These factors have been shown to be important for effective local management of natural resources (Dietz, Ostrom, and Stern 2003). Historically, pagos served as public rituals that communicated meaning and the expectation of certain behaviors. Such rituals can reinforce people's mutual trust and affirm their belief system (Watanabe and Smuts 1999). In the present, cooperative efforts to prohibit logging, create a watershed reserve, and maintain water systems have provided a context to affirm intracommunity ties; these efforts emerged in response to threats of resource degradation and scarcity. La Campa's increasing constraints on resource use support the proposition that scarcity of important resources can foster protective institutions (Gibson 2001). In the process, Western conservation ideas have been syncretically incorporated with, and reshaped by, indigenous beliefs and practice. Campeños continue to confront market pressures to expand coffee production and transform their land, but they also realize that they depend on forests and watersheds for their livelihoods. Out of this nexus arise uncertainties and risks, but also opportunities for emergent syncretic beliefs and practices that conserve their natural resources.

The Lenca experience contrasts with the commitment to moral ecologies that inform an indigenous nature-culture, such as Norget (chapter 5, this volume) found in Mexico, and presents a context different from the melding of reforestation with traditional Maya faith that Hallum discovered in Guatemala (chapter 7, this volume). Today, most Lenca people practice modern Catholicism or Evangelism, in part to participate fully in the modern world. In this regard, the Lenca experience resonates with that of the Urapmin, who turned to Christianity and ousted traditional spirits in the hopes of improving their economic opportunities (Robbins, chapter 3, this volume). In other ways, the Lenca experience with deforestation, and their subsequent concern for forest management, has similarities to Zimbabwe's Earthkeepers movement. In Zimbabwe, people intentionally created rituals to support their institutions and tree-planting practices. The rituals added a layer of meaning, which reinforced participants' commitment to protect the trees (Daneel, chapter 10, this volume). The Lenca people's traditional beliefs and rituals did not aim explicitly to protect natural resources, but they did affirm a meaningful relationship with nature.

The effort to understand how religious beliefs, practice, and knowledge interact to influence environmental and social sustainability cannot be based on a single case study. Each case in this volume casts a slightly different light on the challenges that people face, as well as the diverse contexts that constrain their options and motivate their actions. In each case, we find that people's beliefs, knowledge, and experiences shape their connections to one another and their perceived worlds and that these connections evolve as social, economic, political, and ecological contexts change. We discover no simple generalizations about the intersections among religion, science, and nature; we as yet lack systematic comparative studies that might be able to find underlying principles and patterns that explain how interactions between belief and knowledge systems influence certain social-ecological outcomes. Yet all of these cases indicate that human choices and constructions of the world integrate religious-spiritual, empirical-scientific, and practical experiences and perceptions. The research thus implies that if we are to move toward socially and environmentally sustainable societies, we must engage all of these dimensions.

Acknowledgments

I am deeply indebted to the people of La Campa, who welcomed me into their homes, answered my questions, and supported my work. The research was made possible by funding provided by the Wenner-Gren Foundation (Grant 7748) and the Inter-American Institute for Global Change Research (SGP1–015, as well as CRN2–060 through National Science Foundation grant SBR-9307681). The Center for the Study of Institutions, Population, and Environmental Change, Indiana University, and the University of Arizona also provided support. I am grateful to LASA and SAR for sponsoring the advanced seminar and to all the seminar participants for their transformative insights, challenging feedback, and generosity of spirit.

7

Do You Understand?

Discovering the Power of Religion for Conservation in Guatemalan Mayan Communities

Anne Motley Hallum

The workday in Comalapa, Guatemala, was about to begin. The four North American volunteers were eager to begin mixing cement and laying brick in the construction of a fuel-efficient oven for the Kaqchikel Maya family. The new oven would consume half the firewood of a traditional fire and improve the pulmonary health of the family by sharply reducing and ventilating smoke. All of the materials had been delivered by a US non-governmental organization (NGO), and the volunteers and family members were noisily opening the bags of cement when the homeowner came into her kitchen, smiling and excited, holding an incense burner and a bowl of rose petals. The work stopped as the group watched her place rose petals in the four corners on the floor where the large oven would be built. She then slowly waved the smoke from the incense burner over the site while each Guatemalan in turn said a prayer in Spanish or Kaqchikel to bless the home, the site of the work, and the hands of the laborers. The stove building resumed, but with new commitment because the volunteers felt throughout the day that this backbreaking work was indeed holy.

This story recounts one of many examples of the intersection of religion, science, and the environment that are the subject of this volume and the SAR seminar that inspired it. This chapter adds the dimension of how an NGO from another culture may implement environmental projects without disrupting existing religious and cultural supports. It is the story of the founding of a small NGO, The Alliance for International Reforestation (AIR, www.AIRGuatemala.org), which works largely in Kaqchikel communities of Guatemala to share across cultures its work in environmental sustainability. The second section of the chapter looks at examples of the nexus of religious beliefs and conservation, focusing on three specific themes: creation stories, ritual and poetry, and the sacredness of place. The final section returns to the pragmatic questions of how religion and conservation intersect and how NGOs may work across cultures for environmental protection, based on review of literature and lessons from Guatemala. The intention is to use on-the-ground experiences to address the explicit question that confronted each contributor to this volume: Does religion shape or affect environmental practice, and if so, how? Throughout this chapter, I use examples of how and argue that environmental NGOs must be more sensitive to the power of local religious beliefs for environmental protection and restoration.

World-famous biologist E. O. Wilson (2006) has explicitly called for an alliance between science and religion in behalf of the environment, acknowledging that the language of the scientific community is apparently not enough to inspire action. Wilson (2006:163) states, "Science and religion are the two most powerful forces of society; together they can save the Creation." However, actually forming such an alliance across languages and cultures is incredibly difficult. In the 1990s, in fact, some conservation scientists bemoaned the incompatibility of humans and the goals of conservation and demanded a more scientific focus for "protected" areas that would relocate residents (Redford and Sanderson 2000; Terborgh 1999). This approach led to a lively criticism of environmental NGOs and new research examining numerous cases in which *NGOs* are the culprits that inadvertently destroy sacred woods, disregard indigenous rights, and disrupt sustainable practices (Brechin 2003; Chapin 2004; Haenn 2005; Igoe and Kelsall 2005; Walker et al. 2007). Research results are rich in descriptions and criticism of NGOs but somewhat lacking in advice for *how* to work with residents across cultures and for multiple goals.

Other research concerns common-pool resource theory, which is very specific about how environmental sustainability can be achieved, because it is based on close examination of environmentally sustainable cultures. This social science theory, however, seems somewhat uncomfortable regarding the role of religion in its case studies. The theory addresses the importance of norms and values other than self-interest for designing common-property regimes that are sustainable over even centuries of use and renewal. One of the conclusions from fieldwork by political scientist Elinor Ostrom, winner of a Nobel Memorial Prize in Economic Sciences in 2009, is that such regimes succeed partly because of "shared norms and other-regarding preferences" (Ostrom 2005:20). Nevertheless, in one chapter focusing on shared norms and values, Ostrom (2005:132) seems to avoid such words as *religious, sacred,* or *spirituality,* as in the following sentence: "The institutions [human beings] grow up in—families, schools, play-grounds, neighborhoods—differentially reward or punish them over time so that intrinsic and extrinsic motivations are learned and developed over time." That is, she names playgrounds and schools as sites for learning rewards, punishments, and motivations but neglects to mention sacred places or places of worship, which are also centers for learning norms and values and motivations. In the same chapter, Ostrom reviews the work of other theorists on the importance of people's developing a "shared mental model" that will greatly influence their choices. She then writes, "Vivid rit-ual or symbol helps to select one mental model over others. The resulting congruence in behavior and outcomes helps to reinforce that model among those sharing the same culture" (Ostrom 2005:108). It is difficult to contemplate a more powerful framework for "vivid ritual or symbol" than religious belief and practice. Therefore, here we will explicitly examine the role of religion in Guatemala for emphasizing the sacredness of nature—a "mental model" that can motivate human beings to protect the natural environment. Ostrom's observation is that mental models are reinforced "among those sharing the same culture"; alternatively, we ask whether we may share mental models and rituals *across* cultures, finding common themes, negotiating meanings, and then working for a common aim. In an even deeper sense than E. O. Wilson's (2006) science-religion alliance, may we experience a radical pluralism for the sake of environmental survival?

A SHARED UNDERSTANDING

This story begins in late 1990, when I made my first trip to Latin America during a six-week research trip to Guatemala to conduct inter-views for a study of liberation theology. The research eventually resulted in a publication, but I was called in another direction on that first journey: to work against rural hunger and deforestation in the spectacular countryside of Guatemala. Months later in Florida, a friend and I came up with the ambitious name for a nonprofit organization, Alliance for International Reforestation, because we liked the AIR acronym and the idea of using alliances. We knew only that we wanted projects to be *based in the local communities and to include environmental education, as well as tree nurseries,* and we knew we would need 501(c)(3) status from the Internal Revenue Service to make US fundraising possible. The first major donation, however, was made without any tax exemption, solely because the Washington, DC, donor wanted to encourage the community-based approach, which was fairly novel in 1992. In a move that would become standard for AIR's operations in the United States, I found a friend willing to *volunteer* her professional expertise to obtain 501(c)(3) status, which took many months and countless forms.

I returned to Guatemala in 1992 with my daughter Rachel, followed by many more visits until the region of Chimaltenango became a second home for both of us. In 1993, I was given a sabbatical by Stetson University and was able to spend several months in Guatemala hiring staff members, one by one. At one point, I was carrying the expenses of AIR on my credit card, but as the projects grew, so did the interest and support of environmentalists in Florida. I hired Chris Wunderlich as the executive director for AIR in Guatemala. Chris went on to find and hire AIR's first technicians and receptionist in Guatemala and worked as an extraordinary executive director from 1993 to 1998. He established the basic framework for setting up long-term tree nurseries and sustainable farming projects. When Chris left AIR, with some foresight I decided that from then on the leadership and all paid staff would be native to the nation where we worked (Guatemala and later Nicaragua); all others would be volunteers. In 1998, I made the unorthodox decision to elevate Cecilia Ramirez from receptionist to executive director because she was resourceful and hardworking and had a bachelor's degree in business. Undoubtedly, as a woman, I was more willing to test Cecilia's ability to be the director than a male chairman of the board would have been, and it was a correct choice. It was one of many serendipitous decisions that have had strong, positive ramifications for AIR's success.

AIR remains a small organization, but with many years of stability and growing prestige in the regions where we work. AIR now has a staff of eight full-time persons in Guatemala, in the departments of Chimaltenango and Sololá, with plans to expand to another area of the country. All paid staff members of AIR are life-long residents of the areas where they work in Guatemala; four staff members are Kaqchikel Mayas, and one is a K'icheé Maya. Long-term student volunteers from Japan, England, and the United States work for periods of six months to two years and provide valuable research and labor, but these volunteers are under the strict supervision of the Guatemalan executive director. AIR staff and volunteers have constructed well over two hundred tree nurseries in ninety villages (at publication), trained thousands of farmers and schoolteachers in sustainable agriculture, constructed hundreds of fuel-efficient stoves, and planted almost four million trees. Importantly, it has become clear to us over the years that AIR's work is linked to conservation of the Mayan tropical forest far to the north, because rural-to-rural migration is the major source of rapid population increase in the northern Department of Petén (Carr 2004). That is, rural residents in the central and southern areas leave unproductive farms to become farmers in the north, where they often burn areas of the remaining forests in Guatemala for planting. However, if farmers are able to increase their crop yields without expensive fertilizers or pesticides and in a sustainable way—with trees—they are more likely to stay in the place of their birth, which has ramifications for the environment. We return to this topic of stability versus migration later.

Furthermore, AIR technicians are careful to work with preexisting common-property regimes rather than disrupt them, because residents in each community select their own leadership teams and simply incorporate AIR methodologies into their local "rules in use" regarding common properties. The technicians do not disrupt the local system of recognized boundaries, sanctions, and rewards (Ostrom 1990, 2005). In 2004, AIR was named the outstanding environmental organization in Guatemala by the National Institute of Agriculture and Forestry; in 2008, AIR was recognized with a grant from the United Nations Permanent Forum on Indigenous Issues; in 2011, AIR received the J. Sterling Morton Award from the National Arbor Day Foundation.

When I was in Chimaltenango in 2008, a group of us, including Executive Director Cecilia Ramirez, visited several of AIR's oldest reforestation projects, where the AIR team had established tree nurseries and mapped the area for both farming and conservation fourteen years earlier. As we drove into the high mountains, I commented to my AIR companions that it did not look at all familiar to me. The AIR technicians delighted in reminding me that when we had been to the area years ago, there were only bushes on the mountain slopes and now there were forests. They began pointing out forested slopes above and below us that they and the residents had planted in 1994 and 1995, tall trees still standing and shielding the streams below from erosion and mudslides. We met with several families, proud to show us the trees and telling us about their productive crops and asking about "Cristóbal" (Chris Wunderlich). I recognized many faces that day from my visits fourteen years earlier, but one young woman in particular looked familiar to me. After introductions, I realized that I had a photograph of her at age 7 (figure 7.1), which I had used in slide

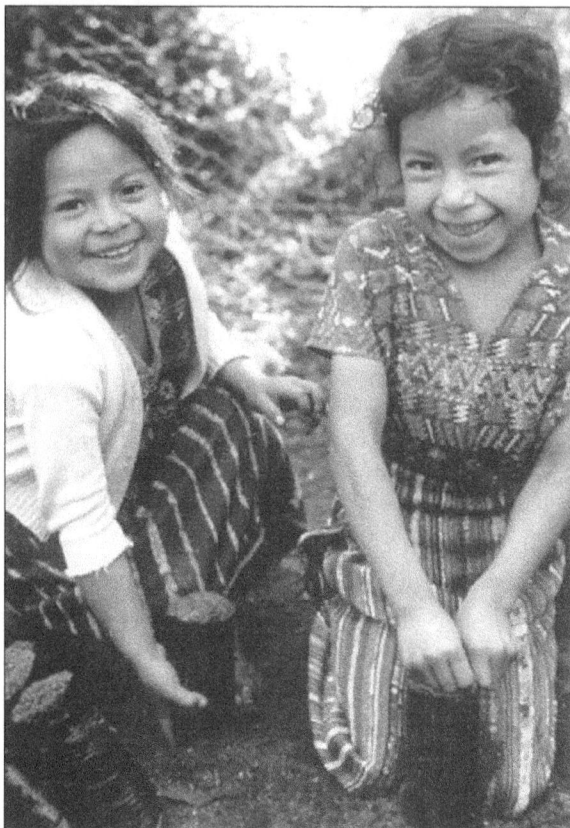

FIGURE 7.1

Children filling seed bags in one of AIR's nurseries, 1994.

presentations. I told her that and thanked her for her beautiful smile, which had helped me raise funds for Guatemala. It was an exciting illustration of a successful cross-cultural partnership over the long term because even though AIR's technician had left years ago, that young woman now has a tree nursery of her own (figure 7.2).

I share the story of AIR's founding in some detail because it reveals what I now believe to be the ironic secret to AIR's success, which is that my total inexperience in creating an organization is what resulted in a successful design, because I almost always deferred to local abilities and leadership, and still do. Similarly, my lack of expertise about Guatemala meant that my attitude has been one of observation and gradual sharing. I made mistakes, especially in the beginning years, but my desire and need to learn

FIGURE 7.2
The young woman is standing in a tree and plant nursery of her own (2008), where she is applying methods her parents learned from AIR technicians in the 1990s. She is the child on the left in figure 7.1.

rather than teach have meant that AIR is really an indigenous organization that just happens to have a US connection. Now that eighteen years have passed, including thousands of email exchanges and dozens of lengthy visits to Guatemala, I look back on the challenges and process of mutual learning I have experienced through AIR's development. On such reflection, it is clear that a key component in AIR's success as a cross-cultural organization has been the discovery of a shared spiritual motivation for the work of conservation and sustainable living. The examples below illustrate the pragmatic power of such motivation, which can overcome setbacks and cultural gaps because of an underlying respect and shared understanding of why we are working so hard together. Lessons I have learned from the Guatemalan participants over the past eighteen years, particularly about the nexus of religious faith and environmental activism, are supported by a growing scholarship, as we see throughout this volume. The examples focus on themes of creation stories, ritual, and sacred places because they are common to religious belief systems around the world and NGO participants will benefit from learning and respecting these beliefs and practices, regardless of the location.

CREATION STORIES

Creation stories are basic teachings transmitted to succeeding genera-tions that can serve as starting points for mobilizing popular support for conservation and environmental restoration efforts. In the related fields of environmental ethics and ecotheology, numerous studies explore environ-mental themes in sacred texts and teachings in the majority of world reli-gions (Anderson 2004; Callicott and Nelson 2004; Coward and Maguire 2000; Daneel 2001; McFague 2008; Northcott 1996; Oelschlaeger 1994). The authors of these studies note that virtually all religions have creation stories about the goodness and giftedness of the natural environment. It is also a widespread belief that defiling nature is an insult to the Creator(s) but protecting or restoring nature is pleasing to the Creator(s).

A particularly bold argument by environmental ethicist Oelschlaeger (1994) is that religious beliefs across cultures can inspire a coalition for environmental protection among religious groups and with scientists. Oelschlaeger offers a specific sociolinguistic framework for forming this alliance, which entails simply reading and listening for common ground among various religions, and for breaking down counterproductive barri-ers that exist between religion and science. Oelschlaeger explains that such an approach is respectful of all religious beliefs and does not require conversion, only listening with respect to stories and worldviews. Thus, he writes, "A merit of a sociolinguistic perspective (that the reading and rereading of texts, that the telling and retelling of stories, defines our specif-ically human beingness) is that no discourse is marginalized. Narratives are simply that, narratives, and not one enjoys a privileged position, not one is 'totalizing.' Not even scientific discourse, such as the theory of evolution, can escape its history, its social construction" (1994:127).

Oelschlaeger emphasizes that the common ground, the mobilizing symbol that is already at least implicit in most religions is "caring for cre-ation." Thus, he seems to offer the usual perspective of "(multiple) cultures interacting with (a single) Nature," instead of the more open *multinatural-ism* that Ivakhiv proposes in chapter 11 (this volume). That is, apparent sim-ilarities may be illusory when cultures have diverse understandings not only of Creation but also of Nature and Caring. This difficulty does not mean that we give up on the possibility of cross-cultural communication, but that we listen with new sensitivity and openness, believing that different under-standings are bridgeable through translation. I shall give specific examples of how AIR staff, residents, and volunteers often discover shared religious-ecological worldviews through working and listening.

The starting point of the creation story for the Mayan people has been written in the sacred Mayan text *Popol Vuh*. Mayan linguists have studied ancient hieroglyphs and Spanish translations of Mayan texts from the 1500s for many years. Tedlock, one of the most prominent linguists, produced an English translation of the primary sacred text in 1985. Although some variations occur in different Mayan language groups (Montejo 2001), I use Tedlock's translation here for the creation story.

In the creation, the gods made the Earth before they made humans. As the *Popol Vuh* recounts, "first the land, the mountains, and the valleys were formed; they were divided by the waters, which ran freely through the hills and separated when the mountains appeared. This was how the earth was created when it was formed by the Heart of Heaven and the Heart of Earth, and that is how they were named when they were first formed" (Tedlock 1985:39, 40). The making of humans was problematic for the gods and required various attempts. First, beings were made of mud, but they were unable to walk or keep their shape and were unable to reproduce and they eventually dissolved into nothing. Second, beings were made of wood, which could walk, talk, and reproduce, but they were not orderly in their actions and they forgot to visit shrines or call upon the gods. They were soon washed away by hurricane flooding (in other versions, they burned up in fires), and their only descendants are the monkeys who live in the jungle today. Finally, one of the female gods, Xmucane, ground corn into fine flour, mixed it with water, and modeled four people from the corn dough (which explains the significance of making tortillas in the same fashion today with every meal). These people are called "mother-fathers," and they serve as symbolic androgynous parents to everyone who follows in their lineage (Tedlock 1985). Humans are to live in harmony and balance and to care for creation and understand its cycles, but according to *Popol Vuh* teachings, two things often get in the way to make man perverse: riches and power. The Long Mayan Calendar says that in the year 2012, the era of the people of corn will end and humans will enter into a fourth era, the era of light, which will be better (Gaspar Pedro González, personal communication, 2007).

Creation stories are the primordial myths of origin and, as such, have "culture-forming power" (Oelschlaeger 1994:222). The significance is not because they are taken literally (although they may be) but because of what they teach: creation is good, and we have a responsibility not to impair the creation. The *Popol Vuh* story emphasizes agriculture and the rhythms of nature, the separate but apparently egalitarian roles of men and women, the evolution of humans through eras of formation and destruction, and the desire of the gods for homage. The creation story also shows the sacredness of maize (corn), in which the maize life cycle of clearing, planting, harvesting, grinding corn, and cooking and eating tortillas is at the center of Mayan beliefs. Thus, the sacredness of maize is about more than agriculture—it is about rhythm and balance between the physical and spiritual worlds and the unity of humans with nature. The four cardinal directions in the Mayan cross, for instance, are represented by the four colors of maize—east is red, west is black, south is green or yellow, and north is blue—with a Ceiba tree in the center connecting the different planes of existence. In the famous memoir of Rigoberta Menchú, winner of the 1992 Nobel Peace Prize, she includes a passage that describes the ten days of ritual before planting the sacred maize crop:

> We make our vows for ten days so that you concede us permission, your permission, Mother Earth, who are sacred, to feed us and give our children what they need. We do not abuse you, we only beg your permission, you who are part of the natural world and part of the family of our parents and our grandparents....
>
> The sun, as the channel to the one God, receives the plea from his children that they should never violate the rights of all the other beings which surround them. This is how we renew our prayer which says that men, the children of the one God, must respect the life of the trees, the birds, the animals around us. [Menchú 1984:57–58]

A significant point about Menchú's description is the common practice of asking permission of the Earth before it is cultivated, because the Mayas do not consider themselves owners of the land in the deepest sense.

The complex topic of syncretism in Guatemala is beyond the scope of this chapter, except to note that traditional Mayas have developed over centuries a sophisticated combination of Catholic liturgy and Mayan spirituality. Most devout Kaqchikel Mayas easily bring offerings to Catholic saints, as well as to the Heart of Heaven and the Heart of Earth, and *cofradia* street processions include figures from the *Popol Vuh*, as well as from the Christian Bible. Menchú, like the majority of AIR staff members and the farmers with whom AIR works, is a Roman Catholic and a Maya, and I have frequently observed that the staff members and farmers use elements of both belief systems easily. Given the Mayan emphasis on connectedness, perhaps we should not be surprised that blending of two different religions often occurs. Dualism is artificial in this cosmology, which often translates into religious pluralism.

In the difficult summer of 2010, I witnessed a particularly dramatic example of the belief that defiling nature is an insult to the Creator but

FIGURE 7.3
Farmer in Xiquin Sanai after ceremony at shrine in field, 2010.

restoring nature is pleasing. That summer, central Guatemala suffered from intensive rains and mudslides. Invariably, deforested slopes had the worst mudslides and established trees prevented them. AIR technicians had just begun to work in the community of Xiquin Sanai, and they received an urgent request from the group leader to bring volunteers to help plant trees. On their arrival, the farmer explained that he had cut all the trees to plant his crop and the Creator was angry at this destruction and the bottom half of his crop had collapsed into a mudslide. He showed us a shrine in the field where the family had sacrificed chickens and performed a ritual asking forgiveness for cutting the trees, thanking God for not destroying the entire crop and pledging to reforest the hillside that day, which we did (figure 7.3).

POEMS AND RITUAL

Creation stories, then, contain morals—about maintaining the harmony, balance, and rhythm of life, about being temporary guardians rather than owners of nature's resources. Rituals flow from such creation stories and beliefs, as we see in the example from Xiquin Sanai. As evidence of the commonality of a creation-care ethic and rituals, note the illustration from another continent—Africa—in chapter 10 of this volume. There, Daneel recounts how the Earthkeepers' reforestation efforts in Zimbabwe in the 1990s always incorporated ecumenical religious ceremony. The participating organizations framed the work with Mass, dance, liturgy, and prayer written by local religious leaders and meeting the people in their own lives. In sharing experiences during the SAR seminar, Daneel confirmed that the rituals and beliefs were *the language* of the Earthkeeping movement in Zimbabwe. He also hypothesized that the demise of the movement arose from human greed and envy within the organization, as well as the political upheaval, indicating the need for compelling rituals to help combat human frailties.

The powerful scholarship on ritual by anthropologist Rappaport (1993, 1999) notes that rituals are events that in their doing accomplish what they intend and also *commit* the participants to that outcome. Thus, in planting trees ritualistically, participants gain more than the outcome of trees: they gain a heightened social sense of being with one another, and the activity is ingrained with meaning (Joel Robbins, personal communication, 2009). The chapters in this book by Scanlan Lyons, Robbins, Tucker, Schnell, and Daneel (chapters 2, 3, 6, 8, and 10, respectively) similarly illustrate the importance of ritual in diverse geographic contexts. Rappaport (1999) goes further to suggest that the practice of ritual is linked to our very humanity, and he writes with urgency about the need for science and religion to be reconciled, to perpetuate the rituals that science often discounts.

This concept seems to be a wisdom that the indigenous Mayas have as a second nature, because they constantly imbue the environmental work with AIR with a ritual meaning, even when the North American or European volunteers must be reminded to include the ceremony. One memorable example of a cultural divide was when a forestry graduate student from Spain volunteered with AIR for six months. Bothered by the time-consuming blessing of a work site before we began planting trees, he began to lecture the group on the mountainside about the need to embrace science and move beyond backward superstition. The residents were angered, baffled, or amused—but this attitude is precisely the type of disrespect and proselytizing AIR seeks to avoid.

The common practice of the AIR technicians is to encourage and make time for religious rituals throughout the day—as in blessings before meals. Occasionally, residents will even create a new ritual when inspired, which occurred in Acatenango, Guatemala: a volunteer simply asked our

Guatemalan hostess what the environment meant to her, and Doña Santiaga responded that her feelings were "complicated" and she would reply later. The next day, as we were planting trees on the mountainside, she asked for time to recite her poem to all of us to express how she felt about the *Creación de Díos* (translated by author, 2008):

> Sacred environment
> Monument of Creation
> God, God has designed you as a
> Model and a Blessing
> Walking, walking
> Today I could not see
> Those immense trees where
> I once used to play
> Walking, walking
> The fresh air embraced me
> And the water calmed me
> Together, let us save
> The Environment

In her poem, Santiaga clearly shows that the fields are more than a place of work for her; she stresses that the connection she has with the environment is not only physical but emotional and spiritual as well—in the holistic view that one encounters frequently. For Santiaga, the fields are a sacred place, a "Monument of Creation." Santiaga goes on to say that to do harm to the environment is to commit a sin and that the deforestation she sees around her causes her grief that she feels "in [her] heart and in [her] spirit." But also note that Santiaga was not content simply to write the poem and give it to the volunteer who had asked her the question; rather, she desired a ritualistic sharing of the poem, a performance, that would heighten the commitment to the day of tree planting for the entire group.

A similar illustration of turning an analytical question into a profound experience occurred for me in my home. Don Eladio Iquique Socoy, a Kaqchikel Maya from the town of Cerro Alto, visited our home in Florida for several weeks in 2001. Don Eladio is a respected community leader in Cerro Alto, and because of this respect, as well as his knowledge of fruit tree grafting and agroforestry, he became the first technician we hired. He worked with AIR in dozens of villages for ten years, until an injury forced his retirement; his son Luis continues as an AIR technician.

Knowing how eloquent Don Eladio is on virtually any subject, I asked him during his visit simply to write some thoughts explaining "why he worked for the environment" (see also Hallum 2003). He chose the title *The Relation between Natural Resources and What It Is to Be Human* for his words (my translation):

> *The relation between natural resources and what it is to be human:* When we are in a forest and where we see and listen to the songs of the birds, the sound of the rivers, when we feel the fresh air, enjoy the beauty of nature, then we ought to think that God is there because it is His creation and He desires that we are able to be happy. But also, we have the responsibility to have a very tight relation with her, so He wants to say that we ought to care for her because our children and our grandchildren and all the generations that come after also have a right to enjoy these natural resources that God has created.

> To love God, then, is to love nature....When you work for nature, you are working for the people—directly. There is no separation between helping Nature and helping people. *Do you understand?* God manifests Himself in nature. He shows Himself to us in nature, and also, He shows Himself to us in every face. [Don Eladio Iquique Socoy, personal communication, 2001]

A few striking themes emerge from this brief essay. One is the urgency of Don Eladio's words to me and his desire to teach me (*"Do you understand?"*) and to meet me in my own life of perhaps not understanding the tight connections among God, nature, and humanity. He wrote these words during his first trip outside Guatemala, where he noticed, among other things, that "the people live in the cars!" Although most understand the systemic interconnectedness within "nature," many of us seem to have forgotten that we are a part of nature and rather view it as accessible to scientists only or as an outside system we occasionally visit—a disconnect Don Eladio observed. His words teach, and they also explain away the conflict often found in scholarly and activist literature of conservation versus development of livelihoods (Brechin 2003; Redford and Sanderson 2000; Terborgh 1999). In the cosmology offered by Don Eladio, there is no conflict. He explains that the linkage between helping nature and helping people is not even indirect; rather, it is direct, because all of life is from one source.

THE SACREDNESS OF PLACE

Until recently, the knowledge, beliefs, and sustainable practices of the indigenous Mayas have remained remarkably in place despite centuries of conquest, civil war, and discrimination. For instance, mapping by anthropologist Mac Chapin and the Center for the Support of Native Lands (Lovgren 2003) has confirmed that intact forest lands coincide with the most stable indigenous populations. The environmental benefits of indigenous sacred places are now being recognized by the Convention on Biological Diversity and by the International Union for Conservation of Nature (IUCN). At recent conferences, both institutions called for sacred places—now dubbed indigenous and community conserved areas (ICCAs)—to be assessed for inclusion in protected areas (Berkes 2008a). But the corollary is to guard sacred places from disruption in the first place, if at all possible, to avoid the movement of populations to places far away from ancestral homes and sacred areas. When they move into unfamiliar territory, the ancient desire for harmony with ancestral land is weakened and deforestation accelerates. The environmental impact of displacement of indigenous populations because of war, or lack of land title, or crop decline, or any other reason is severe. Migrant residents often feel they have not only lost ancestral ties but have lost their cultural and religious identities as well because these identities are centered on the places left behind. Certainly, if the African population in Zimbabwe had not been pushed into refugee status by the heavy-handed actions of dictator Robert Mugabe, the reforestation efforts could have deepened and spread. In Guatemala, there has been a massive influx of new residents into the northern Department of Petén since the end of the civil war in 1996. The population there in 1960 was approximately twenty thousand people, and the massive rain forest was intact, but the Petén population is now well over five hundred thousand. Swidden farming (often called "slash-and-burn") by thousands of these families is occurring too rapidly for regeneration, even within the legally "protected core" of the Maya Biosphere Reserve.

Anthropologists Kay Warren, in her studies of the Kaqchikel Mayas, and Richard Wilson, in his observations of the K'icheé Mayas, have uncovered many of the same themes regarding sacred places. Richard Wilson (1995) asserts from his field research that the Mayan identity is based most strongly on religion rather than ethnicity or any other dimension of culture or class. A major portion of his research describes the rituals surrounding thirteen sacred mountains called the tzuultaq'as, demonstrating the centrality of place. The belief is that the Creator placed the people and their ancestors on a particular piece of land, where guardian divinities live inside a particular mountain group. Thus, the mountain group defines the family identity. If trees are to be cut from the mountain or crops planted on it, the activity is done with reverence and with permission because the "master of the mountain" divinity may also become angry. It is still common for Kaqchikel Mayas to ask permission of the tree and mountain guardians before a tree is cut for firewood. It is common for farmers in Chimaltenango to give poems for trees that "make music for our ears" or to say that "trees are our sentinels, our guardians, our friends on this journey" and "to kill a tree is to kill the presence of life here." In a day of reforesting a farmer's field, the owner told us how he had wept when he first cleared the hillside of trees for firewood and planting, because his father and grandfather had planted the trees.

Warren (1998:167–169) emphasizes that within the narrated ritual poems honoring creation and ancestors, there is also a great deal of anxiety, as in this example:

> Our mothers came,
> Our grandmothers,
> Our grandfathers,
> In ancient times,
> With ancient history.
> They had good words.
> Good words were in their thoughts.
> They knelt before the Earth....
> Perhaps the word will continue,
> Perhaps the voice will continue,
> But now we cannot express ourselves well
> In the presence of the Earth.

This ominous poem offers a foreshadowing of what happens when younger generations become alienated from their ancestors and from their guardian mountain. One can argue that the residents of the migrant communities in Petén and other places in Guatemala may feel less reverence for the Earth because everything is so uncertain and because it is not the *place* of their ancestors who were left behind. When indigenous communities and generations are torn apart by war or forced migrations from lack of land, the ethic of treating the religious topography with reverence also begins to unravel. If AIR and other NGOs can help to make farming sustainable and crops more productive, families will experience less pressure to leave their ancestral homes; indirectly, the NGOs help to protect the undeveloped forests in other regions.

CONCLUSION

This chapter begins with a glance at social science literature about NGOs, common-pool resource regimes, and examples of environmental ethics and ecotheology literature. Another interdisciplinary field relevant to analysis of the nexus between religion and conservation is traditional ecological knowledge (TEK), primarily consisting of case studies of indigenous cultures. Because scholars influence one another, it is not a coincidence that these overlapping specializations, as well as new appreciation of indigenous peoples, criticism of NGOs, awareness of common-pool regimes, and urgent calls for sustainability, seem to have emerged around the same time: the mid-1980s. For instance, the IUCN sponsored a series of workshops on TEK from 1984 to 1989 that were a springboard for several case-study publications. Probably the most prolific scholar in this field is Canadian biologist Berkes (2008b:7), and his layered conceptualization of TEK is most helpful: "Traditional ecological knowledge [is] *a cumulative body of knowledge, practice, and belief, evolving by adaptive processes and handed down through generations by cultural transmission, about the relationship of living beings (including humans) with one another and with their environment.*"

Given the holistic sensibilities of indigenous knowledge throughout the world (Callicott and Nelson 2004; Daneel 2001; see also citations to ecotheology literature earlier in this chapter), this layered definition makes sense. It does not divide the empirical observations of knowledge (taxonomies, life cycles, distribution) from practices (tools, rules, techniques) or from beliefs (worldviews, ethics, rules, motivation). Rather, they are all reinforcing aspects of local decision making. Berkes stresses the vital distinction between TEK and Western thought: the holism of one versus the compartmentalization of Western thinking. Recall the words of Don Eladio, who automatically refers to creation as female, stresses the seamless interconnection of God, humanity, and nature, and removes the issue of a hierarchical priority or conflict over whether to serve humans *or* nature.

The unity of most non-Western traditions means that it is nonsensical to talk about preservation of nature *without humans* (except perhaps for the most sacred sites of rituals), because human society is as much a part of nature as anything else living. The wilderness and rainforests are not places to visit or research—they are home. Therefore, even the concept of an "off-limits" zone in a biosphere reserve makes little sense. I do not mean to say that no conservation ethic or practice exists among indigenous people, but it is an ethic of sustainable use and restoration rather than exclusion. Many case studies from the commons literature demonstrate that TEK, the complex of knowledge-practice-belief, can produce institutions that provide sustainability for living things for centuries (Berkes 2008b:235–238; Moran and Ostrom 2005; Ostrom 1990, 2005). A final point about Berkes' (2008b:23) TEK definition is that this knowledge is "evolving by adaptive processes"; not permanent knowledge that can be placed in a reference book, it is "lived knowledge" for indigenous people, which we can never get through a publication. The hubris of thinking that scholarship alone can lead to understanding of traditional knowledge has led to inaccurate stereotypes of indigenous people relative to the environment.

We are not essentializing indigenous beliefs here to make a simplistic argument that the Mayas, for instance, are automatically wise conservationists, at one with nature. Few, if any, anthropologists today hold such a view, recognizing that the indigenous vary in their sensibilities and values, just as other ethnic, racial, or cultural groups vary. There are examples from archaeology of indigenous cultures that hunted numerous species to extinction, and we have the infamous example of Easter Island, where the gradual deforestation by the ancestors of Polynesians was so severe, ecological collapse occurred. Nevertheless, the common indigenous perspectives of holism, the sanctity of nature, and the attachment to a particular ancestral place are in general more aligned with an ecological worldview than the Western tendency to compartmentalize.

This recognition leads us to the question we have been addressing throughout this chapter and which is often overlooked in the literature cited here: *How may an outside NGO best support environmental efforts in other countries, that is, work cross-culturally for a common goal of sustainability?* We are, at last, understanding through sharing research from anthropology, mapping, TEK, ecotheology, and common-pool resource theory how vital indigenous wisdom is for conservation—and how indigenous practices have been disrupted by war, migration, land seizures for economic profit, neoliberal free trade, and many other external factors. For the sake of conservation and livelihoods, how are we to respond as an outside culture?

After years of working with AIR in Guatemala—and seeing hundreds of tree nurseries and agroforestry systems established, 750 stoves constructed, and whole mountainsides reforested—I have two answers to this question. First, NGOs need to have an institutional design that defers to local leadership from the very beginning of the projects (not simply tacked on at the end, as a "supervisor"). Second, NGO members need to have an attitude of learning that embraces or, at least, respects local wisdom and religious ritual. One brief example further illustrates this local leadership and openness and involves AIR's addition of medicinal gardens in several of the Mayan communities. Such gardens were not part of the original ideas for the communities; however, some leadership groups began planting medicinal plants adjacent to the tree nurseries and began teaching the AIR technicians about the benefits of each plant. They explained to the staff that such plants were gifts from the Creator to humans and it would be an insult if the plants were not used for human health. Now, AIR has assisted with several new gardens, a demonstration medicinal garden was planted at the AIR Training Center, and this TEK is being shared with anyone who will listen.

On a deeper motivational level, a central variable that contributes to the success of the majority of AIR's projects is the spiritual understanding about caring for creation that is so easily shared in Guatemala. One may argue that a deep-seated religious *faith* is especially important for environmental work because it takes a long time to see the results of the labor and self-interest is not immediately apparent. This argument is similar to the idea of faith as an attitude of perseverance presented by Ballestero (chapter 9, this volume), but with more of an optimistic trust that we are part of a cosmology. The belief in the sacredness of creation and the interconnectedness of humanity and nature thus contributes to the faithful patience necessary for environmental efforts. I can personally add that the long view of faith and hope is as important for the administrator and fundraiser as it is for the technicians and farmers planting trees.

All the vivid rituals, symbols, and stories examined in this chapter are examples of the shared "mental models" that reinforce normative rules for sustainability in particular situations (Ostrom 2005:108). With care, an NGO can enter into such a system and enhance the sustainability. Thus, the Guatemalan staff of AIR has a close relationship of mutual trust and respect with the Kaqchikel and K'icheé Mayas that encourages the villagers to implement these new agroforestry methods over the long term. This relationship is strengthened because of a few variables already noted: the staff members are Guatemalan, they work with each village for a minimum of five years, they defer to the residents often, and they encourage preexisting common-property regimes with local leadership and rules.

The relationship with residents is also strengthened because the staff members use a vocabulary filled with familiar cultural and religious symbols and stories. It does not take much observation to notice the ease and frequency of religious references among the residents and the AIR technicians as they work in tree nurseries, fields, or training classes—prayers before travel and meals, blessing of work sites, hymns while working. Volunteers from an outside NGO need to set aside the notion that nature belongs only to the realm of science and instead bring a heightened sensitivity, respect, and sharing in the religious values and rituals that animate environmental efforts.

8

Believing Is Seeing

A Religious Perspective on Mountaineering
in the Japanese Alps

Scott Schnell

Do the environmental problems that now confront us call for basically scientific and technological responses, or are we also in need of images and concepts that inspire more ecologically mindful ways of living? In a critical assessment of the American environmental movement—specifically, its failure to reach beyond the limits of a special interest group—Shellenberger and Nordhaus (2004) offer several suggestions for appealing to the broader public. One such suggestion is that environmentalists "tap into the creative worlds of myth-making, even religion, not to better sell narrow and technical policy proposals but rather to figure out who we are and who we need to be" (2004:34).

This seems to underscore the mental dimension of environmentalism—the realm of conceptualization. Religion, after all, remains one of the principal means by which people order the world around them and ascribe meaning to their experiences. Understandably, however, many environmental advocates are wary of dogmatic assertions that cannot be empirically verified, such as a supernatural presence or design. But strict adherence to dogma is by no means the exclusive province of religion, nor does religion, in all its diverse forms, necessarily presuppose a supernatural entity. Geertz's (1965:4) definition of religion—one of the most widely cited in the social sciences—makes no specific mention of the supernatural per se; in fact, it seems to apply rather broadly to *any* school of thought, religious or otherwise, in terms of "(1) a system of symbols which acts to (2) establish powerful, pervasive, and long-lasting moods and motivations in men by (3) formulating conceptions of a general order of existence and (4) clothing these conceptions with such an aura of factuality that (5) the moods and motivations seem uniquely realistic."

But how are the moods and motivations instilled, and how are the conceptions enacted such that they register a positive impact in the material world? The answer, I suggest, is *ritual*, considered here in the most fundamental terms as any activity that expresses or conveys symbolic meaning. Although ritual is a prominent element of traditional subsistence technologies (Anderson 1996; Berkes 2008b; Lansing 2006; R. Nelson 1983), it seems to have been all but eliminated from industrialized food and forest production. Recently, however, William R. Jordan III has incorporated ritual into his ecological restoration work at the University of Wisconsin Arboretum. Through his exposure to anthropology, Jordan (2003:5) recognizes ritual not as formulaic or prescribed behavior so much as an ongoing creative process: "At the deepest level, ritual offers the only means we have of transcending, criticizing, or revising a morality or [an] ethical formulation prescribed by authority or handed down by tradition. Most fundamentally, it is the means by which humans generate, re-create, and renew transcendent values such as community, meaning, beauty, love, and the sacred, on which both ethics and morality depend." These values, in turn, exert an influence on more mundane activities, such as our daily interactions with the landscapes we inhabit.

Jennings (1982:117) takes the potential for creativity a bit further, describing ritual "as a way of coming to know, that is, as a way of searching for and discovering knowledge." While the movements themselves may be prescribed, their inherent meanings are often left for the participants to discover on their own, and it is by performing the movements that certain attitudes are formulated, certain realizations achieved. From this perspective, knowledge does not precede ritual; rather, it is through ritual that knowledge is acquired.

These ideas suggest that focusing only on the outward manifestations of ritualized activity is missing the point; we must also consider ritual's effect on the heart and mind of the individual participant. I shall illustrate using a simple example. Several years ago I was invited by a group of rock climbers to help pick up the trash that had accumulated at one of Iowa's state parks. As we moved out across the landscape, gathering up discarded items ranging in size from cigarette butts and bottle caps to old automobile tires, I remember thinking how futile our efforts seemed to be. After all, uncaring visitors would soon return to deposit more of their refuse, and in a few weeks the trash would be right back in place. Also, considering the vastness of the earth's surface and all the garbage that has been dumped upon it, what impact would our limited actions have in improving the quality of the environment? Then it suddenly dawned on me that I was focusing too narrowly on the material effects of our efforts and not enough on the experiential—that is, the mental and emotional. By engaging in this activity, we were impressing upon ourselves and one another the importance of environmental stewardship, of caring for the landscape. Moreover, since littering itself would surely continue, our cleanup efforts had to be ongoing—stewardship implied continual vigilance. There was even a sense that, since I had come to this realization while others perhaps had not, I had to be doubly dedicated in order to offset their indifference. Each act of picking up an item of garbage and depositing it in the proper receptacle further ingrained these ideas, and the lessons were registered upon my person through physical exertion and fatigue. An obvious social element was present as well; while working, I began to converse with other participants, and, not surprisingly, we discovered that we shared an interest in ecology and a concern for the environment. Soon we were exchanging contact information, sharing ideas, and suggesting relevant books to read. In a sense, our attitudes and perceptions were being mobilized toward environmental activism. "The hand teaches the heart," as the old saying goes, meaning that activity in the service of an ideal, such as Daneel's tree-planting sacrament (chapter 10, this volume), will ingrain the ideal more deeply and enhance the actor's commitment to it.

Of course, picking up trash hardly fits the concept of ritual as it is normally construed. When ascribed with a higher ideal or motivation, however, even a mundane activity may be said to contain a ritual aspect. Reader (1995), for example, describes how the common chore of sweeping in Japan becomes a metaphorical enactment for ridding the mind of counterproductive images and imposing order on a seemingly chaotic world. Thus, "actions which appear, at least on the surface, to be ordinary and everyday ones, may assume the status of rituals endowed with inner symbolic meanings" (1995:228). Reader recalls how, during his sojourn at a Zen temple, he and some of the resident monks were assigned to sweep the temple garden every morning even when it was largely devoid of leaves and debris. This, to him, initially seemed like a waste of time. But watching the monks unquestioningly rise to the task led him to an important insight into the nature of Zen discipline—that even an ordinary activity like sweeping can become a kind of meditative exercise:

> The importance of work, in this respect, was in the performance of an action rather than with its practical ends.... [T]he central issue was of going through the motions, with a ritual performance that stated both to themselves and to all around that they were doing the right thing in the proper way at the correct time. Cleaning and sweeping the garden was a ritual performance and hence, as with ritual in general, its importance need not primarily, or at all, be with the external actions involved but with the inner meanings they symbolized. [Reader 1995:230]

Is there a place for ritual—or religion more generally—in the contemporary world dominated by science and technology? It has long been theorized that science will eventually replace religion as the preferred explanatory framework, its superiority being routinely demonstrated through empirical observation (for example, Berger 1967; Dawkins 2006; Frazer 1890; Freud 1927; Tylor 1920). So far, however, the displacement of religion by science has yet to transpire. Of course, challenges to the theory of religion's demise have been equally persistent, one of the best known being an essay by Evans-Pritchard (1937) titled "The Notion of Witchcraft Explains Unfortunate Events." Its argument is that while science can address the question of *how* things happen—misfortunes, for example—it cannot offer satisfactory explanations for *why* they involve certain people or occur at particular moments. Religious belief, in Evans-Pritchard's case witchcraft, supplies the missing information. However, it is not just negative events that religion helps to situate within broader fields of meaning, as several of the contributions in this volume attest (see, for example, Norget, Hallum, and Daneel, chapters 5, 7, and 10, respectively). At the very least, religion offers some emotional support under trying circumstances or a moral compass for negotiating difficult situations. Thus, religion will likely persist even as science and technology proceed.

Here again, Japan, the locus of my own research, offers an instructive example. Japan is widely considered one of the world's most technologically advanced and well-educated postindustrial societies. And generally speaking, the Japanese people, too, are skeptical of dogmatic religion, having witnessed firsthand how easily it can be manipulated in support of militaristic tendencies. Yet this does not stop them from flocking to Shinto shrines and Buddhist temples on certain occasions (such as the New Year holiday), nor from praying for success in their endeavors, buying protective amulets, and commemorating the souls of their ancestors.

Reader and Tanabe (1998) explain this seeming discrepancy by distinguishing *cognitive* belief (or what I would call *literal* belief)—that which appeals to the intellect—from *affective* belief, that which appeals to feelings or emotions. Affective belief is a reflection not of what one knows to be factually accurate, but of the way one thinks and feels about things. Thus, a person can literally be a rocket scientist yet find no incongruity in visiting a shrine to offer prayers for the success of a mission and the safety of the crew. The ritual is a way of physically enacting one's sincerity and commitment, directed inward toward the self as much as outward toward some supernatural authority.

In expanding on this notion of affective belief, I would like to reverse the order of another well-known adage by suggesting that *believing is seeing*; in other words, what we refer to as "religious belief" is not so much an assertion of factuality as a favored way of envisioning or perceiving the world. As Guthrie (1993:42), citing Wittgenstein, reminds us, "we never merely see, but always 'see as.'" *Perception*, then, is simultaneously an act of *interpretation* based on our own preconceived notions—our "beliefs." I use "seeing," therefore, not in referring simply to visual perception, but to opinions and perspectives—the way one "sees" an issue—which can change over time, given the right opportunity or inspiration.

I do not mean to reduce religion to a mere psychological process, because the difference between perception and revelation will always be moot. To extend Evans-Pritchard's (1937) assertion, science can explain the mechanisms by which a vision is received but cannot predict the meaning or significance it will assume in the heart and mind of the recipient; *that* is where the religious dimension comes into play.

I illustrate these ideas by presenting two competing conceptual approaches to mountaineering in the Japanese Alps. One involves climbing as a recreational activity; the objective is simply to reach the top and return safely, enjoying the challenge, the sense of accomplishment, and the view along the way. This is often accompanied by assertions of mastery over nature such as "conquering" a mountain or staging a "final assault" upon the summit. The alternative, however, sees climbing as an act of devotion—an expression of humility, respect, and gratitude to the mountains as the source of one's sustenance, with the emphasis not on asserting mastery over—but rather reestablishing a sense of unity with—nature.

"OPENING" THE MOUNTAINS

In conducting ethnographic fieldwork, anthropologists are often drawn toward what they inwardly admire and perhaps find missing in their own experience. For me, that coveted missing aspect was the opportunity to engage in a kind of animistic veneration of the natural landscape. As a youth, I often wondered why people worshipped within the human-made confines of a church or temple building when they could immerse themselves instead in nature's grandeur and thereby recapture the sense of awe and mystery that must surely lie at the heart of religious experience (see Norget's discussion of "the numinous," chapter 5, this volume).

The Japanese seem to have recognized this, at least within their philosophical and literary traditions. That recognition is what drew me to Japan as my focus of ethnographic inquiry and to the rugged mountains that compose its interior. Mountains are by their very nature ethereal and mystifying. They reach into the clouds, blurring the distinction between earth and sky. It is little wonder that the Japanese, like people all over the world and throughout history, looked to the high mountains in seeking to transcend the realm of ordinary experience and routine.

But again, contemporary Japan is a highly urbanized, postindustrial society, having achieved economic and technological parity with the most prosperous nations of the West and in some respects surpassing them. Too often this has meant abandoning its own traditions in deference to the standards of Europe and North America, which in terms of modern economic and cultural development have long dominated the global arena.

Thus, despite Japan's long historical tradition of venerating the mountains, the most celebrated figure in the history of Japanese mountaineering, ironically, is an Englishman named Walter Weston (see Ion 1999). While serving as an Anglican missionary based in Kobe during the 1890s, Weston succeeded in summiting the highest peaks in a range of lofty mountains now popularly known as the Japanese Alps, or Northern Alps (figure 8.1). For this he is attributed with having "opened" the area to recreational climbing and is widely described as the "father of modern mountaineering" in Japan. Every year on the first Sunday in June, a festival is held to honor his memory at Kamikōchi in Nagano prefecture, the most popular point of access to the rugged Northern Alps.

Weston's heroic stature has been fostered in part by his own prolific memoirs, wherein he consistently portrays himself as an explorer of regions yet unknown—from a European perspective, that is. A case in point is his account of ascending a high and majestic-looking mountain called Kasagatake (Mount Kasa), which now lies within the boundaries of

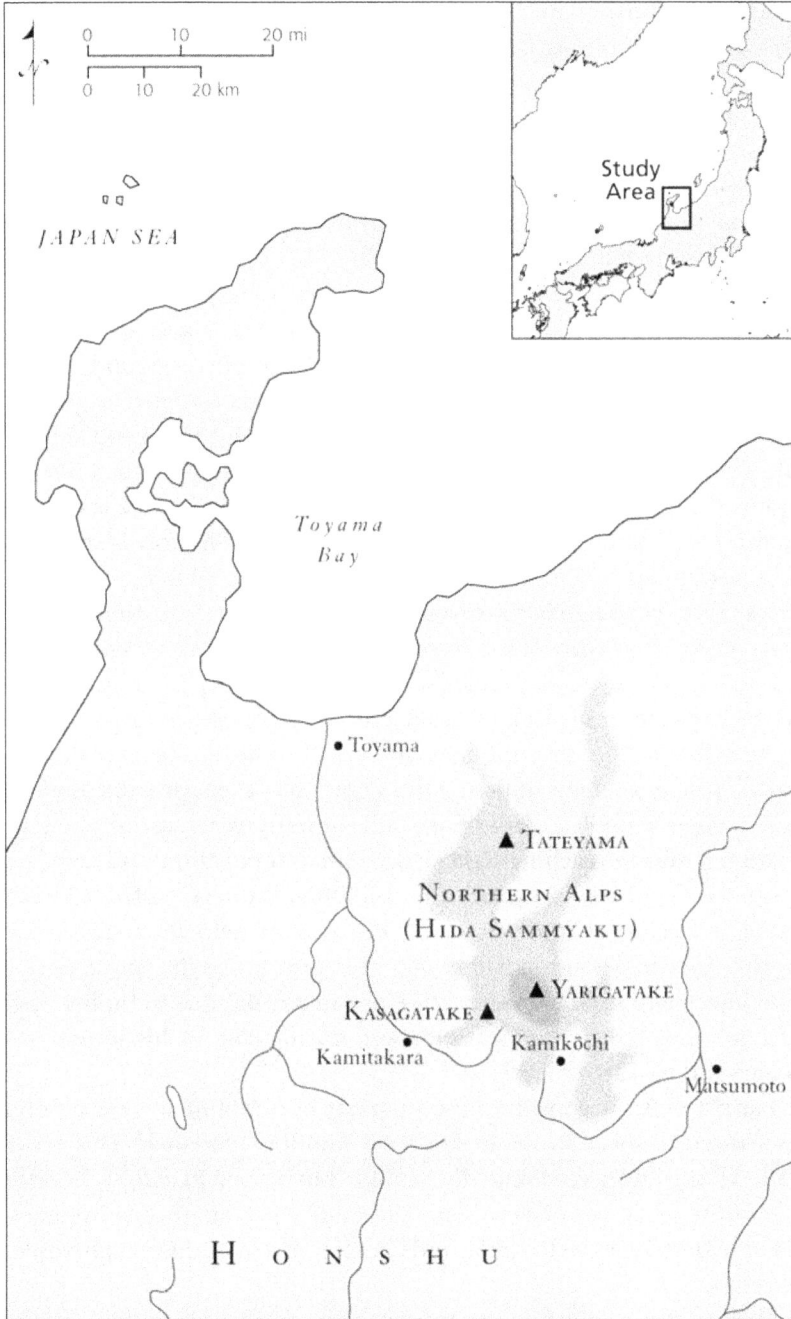

FIGURE 8.1

Map of central Japan showing locations mentioned in this chapter.

Kamitakara township in Takayama, northern Gifu prefecture (Schnell 2007). After overcoming a series of challenges posed by thick vegetation, slippery rocks, and generally rugged terrain, Weston and two companions finally arrive at the summit, guided by a pair of local hunters. He writes, "We found a tiny cairn, erected by the hunters on some former visit." To this he adds, "Excepting themselves—or some of their comrades—they told us we were the first climbers, European or Japanese, to set foot on the top" (Weston 1896b:249).

As is true for any of us, Weston was largely a product of his era. Here we can perceive the typical attitude of a Western colonialist adventurer in a foreign land—the desire to explore uncharted territories and describe them for an inquisitive and admiring public back at home. Thus, despite his status as a member of the clergy, Weston's desire to ascend the lofty peaks seems to have been driven more by personal ambition than religious motives. This is demonstrated by his proclamation "Yarigatake is ours!" in achieving the summit of another famous mountain (Weston 1896b:93). It was important for him to have been *first* to climb a mountain, to *conquer* or *claim* it in the language of European mountaineering at the time.

As to the singularity of his accomplishment, however, Weston was misinformed. Perhaps he had failed to understand what his hunter-guides were saying, due to his lack of proficiency in Japanese; perhaps they had simply told him what they thought he wanted to hear. Whatever the case, as local residents, they undoubtedly knew that a charismatic Buddhist priest named Banryū (1786–1840), fully seventy years earlier, had succeeded not only in reaching Kasagatake's summit but also in blazing a trail for others to follow, complete with Buddhist statuary, called *ichirizuka*, located at distanced intervals along the way to help them mark their progress. Indeed, if Weston had bothered to look inside the "tiny cairn," he would have discovered a bronze statue of Amida (Buddha of Infinite Light and Life) that Banryū had placed there during one of his several visits (Hokari and Hokari 1997:57).

Banryū's efforts constitute the opening of a mountain in a different sense, referred to as *kaizan* in Japanese Buddhist parlance. This activity entailed not simply reaching the summit but rather placing a Buddhist statue there as an act of devotion. The entire mountain thus becomes a kind of pedestal for the Buddha, and climbing it a quest for enlightenment and reunion.

Nor was Banryū the first to consecrate this particular mountain in such a manner. Evidence shows that a priest named Dōsen had climbed Kasagatake as early as the 1260s or 1270s, and the itinerant priest Enkū left one of his now famous wood carvings at the summit sometime during the late 1600s (Hokari and Hokari 1997:28–29, 35–36, 51–56). In any case, Banryū never claimed priority in attaining the summit. His own memoir, preserved to this day in a local Buddhist temple, is titled *Katagatake saikōki*,[1] or "Account of the *Re*-Opening of Mount Kasa" (emphasis added), thus readily acknowledging that he was not the first.

Moreover, it is likely that these Buddhist ascetics relied heavily, as the Weston party had, on the guidance of hunters and timber cutters, the only people with extensive knowledge of the high mountain terrain. According to local belief, the upper reaches were occupied by the *yama no kami*, a spirit or deity of the mountains who seems to have been conceptualized as either male or female depending on a person's occupation. Hunters, for example, identified the yama no kami as female and venerated her as both their guardian and benefactor. It was customary among them to seek her permission before entering into her realm, to humbly thank her for the gifts she bestowed upon them in the form of edible vegetation and game animals, and to avoid incurring her displeasure by abusing the privilege. Confident in their favored relationship with the yama no kami, they alone could enter into the upper regions with equanimity. In fact, the hunters appear to have functioned as intermediaries between mountain (personified by the yama no kami) and village, or "wild" and domesticated space, and were regularly enlisted to ascend the highest peaks and offer prayers for rain in behalf of the farmers below (Weston 1896b:160–162, 1918: 141–142).

Banryū had been raised in a tiny village lying just to the west of Tateyama, one of the most venerated mountains in all of Japan and long a center for mountain ascetics. As the second son in a household subject to the rules of primogeniture, the young Banryū was eventually obliged to leave home and make a living on his own; he thus became a Buddhist monk (Kurono 1997:2). There is little doubt that throughout his early life he came in daily contact with the hunters and timber cutters who made their living in the surrounding forests, and his later acquisition of Buddhist concepts was likely seasoned by their beliefs (Kurono Kōki, personal communication, November 16, 2006).

Although he went on to be ordained as a priest and eventually founded a number of Buddhist temples, Banryū himself eschewed the confines of temple worship, preferring instead to engage nature directly on its own terms as the ultimate expression of the Buddha's wisdom. His was a solitary practice, but one that he encouraged others to adopt. The *yamabushi* of the Shingon and Tendai traditions were rather secretive and exclusive, but

Banryū was a proponent of Jōdo-shū, or Pure Land Buddhism, which enjoyed widespread appeal among the common peasantry. Thus, his primary concern lay with ordinary people who had neither the means nor the opportunity to devote themselves to esoteric study.

Banryū described himself as a *nembutsu gyōja*—a practitioner of a form of asceticism that drew on Jōdo-shū conventions. As far as I can determine, his ascetic practice in the mountains consisted of (1) chanting the nembutsu, an expression of faith in and gratitude to Amida Buddha; (2) otherwise remaining silent (*mugon*); (3) subsisting on a "tree diet" (*moku-jiki*—the consumption of nuts, fruit, and other edible products of raw nature, as well as buckwheat flour mixed with water, but no cultivated or processed foods such as rice or miso); and (4) simply "merging with nature" (*shizen to ittai-ka suru*). The latter compelled him to seek ever more remote and challenging terrain, eventually leading to the summit of Kasagatake and other high-altitude destinations. The goal in this practice, it seems to me, was to shed all vestiges of society and culture that insulate humans from their natural surroundings and thereby to reestablish an intimate association with the essence of life as reflected in the image of Amida Buddha. That he succeeded in this effort is attested by his own written account, the *Katagatake saikōki*.

MIST AND MYSTICISM

The *saikōki* is an obscure but important document—perhaps the only existing firsthand account of opening a mountain in the Buddhist sense. Banryū, as its author, first explains his interest in Kasagatake and gives a brief accounting of others who had climbed it. He then describes his own initial ascent, crossing ridges and streams, then higher up "over crags and pinnacles so precipitous that words could not describe them." Upon reaching the summit, his immediate act is to chant the nembutsu. He notes also that he looked for signs of anger from the mountain spirits but that none was forthcoming. There follows a testament to the remarkable view: "To the south I could see the provinces of Mino and Ise, to the north Etchū and Kaga, to the east I prayed to Mount Fuji, as well as to Tateyama, and Hakusan. To the west I worshiped the sun setting over the Inland Sea" (handwritten manuscript, temple archives at Honkaku-ji, Kamitakara).

Upon returning to the realm of human settlement, Banryū determines to open a route to the summit for ordinary villagers to follow. After obtaining the blessing of local leaders, he organizes a party of sixteen villagers from Sasajima, located at the base of the slopes leading up toward the mountain, to help him mark the trail. After three days, they successfully

FIGURE 8.2

Painting by Banryū of his visionary experience in the mountains.

arrive at the summit. It is there that the most remarkable part of the narrative unfolds, namely, that while Banryū and some of the villagers are chanting the nembutsu, Amida Buddha suddenly appears to them "from the midst of the clouds" (figures 8.2 and 8.3). Banryū describes the image of Amida in some detail, its head and shoulders encompassed by a multicolored halo.

This visionary experience almost certainly derives from a natural phenomenon that sometimes occurs along the ridges and at the summits of the high mountains when the mist rises up from the valley below, but only in the early morning or late afternoon, when the sun is low in the sky. Standing with the sun at one's back, it is possible to see one's own shadow projected onto the mist as a kind of ghostly apparition, the head and upper body encircled by concentric, multicolored rings. In Europe this phenomenon is known as the "Brocken spectre," named after Mt. Brocken in the Harz Mountains of central Germany, where it is regularly sighted. But in Japanese Buddhist idiom, it is referred to as *goraigō*—an appearance or a manifestation of the Buddha. Banryū thus understood the encounter as Amida appearing before him—an expression of

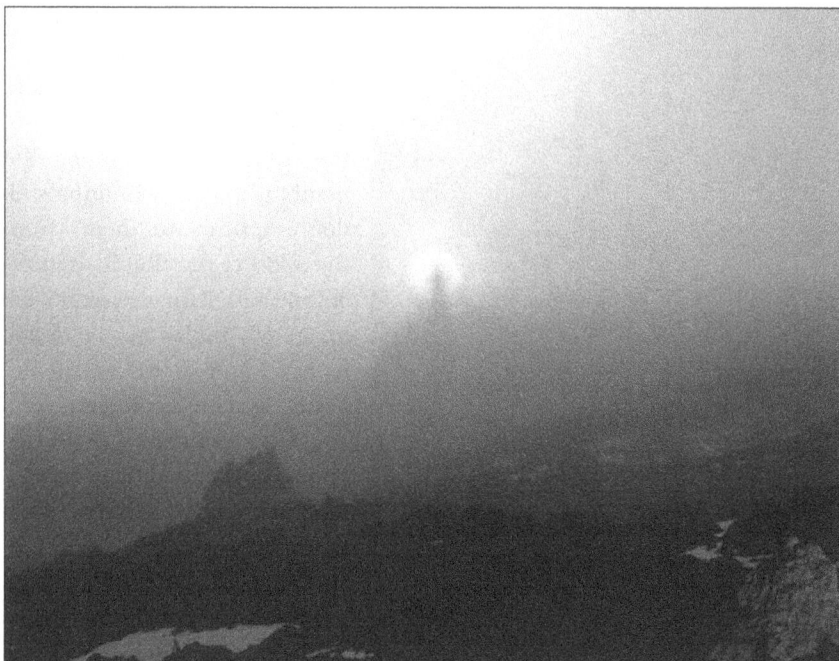

FIGURE 8.3

The Brocken spectre, as seen in the vicinity of Roque de los Muchachos Observatory in the Canary Islands. Photo courtesy Dr. Stefan Binnewies and Josef Pöpsel of the Capella Observatory, http://www.capella-observatory.com.

approval for having reopened the mountain and thereby affording the same mystical or numinous experience to others as well.

It is significant here to note that, since an individual must be positioned directly between the sun and the backscattering mist in order to observe the phenomenon, several people may be standing abreast but each will see only a single image—namely, a projection of his or her own body. Of course, one can wave one's arms about and immediately recognize that the image does the same, but if Pure Land Buddhism encourages us to discover Amida in ourselves, this would not necessarily negate a religious interpretation. In any case, the immediate reaction of Banryū and his followers would undoubtedly have been to clasp their hands and bow, meaning that the image would simply have reciprocated in an expression of mutual respect.

It is noteworthy also that Banryū does not deny the validity of local beliefs but rather draws them into a comprehensive Buddhist framework.

Indeed, the image of Amida that Banryū encountered is reminiscent of the yama no kami concept, as both may be considered personifications of *daishizen*, or "all-encompassing, all-pervasive nature" (Buddhist priest, personal communication, Toyoshina, Japan, June 8, 2004). As Pals (2006:200) explains in his chapter on Eliade, "however the sacred is conceived, the role of religion is to promote encounters with it, to bring a person 'out of his worldly Universe or historical situation, and project him into a Universe different in quality, an entirely different world, transcendent and holy' [quoting Eliade]."

Despite his revelatory experience on Kasagatake, Banryū's most celebrated accomplishment came a few years later in relation to a different mountain—none other than Yarigatake, which, with its distinctive spear-shaped peak and an elevation of 3,180 meters, is easily the most recognizable symbol of the Northern Alps and therefore of Japanese mountaineering in general. Banryū spent years establishing a route to its summit from the vicinity of Matsumoto. Although suffering frostbite and nearly perishing in the effort, he eventually succeeded in placing a Buddhist icon at the top of Yarigatake, even attaching an iron chain along the precipitous final ascent to ensure that others could reach the top in safety. Such efforts have earned him the title of *shonin*, which in Pure Land Buddhist tradition is reserved for a great teacher or exemplar. It is here that my research enters into contemporary times, looking at how the image of Banryū has recently been resurrected and redeployed in support of a mountain-oriented aesthetic of humility and respect.

REDISCOVERING BANRYŪ

Throughout the twentieth century and largely owing to Weston's impetus, hiking and climbing in the Japanese Alps became hugely popular pastimes. They now attract thousands of visitors every year and, along with skiing and hot spring resorts, are mainstays for economic development in the area. The highest peaks reach to around 3,000 meters in elevation, which does not seem impressive by European standards, but considering that the climber starts out at an elevation of perhaps 600–700 meters, the trek to their summits is demanding. The summits are linked by a well-marked trail network, and while the steep slopes can be treacherous during the winter months, technical climbing is not required for most major routes during the peak climbing season of July and August. For an average visitor, in other words, the climb is something on the order of a very steep hike. The trail network is dotted by a number of well-maintained lodges that provide overnight accommodation and hot meals, greatly reducing the amount of weight a climber has to carry. Consequently, the summits are accessible to young and old alike, and varying levels of physical ability are well accommodated.

Yarigatake, often described in tourist brochures as "the Japanese Matterhorn," occupies a strategic location at the intersection of several popular trails. For three generations, the Hokari family has owned and operated the mountain lodge located just below the summit, which is host to thousands of mountaineering enthusiasts every year. It thus serves as a kind of clearinghouse for information about the mountains. In the common dining area on the lower level of this lodge, there is an altar rather conspicuously devoted to Banryū Shonin, complete with a bronze statue. Furthermore, the Hokaris are the authors of the only significant scholarly work on the life of Banryū Shonin (Hokari and Hokari 1997), an ongoing project that has been decades in the making. It is largely through their efforts that Banryū has come to the attention of a wider public outside the local towns and villages he once inhabited.

Indeed, Banryū's memory might well have been lost if not for the efforts of several dedicated groups of followers scattered throughout Gifu, Nagano, and Toyama prefectures. These include the priests at various temples with which Banryū was affiliated, the members of several *ko* (lay) Buddhist associations, inspired by Banryū's teachings, and residents of Kamitakara township in northern Gifu prefecture, where Banryū practiced his austerities and first began his forays into the high mountains. Most influential of all, perhaps, is an artist, historian, and inveterate Banryū promoter named Kurono Kōki, who drew them all together into an advocacy network—Network Banryū.

To many mountaineers, evidence that Banryū had preceded Weston in ascending the lofty summits has been welcome news indeed, and he is now on the verge of becoming a kind of patron saint for the Japanese climbing community. In 1986, a statue commemorating Banryū and his achievements was erected in the plaza outside the main railway station in Matsumoto, one of the major gateways for visitors to the Japanese Alps. Every year in early September, the head priests of two key temples in the Matsumoto area lead a pilgrimage to the summit of Yarigatake to commemorate Banryū's efforts and raise awareness of his nature-oriented spiritualism. Having joined in this event myself on two occasions, I can assure the aspiring participant that it does not require the kind of austerities to which Banryū subjected himself. It does, however, involve chanting the nembutsu at regular intervals. As I have come to understand it, the chant is meant to remind oneself of one's own association with Amida—that is, with a personification of all-encompassing, all-pervasive nature—to remove or break through the artificial/cultural barriers we have created between ourselves and the sources that sustain us, and to rediscover our connection to or place within the natural world.

Meanwhile, over in Gifu prefecture on the range's western slope, the township of Kamitakara began conducting an annual Banryū celebration of its own to mark the opening of the climbing season in mid-May. This creates an interesting counterpoint to the Weston festival held in Kamikōchi (on the eastern side), mentioned earlier. The principal of a local elementary school insisted to me (correctly) that the official name for the Northern Alps is Hida *sammyaku* (Hida mountain range) and that this was the term that should be used. "Japanese Alps," in his opinion, was derivative of European colonialism.

An inspired group of Kamitakara residents is now hard at work trying to reconstruct Banryū's devotional climbing route to the summit of Kasagatake, where he had his first visionary encounter with Amida. One of the members of this group is a venerable old bear hunter and former chief of the local mountain rescue squad. As both a hunter and mountaineer, his insight into identifying the most probable route over the rugged terrain to the summit is particularly valuable. So far the group has discovered five of the eight original ichirizuka that once marked the way, and the lower section of the route at least is now well understood.

Banryū's reopening of Kasagatake is especially meaningful to the people of Kamitakara for several reasons. First, Banryū had based himself there during his initial preparations, living in a cave located at some distance into the foothills. Second, the route he created lies entirely within the township, including its starting point at the village of Sasajima. Third, the mountain itself sits majestically at the head of the drainage system and dominates the entire landscape. Late in spring, a patch of snow melting on its western slope temporarily forms the image of a huge white horse; farmers in the region traditionally relied on the appearance of this image as a signal to tell them when temperature conditions and water availability were conducive to spring planting. Finally, unlike most of the other major peaks that lie along the border between Gifu and Toyama prefectures on the west side and Nagano prefecture on the east side, Kasagatake is located entirely within the boundaries of Kamitakara and in this sense is distinctively their own.

I recall vividly a comment made by a senior woman of Kamitakara following a local presentation on Banryū's legacy. She happened to be the mother of the resident priest at the nearby Buddhist temple that houses the *Katagatake saikōki*. She relayed to the audience how every evening she climbs up the temple's bell tower to ring the bell eight times at sunset and as soon as she reaches the top, she faces the summit of Kasagatake, which is visible in the distance, then puts her hands together and offers thanks to the mountain for bringing her safely through another day. This illustrates again the significance of ritual, not necessarily in effecting an outcome in the outer world, but in conditioning one's own thinking toward greater respect and appreciation. The woman concluded by underscoring an important point—that Kasagatake was not just any mountain. She found phrases like "conquering" a mountain (*seiha suru*) or "setting foot upon" the summit (*fumitsukeru*) to be offensive—not to her personally so much as to the mountain itself. She urged the audience to follow Banryū's example by treating the mountains with respect and veneration. Indeed, although she did not mention it at the time, Banryū never referred to his own ascents as climbing; rather, he preferred to use the term *sankei*, which is usually reserved for visiting a shrine or temple.

Weston and Banryū can perhaps be seen as opposite ends of a continuum. In Japanese parlance, Weston represents *supōtsu tozan*, or sport mountaineering, the recreational form with which most of us are familiar. Banryū's approach, on the other hand, is best described as *shinkō tozan* (devotional mountaineering) or *tohai* (climbing as a form of veneration). Most people would fall somewhere between these two poles—closer to one way of thinking, perhaps, but not entirely devoid of the other. Indeed, the same could probably be said of the two "polar opposites" (Weston and Banryū) themselves.[2]

Part of Banryū's renewed appeal undoubtedly derives from the fact that he was Japanese, not a foreigner like Weston. We should be wary, however, of the tendency for nationalistic pride to inspire false dichotomies. Take, for example, the following item, which appeared in the newspaper *Yomiuri Shimbun* (2004) as part of a special feature on Kasagatake. It begins with a quote from the *saikōki*:

> "Amida Buddha appeared from the midst of the clouds...."
> Banryū is said to have encountered Amida Nyorai [Amida Buddha] several times on Yarigatake and Kasagatake. It is thought that he was seeing a phenomenon that occurs at sunrise or sunset, when, standing with the sun at your back, you can see your own shadow with a rainbow-like halo projected onto the mist. In Japan this is revered as goraigō, but in the West it is given unfortunate names like Brocken spectre (Brocken phenomenon), taken from the name of the German mountain where it is

often seen. This seems to be a cultural difference compared with Japan, where from long ago mountains have been treated as objects of devotion.

I would argue that the two contrasting attitudes—which I have rather simplistically represented in the persons of Walter Weston and Banryū Shonin—cannot be attributed so easily to some gross distinction in national character between Japan and the West. In fact, the vast majority of Japanese climbers employ the term *burokken genshō* (the Brocken phenomenon) rather than goraigō; many do not even recognize the latter term. And the final ascent of Yarigatake—its precipitous spear-shaped peak—is often described as an attack (*atakku,* employing the English loanword). The "Westonization" of Japanese mountaineering, as Ireland (1993) described it, could not have occurred without a willing and receptive public (Wigen 2005).

Rather, preference for one or the other approach has more to say about the individual climber. The image of Weston appeals to the sport mountaineers—people who look to the mountains as a place to foster an indomitable spirit through physical challenges and exertion, where landscapes serve as settings for their own adventures. Banryū's example appeals to people who see the mountains as sacred—a revelation of the mysterious and divine, from which their very sustenance derives. Both types can be found within or outside Japan, regardless of nationality. Banryū's perspective, *or something like it*, may find increasing appeal around the world as we struggle with the consequences of industrial excess.

And that is one of the most lasting impressions I took away from my participation in the SAR seminar from which this volume derives. At first I felt a bit out of place as the only participant dealing with a religious tradition outside the realm of Christianity. Through my interactions with the other members, however, I began to recognize how closely some of their field examples paralleled my own. The general pattern involved a world religion (in this case, either Christianity or Buddhism) being adapted at the local level through the incorporation of indigenous or home-grown perspectives, producing a synthesis that was more finely tuned to a particular environment or more compatible with existing needs and preferences. I came to realize that, as a framework for environmental ethics, the problem with a world religion is precisely its global expansion and appeal; the wider it spreads beyond its place of origin, the less meaningfully it speaks to a particular landscape—*our* mountains, *our* rivers and forests, right here in *this place.* Localized popular belief—the ancestral guardians of the land in Zimbabwe (Daneel, chapter 10), the Mayan *Popol Vuh* (Hallum, chapter 7), the moral ecology of the Chinantec in Oaxaca (Norget, chapter 5), even the strategic assertion of desiccation theory by indigenous Mexican forest communities (Mathews, chapter 4)—reinstills the missing relevance.

The Urapmin of Papua New Guinea (Robbins, chapter 3) are the exception that proves the rule; their efforts to disenchant nature coincide with their embrace of industrial development, as happened in the West during an earlier era (Merchant 1989). If expelling spirit from the land is a correlate of our own isolation from nature, perhaps reintroducing spirit to the land is a necessary step in uniting us again. The contributions to this volume give us some idea of how that might be achieved.

RECREATION OR REVERENCE?

In conclusion, I am by no means suggesting that Weston is unworthy of the special esteem he has been given. Rather, I maintain that Banryū offers a more useful and instructive example for a public increasingly concerned about the impact of human activity on the natural environment and increasingly aware of the ecosystemic relationships that integrate and sustain us. As objects of reverence, personifications of nature such as the mountain god—or, in this case, Amida Buddha as a manifestation of dai-shizen—offer potentially useful images to a world sorely in need of restraints on environmental abuses. In the words of theologian and philosopher Leonardo Boff (1997:118), "only a personal relationship with Earth makes us love it." Ritual is a way of enacting such a relationship, and personification through ritual makes it easier to imagine and articulate, easier to *conceive*.

Mr. Kurono, the founder of Network Banryū, once told me that when Westerners see the Japanese offering prayers in the direction of a Buddhist image and interpret this as worshiping idols, they are making a mistake. The image is merely a focal point, a device that renders a complex web of interactions into a more readily comprehensible form. He also noted that the image of Amida represents different things to different people, so the equation with dai-shizen is a reasonable one to make (personal communication, Irigawa, Japan, September 20, 2006). As with ritual, the form may be prescribed, but its meaning is negotiable. The same may be said of chanting the nembutsu.

Of course, it is open to conjecture whether conceptualizations like these will encourage more sustainable interactions with the environment. But it is clear from the conservationist ethos of traditional hunters all over Japan (as expressed through their veneration of the yama no kami) that such was the case at one time, so at least the potential is there. As Rappaport

(1979:100) suggested, "to drape nature in supernatural veils may be to provide her with some protection against human folly and extravagance." From this perspective, animism—that is, ascribing awareness and sensitivity to the environment (R. Nelson 1983:31)—emerges not as superstitious and backward but as a truly enlightened point of view.

In the artificial worlds we have created, so cut off from our natural surroundings, Banryū's example of merging with nature is well worth emulating. After all, direct personal interactions with the landscape can be highly moving and memorable experiences. This was impressed upon me during my own ascent of Kasagatake in October 2006, when the goraigō/Brocken spectre suddenly appeared before me "from the midst of the clouds." I found that my prior understanding of the physics behind the phenomenon did little to dilute its mysterious effect. Like Banryū, I see it as an expression of encouragement and favor—from nature personified in my own projected image.

Notes

1. This is an alternative rendering of the mountain's name, Katagatake rather than Kasagatake, as it is more commonly known in the present day.

2. Weston, of course, was not entirely devoid of religious inspiration from the mountains (Weston 1896b:88), nor was he oblivious to the threat of recreational mountaineering (Weston 1896a:146). And in some of his later writings, he seems to espouse a more sympathetic attitude toward the spiritual power of the mountains (Weston 1918:157).

9

The Productivity of Nonreligious Faith

Openness, Pessimism, and Water
in Latin America

Andrea Ballestero

The trip my friend Eduardo and I took in 2007 to Guanacaste, a province in the northwestern part of Costa Rica and the driest region of the country, was long and afforded us plenty of time to talk.[1] A lawyer, like me, Eduardo had become disenchanted with the profession and had moved to other walks of life, in his case, music and philosophy. At the time, he was working on a new CD, writing his thesis on Spinoza and the law, and had a full-time job with CEDARENA, a small environmental law NGO that was involved in environmental struggles and legal actions around the country.

The purpose of our trip was to hold a meeting with local communities to discuss the contents of a new water law that CEDARENA was involved in writing. During the drive, Eduardo gave me some background about the law writing process and explained that it was taking an inordinate amount of time for the committee to produce any results. "That is something that we always have a hard time explaining to the communities," he said. "They always wonder why the work of these committees takes so long" (personal communication, February 8, 2008). I also wondered about that. This law had already consumed more than four years of negotiation, a long time even for Costa Rican policy-making rhythms, which are known to be extremely slow. Eduardo's narration of the process and his descriptions of the committee were colored with a sense of pessimism and frustration. He told me that he did not expect the product that was to come out of the "minister's committee," a qualification showing who he believed had control over the process, to be beneficial at all. He did not believe that his NGO was going to be able to exert enough influence over the process to make the outcome acceptable as a "good" law.

CEDARENA had been involved in the negotiations of this new water law since the first version was drafted in 2002, and here we were in 2007, driving on a highway and talking about how this process was still unfolding. Curious about what kept Eduardo and the other NGO members committed to this process, I asked him why they were still attending the meetings, providing feedback, and reading drafts. "Well," he said, "I don't believe anything is going to come out of it, but one has to have faith that the unexpected might happen." This answer immediately sparked a number of thoughts for me. What kind of faith was he speaking about? How was this faith entangled with technoscience and nature in the governance of water? How did faith coexist with pessimism and even disbelief?

These questions were also at the core of the explorations that we conducted during our SAR seminar. Our discussions confounded clear-cut distinctions between science, nature, and faith (religious and nonreligious), and precisely because of that, the conceptual territories we explored in our conversations remained not only open but also inclusive of the differences between our thinking. This chapter replicates that openness conceptually and structurally. I experiment with a counterintuitive form of faith that does not rely on belief or religion as its primary location. I put forward a notion of faith as a collective disposition to enduring involvement, despite the lack of clear results or planned outcomes, in the context of political processes of collective decision making. Faith, in this sense, is a form of relating to others, a pragmatic disposition that breeds an open-ended engagement with time and nature, which makes possible, although does not guarantee, change toward more democratic water use and distribution. For this type of faith, incompleteness and difference are intrinsic conditions rather than problems to be solved.

In developing this notion of faith, I benefited from the sense, shared by participants in the seminar, that the most productive spaces for our discussions were those of intersections, entanglements, and gray zones between categories such as belief and disbelief, rationality and affect, optimism and pessimism, religion and nonreligious forms of life. This chapter inhabits these gray zones by interweaving ethnographic material with conceptual possibilities in order to suggest that faith, as a form of engagement across difference and as a disposition to "keep going," is a productive way of understanding the politics of nature, science, and governance in Latin America. With that purpose in mind, I put Eduardo's insight at the core of my analysis to ask, What kinds of processes and technical discussions make actors "have faith that the unexpected might happen" amidst the asymmetries in power, knowledge, and resources that exist in all political processes? In these cases, faith emerges from the day-to-day frustrations of working for political change through the "awkward, unequal, unstable, and creative qualities of interconnection across difference" (Tsing 2005:4). The task of this chapter is to find ways to remain attentive to the specific, subtle, and often unnoticed ways in which those asymmetries are made unstable by refusing "powerful" players any certainty about the final outcomes of a process. My purpose is to replicate the sense of political involvement as it is experienced in real time, not from a post-event perspective in which actors, politics, and results are clearly identifiable. My attempt to replicate that experience is akin to the notion of a cosmopolitical project that requires one to "slow down" in the creation of morally desirable outcomes so that when imagining alternatives, one does not reproduce the oppressive or exclusionary world one is attempting to change (Stengers 2005; see also Ivakhiv, chapter 11, this volume).

The chapter presents two modest and unfinished encounters occurring in Brazil and Costa Rica, two countries presented as exemplary of sound water policies by international institutions; Brazil became known because of the far-reaching institutional transformation of its water sector in the 1990s, and Costa Rica because of its success in securing access to improved sources of water for virtually all of its population. In those locations, I follow the work of two heterogeneous committees, one making decisions about water allocation and the other writing a new water law. In the Costa Rican committee, the lack of technoscientific information about water availability makes participants create additions, in the form of dissents, to a text that is never finalized or fully adopted. In Brazil, technoscientific information is available but local residents reject it squarely and, since agreements depend on the use of such data, collective decisions are endlessly postponed. As a consequence, they schedule new encounters to create more opportunities for future conversations between state representatives and local communities and to redress the traditional imposition of "technical" state knowledge on local interests and positions. In both cases, the "unexpected outcome" is not so because it is unknown, but because it never arrives. The unexpected is a desired resolution that seems impossible to achieve.

Conceptually, this chapter is also an experiment in borrowing and recontextualization. I borrow Eduardo's insights about faith and the potential for the unexpected and use them as analytic resources to understand the work of Brazilian state bureaucrats. This move is analogous to the one performed by the Urapmin in Papua New Guinea when they appropriate spiritual warfare (Robbins, chapter 3, this volume) and by indigenous groups in Oaxaca when they redeploy desiccation theory (Mathews, chapter 4, this volume). As these three chapters show, what is of relevance is the new and often unanticipated uses and meanings that these epistemic objects—spiritual warfare, desiccation theory, and faith—are given, not what we presume each of them represents. There is, however, one difference between my case and those of Robbins and Mathews. In this chapter, it is the anthropologist who takes the lead from her informants to perform the recontextualization by projecting Eduardo's notion of faith to understand the Brazilian and Costa Rican events. In this sense, this is also an experiment in the creation of knowledge alongside informants and through their folk categories (Bunzl 2004; Holmes and Marcus 2005; Maurer 2005).

The chapter is structured in three sections. I first outline the workings of the Costa Rican committee that Eduardo's NGO is part of. In that setting, technical and legal dissents about the law are multiplied to the extent that a final text is never produced. This proliferation of dissent creates a lack of closure to a process that otherwise would be easily colonized by powerful economic interests. One key issue in this case is the long history that precedes the committee's work and the sense of pessimism that history creates. Second, I present the case of Feitiçeiro in northeast Brazil where, in a gathering to allocate water, the dominant logic of numbers and hydrological models is broken. That rupture creates more than a failed meeting; it produces the need to have another encounter to provide continuity to conversations and makes the rejection of technical data a viable means for retaining political connections. Third and finally, I outline three of the qualities that make faith a distinctive form of relating to others: epistemological failure, embracing pessimism, and commitment to an open-ended future.

FAITH AS THE MULTIPLICATION OF DISSENT: MAKING THE LAW IN COSTA RICA

At the World Water Forum in Mexico City in March 2006, a World Bank official presenting state-of-the-art water reforms in Latin America showed a slide with a map of the entire region. In the map, countries that had reformed their water laws in the preceding ten years were displayed in green, and countries that still retained "outdated" laws were colored in red. Costa Rica was one of the red nations. After the presentation, about ten people from the audience gathered in the hallway outside the room where the panel had taken place to comment on what they saw as an unjustified shaming by World Bank officials. They were all Costa Ricans who had been part of the many attempts to transform the Costa Rican water legal structure. Although still red in the World Bank classification, Costa Rica did not suffer from any lack of attention to water. Since 1980, twenty-five draft water laws had been introduced in Congress, yet none had passed; the 1942 Water Law was still in effect. Although many institutional and policy changes had indeed occurred since 1942, environmental organizations and social movements were still invested in passing a new law. NGOs were worried about the possibility of private ownership of water due to trade liberalization reforms and believed a law could prevent that from happening. Furthermore, they shared with other organizations a preoccupation about the fourfold increase of Costa Rica's population and the rapidly growing demand for water (Aguilar Schramm et al. 2004; Bonilla-Carrion and Rosero-Bixby 2004; B. Wilson 1998).

A couple of months later, the people I had met at the forum in Mexico invited me to attend the sessions of an intersectoral committee set up by the Environment Ministry to work on "a new water law" proposal. The text the committee was discussing had a long history that went back to 2002 when three different draft laws were introduced in Congress. Given this heightened interest in water, the permanent Environment Commission, in coordination with the Global Water Partnership,[2] had organized the First National Water Forum and launched a major consultation process to merge the three 2002 proposed laws and incorporate the opinions of citizens and institutions. During 2003, representatives of the commission traveled around the country to present the merged text in different locations to promote discussion and incorporate new ideas from local communities, water users, and public institutions. According to their report, four hundred people participated in the hearings, an accomplishment that made one of the leaders of the process, a congresswoman especially interested in water issues, proudly tell me that "never in the history of [Costa Rica] had a law been consulted as much as this one" (personal communication, April 29, 2008). All of this activity created a generalized feeling among Congress representatives, NGOs, and public institutions that a new water law was finally going to be approved.

Soon after the end of the consultation, the commission produced a text that was reintroduced to Congress for a vote. While the proposal moved up through Congress's agenda, word about its contents spread, and the largest newspaper in the country published a piece titled "Plan prohibits agriculture in 75% of the territory" (Loaiza 2005). The piece underscored Article 125, which the journalist described as establishing "a prohibition to change land use in any area with water recharge potential." Although clearly alarmist, the headline was not completely incorrect. Geographic and climatological conditions give most of Costa Rica's territory underground water recharge potential, but the text of the law explicitly established that in order to be recognized as such, those areas would have to be formally designated by the government. The reporter also included in her piece the objection of representatives from the Costa Rican Construction Chamber, who argued that the wording of Article 125 was a risk to any simple homeowner, who could end up in prison for two to six years just for cutting the grass on his or her property. The effect of the article on public opinion was immediate. Private interests mobilized and lobbied Congress and the environment minister for more prominent participation in the crafting of the law. NGOs and public institutions saw the newspaper article and ensuing letters, meetings, and conversations as a political maneuver by private interests to control what they considered potential obstacles to their business activities. Responding to public opinion pressures and business's sudden interest in having a more active role in the writing of the law, the environment minister convened another committee in late 2006 to review the text of the law, this time with a sizeable representation of private interests. Representatives of NGOs working on water issues and environmental justice were also invited and shared the space with lawyers from public institutions such as the health and environment ministries, the public water utility, the public irrigation facility, and the national electricity institute. As is customary in Costa Rica, participation in the committee was voluntary and by invitation. For the smallest organizations, such as CEDARENA, involvement was quite onerous since researching international trends on water laws, preparing for the discussions of the text, and constantly assessing possible changes in the positions of the actors demanded considerable time.

I provide this historical background to highlight how complicated and slow the process of writing this law had been and why the prospects of a prompt outcome were very weak. After joining their weekly meetings in 2006, I became puzzled by the committee's "working methods." I had expected to find powerful actors, such as business representatives and state institutions, dominating discussions and subtly imposing their perspectives. I had also expected heated discussions and intense pressure to produce a final and detailed text in order to present it to the minister. Surprisingly, I found a working process that fomented difference, lack of consensus, and very few textual outcomes; it is to this working style that Eduardo was referring when he later talked to me about faith.

Although the site of their weekly meetings usually changed, the most recent four had taken place at the Chamber of Commerce headquarters. Most members of the committee were lawyers, although several engineers also took part. They all seemed very comfortable working, arguing, and joking with one another. The conflicting visions that I knew they held did not seem to make the working environment tense in any way. The table and chairs in the meeting room were organized in a half-circle, and each seat had a microphone that we were supposed to activate whenever we spoke. After saying hello and entering the room, almost everybody spotted a location to sit near people they already knew. This meant that there were clusters of NGO representatives, private businesses, and public institutions gathered throughout the room. With a view of bright green mountains, laptops, and business suits setting the tone, our meeting commenced. On a large screen hanging from the wall was a projection of a two-column document. The left column contained text that merged the three 2002 proposed laws with the comments collected during the consultation process. The right column had a series of newly proposed revisions that this committee had worked on in previous meetings.

The group's technical work was presented by a moderator, usually the environment minister's representative, who would read an article and ask for comments from the table. For most articles, there was no feedback and we moved on, but a few articles incited broad and lengthy discussions. Article 48, about water permits and charges, was one of them, and it ignited a heated technical discussion about good legal practice and water monitoring systems. The specific question we were considering that day was how to deal with the lack of data about water availability in a manner that was consistent with the principle of *seguridad jurídica* (legal predictability). This principle allows lawyers and judges to "present their innovations as the expression of a principle that was already in existence," creating a situation in which new events make the legal system even more "the same" than it was before (Latour 2004b:93). This principle requires any event in the future to be a continuation of existing legal tenets and ensures commensurability, if only symbolically, between future events and existing laws. Thus, making a law requires an ongoing reflexive examination of normative ideas in connection to a world that is future and uncertain. Even though technoscience is supposed to reduce that uncertainty, it is never fully able to do so, from a legal perspective, because the world always exceeds what techno-science can predict or control. Hence, the law needs a principle such as seguridad jurídica to secure its own continuity in the face of unpre-dictability and uncertainty. One of the ways in which predictability is cre-ated is through the granting of licenses and permits. These legal instruments are supposed to delineate and control the use of public resources by private citizens and to make public agencies account for their policies on resource allocation and management.

After a short lunch, we continued discussing Article 48 and its implica-tions for water use, the acquisition of water permits, and the environmental and economic logic according to which permits should be extended. The conflict between predictability and uncertainty was directly addressed when the representative of the State Irrigation Facility (SIF), an engineer who manages water projects with farmers in the northwestern part of the coun-try, posed the issue of a lack of available knowledge. The area he works in had experienced a drastic surge in construction of large-scale international resorts and other tourism projects, resulting in a skyrocketing demand for water. He argued that the problem of knowing how much water was avail-able for allocation presented an issue of high uncertainty. Article 48 would require the agency granting water permits to calculate a balance between the basic water-flow needs to maintain ecological processes and existing water permits within the parameters of current and future water availability. That calculation became complicated only because of the lack of systematic and trustworthy data. "We can give permits," he argued, "but we don't really know how much water we are going to have in five or ten years, especially with climate change. I can think of at least two examples of rivers that have drastically changed their water levels. How can we make sure that the system we are putting in place with this law creates the necessary seguridad jurídica for the users but also for the State to protect the resource?" (fieldnotes, August 17, 2007). The question unleashed a discussion about the decay of the public research infrastructure of the country, the insecurity this creates for private investment, structural adjustment programs of the 1980s and 1990s, and the growing water conflicts between local communities and resorts in Guanacaste. But the discussion did not lead to any final solution for establishing a mechanism to calculate water quantities to grant permits. Although projections of water availability probably existed in public agen-cies related to the topic, they were not readily available at the meeting, and not having the data was the same as not knowing.

After it became clear that the information gap could not be filled, Lucía, the representative of the Chamber of Industries, proposed a break.

She suggested that we have some coffee, talk about it informally, and come back to discuss the next article with the awareness that we could return to the unresolved discussion later. Lucía insisted that it was not necessary to clearly define how predictability related to the amount of water and the permit system right then. Following her suggestion, we got up from our leather chairs and walked to the side of the room where individual plates with pastries had been meticulously arranged by one of the cleaning ladies, who had quietly entered the room while people remained focused on the screen. During the coffee break, our conversations shifted to various matters: the last soccer game, how many months left until a colleague who was pregnant would give birth, and the suspicion that the minister was not going to take the committee's results seriously. After about twenty minutes, we went back to our chairs.

Lucía turned on her microphone and proposed that we note a dissent in the right column of Article 48. She said it would be a good idea to list the organizations holding different opinions and that we should move on to discuss the next article. CEDARENA's representative suggested also pasting the text of the original article to show concretely what participants with a different view wanted to see in the final version. The Environment Ministry representative, on whose laptop the projected document was saved, proceeded to type *Disenso* (Dissent) in red under the new text (table 9.1). Then he copied the text from the left column into the right one without making any changes and listed the organizations that supported this version of the text. Since no one complained about his rearrangement or about the additions he made, it was understood that we were all in agreement, and we moved on. As time went by, the right column became a repository of alternative texts and lists of organizations that objected to parts of the law. The proliferation of dissents did not seem to trouble the participants; in fact, quite the contrary, this was the solution they had found to the multiple disagreements they had with one another. It was striking to me that after four years of work, the right column of the document projected on the screen was once again populated with notes of dissent. Based on the history of this project and given all the notes in the right column of the table, it seemed inevitable that no text would be finalized, let alone adopted, before the two-week deadline for the committee to present its results. But committee members, as Eduardo would note later, were still engaged in doing the work and thinking through the text despite their generalized feeling that nothing would come out of the process.

After hours of discussion, we finally returned briefly to Article 48, but we still had no agreement and the energy level was low. Implicitly, we all

TABLE 9.1
Working document for the new law text

PROYECTO DE LEY DEL RECURSO HÍDRICO EXPEDIENTE 14585	
TEXTO PROPUESTO	RECOMENDACIÓN
ARTÍCULO 48.- Aprovechamiento del recurso hídrico Toda persona física o jurídica, pública o privada requerirá concesión o permiso de uso para el aprovechamiento del recurso hídrico. Las concesiones y los permisos de uso se otorgarán teniendo en cuenta la explotación racional y conjunta de los recursos superficiales y subterráneos y un manejo integral del recurso. Las concesiones destinadas al abastecimiento de población solo podrán ser otorgadas al Instituto Costarricense de Acueductos y Alcantarillados de conformidad con la ley No. 2726 Ley Constitutiva del Instituto Costarricense de Acueductos y Alcantarillados de 14 de abril de 1961, a las Municipalidades, Asociaciones Administradoras de Acueductos y Alcantarillados que crea esta Ley o a las empresas públicas reguladas por ley especial. Para este servicio público no será aplicable la norma contenida en el numeral 74 de la ley No. 7494 Ley de Contratación Administrativa de 2 de mayo de 1995. Dentro del trámite de una concesión o un permiso de uso, la Dirección Nacional del Recurso Hídrico procurará el mejor y más eficiente uso del recurso, sin detrimento de la vulnerabilidad ambiental acumulada y oferta futura del mismo. Debe evaluar el impacto acumulado que la actividad genere sobre el recurso hídrico, los cauces, los ecosistemas y otros aprovechamientos autorizados en la cuenca con base en el orden jerárquico de prioridades establecido.	**ARTÍCULO 48.- Aprovechamiento del recurso hídrico** Toda persona física o jurídica, pública o privada requerirá concesión o autorización de uso para el aprovechamiento del recurso hídrico. Se otorgarán teniendo en cuenta la explotación racional y conjunta de los recursos superficiales y subterráneos y un manejo integral del recurso, procurando el mejor y más eficiente uso del recurso, sin detrimento de la vulnerabilidad ambiental acumulada y oferta futura del mismo. Debe evaluar el impacto acumulado que la actividad genere sobre el recurso hídrico, los cauces, los ecosistemas y otros aprovechamientos autorizados en la cuenca con base en el orden jerárquico de prioridades establecido. Estos derechos deberán tomar en cuenta los principios y orden jerárquico que establezca esta ley, el Plan Hídrico Nacional y el Plan Hídrico de Unidad Hidrológica respectiva. DISENSO **Para ESPH, JASEC, FUDEU, UCR, CEDARENA y Ay A la Propuesta es rescatar la propuesta de la Comisión:** Toda persona física o jurídica, pública o privada requerirá concesión o permiso de uso para el aprovechamiento del recurso hídrico. Las concesiones y los permisos de uso se otorgarán teniendo en

El otorgamiento de toda concesión sobre el aprovechamiento del recurso hídrico deberá tomar en cuenta los principios y orden jerárquico que establezca esta ley, el Plan Hídrico Nacional y el Plan Hídrico Regional respectivo.

cuenta la explotación racional y conjunta de los recursos superficiales y subterráneos y un manejo integral del recurso.

Las concesiones destinadas al abastecimiento de población solo podrán ser otorgadas al Instituto Costarricense de Acueductos y Alcantarillados de conformidad con la ley No. 2726 Ley Constitutiva del Instituto Costarricense de Acueductos y Alcantarillados de 14 de abril de 1961, a las Municipalidades, Asociaciones Administradoras de Acueductos y Alcantarillados que crea esta Ley o a las empresas públicas reguladas por ley especial. Para este servicio público no será aplicable la norma contenida en el numeral 74 de la ley No. 7494 Ley de Contratación Administrativa de 2 de mayo de 1995. Dentro del trámite de una concesión o un permiso de uso, la Dirección Nacional del Recurso Hídrico procurará el mejor y más eficiente uso del recurso, sin detrimento de la vulnerabilidad ambiental acumulada y oferta futura del mismo. Debe evaluar el impacto acumulado que la actividad genere sobre el recurso hídrico, los cauces, los ecosistemas y otros aprovechamientos autorizados en la cuenca con base en el orden jerárquico de prioridades establecido.

El otorgamiento de toda concesión sobre el aprovechamiento del recurso hídrico deberá tomar en cuenta los principios y orden jerárquico que establezca esta ley, el Plan Hídrico Nacional y el Plan Hídrico Regional respectivo.

agreed to adjourn the meeting soon after 4:30 p.m. until the next Wednesday—the last opportunity to add anything to the text before it would be given to the environment minister and then relayed to Congress.

The two-column table the committee produced embodied two alternative logics of legal rationality and democratic decision making. The left column contained a tight and cohesive text following legal custom. The right column held contradicting positions that gave multiple dimensions to each article and showed some of the inconsistencies that derived from people's ideas on how to "improve" the text. Contrary to my expectations, the document made these two parallel and diverse logics hang together without attempting the translation of one into the other. They were convinced that in an uncharted future, it would be possible to resolve differences, lack of knowledge, and dissent in a way that was unimaginable in the present. It was unnecessary to discuss how it would be done or by whom during the meeting. The working style of the committee members, in relating to one another and to the process, became a mechanism to push into an open future the creation of a consensus text that would secure the necessary seguridad jurídica and resolve the dissents without forcing them to clearly outline and plan how that would happen.

RUPTURING CONNECTION TO FOSTER FUTURE ENCOUNTERS IN NORTHEAST BRAZIL

Water policy makers find in mathematical models one of the most promising tools for making decisions about the future. They believe that numbers and models make possible the combination of otherwise disjointed domains—geographical, temporal, and epistemological (Guyer, Khan, and Obarrio 2010; Porter 1995; Pryke 2007). When considering models as cultural objects, one can think of the mathematics behind them as cultural scripts whose meanings are not inherent to mathematics itself but are built through the social interactions leading to their creation and use. The ways different actors read mathematical models differ drastically according to each person's history, relation to water, and political stakes. The existence of such multiplicity gives footing to critiques of science and the state because of how they sanction certain knowledge forms and repress others (Fisher 2000; Jasanoff 2004b; Jasanoff and Long Martello 2004; Scott 1998). This repression often forces local residents and nonexperts to reinvent their positions as "technical" in order to be legible to the state and to dominant technoscience (see Mathews, chapter 4, this volume, for an analysis of how this process takes place). What is of particular interest in this case, however, is what happens when that reinvention does not take place and when difference prevents the creation of agreement. How do these relations across difference remain politically viable and inclusive? In this case, conflicting stories around numbers create a radical disjuncture that, paradoxically, creates a need for future encounters between political actors and keeps them committed to their interactions. This form of engagement can be understood as a form of faith that, although refusing participants any certainty about outcomes, keeps their relations lively and inclusive.

The events I narrate took place in July 2005 in the town of Feitiçeiro—Wizard, in English—in northeast Brazil and, like the Costa Rican case, had a history embedded in longer processes of political reform, state making, and water politics. Feitiçeiro, with a population of about one thousand, has historically had water scarcity problems. The town is located in the state of Ceará and is in the region known in Brazil as the "Drought Triangle," a label that condenses the region's history of droughts, complicated water politics, and barren poverty (Ansell 2010; Lemos 2003; D. Nelson and Finan 2009). With a semi arid environment and a yearly evapotranspiration rate that is higher than its rainfall, Ceará and Feitiçeiro's histories are structured by long-term and perennial water deficits unequally experienced across class and gender lines. To alleviate this situation, the state has invested in a sophisticated network of reservoirs, channels, and technical institutions to manage the state's current and future water crises. The flow of resources for drought relief and water infrastructure to the region has actively shaped politics and clientelistic relations in Ceará. The state's irruption into the international policy arena in the 1990s was propelled by a major institutional reform of the water sector that, with support from the World Bank, would bring water management practices to meet twentieth-century technical and political standards. Organized around the precepts of "modernizing" water institutions, updating the regulatory framework, installing bulk water-charging mechanisms, and implementing a participatory reservoir management program (Ballestero 2004, 2006; Lemos and Farias de Oliveira 2004), the reform has been referred to as a "success case study" by international organizations (Simpson 2003). When local and international experts involved in the reform present the results of their experience, they speak highly of the participatory reservoir management program and of the role it played in changing the entrenched technocratic and politicized water culture of the state (Arons 2004; Lemos 2003; D. Nelson and Finan 2009). The program intended to devolve decision-making control to local populations in order to halt the federal, state, and local political uses of water infrastructure. Although this reform and the reservoir program were launched in the 1990s, the residents of Feitiçeiro only heard about the possibility of managing their own reservoir in 2001.

Feitiçeiro's reservoir is small; its water is used for human consumption by local residents and for agricultural irrigation by a small number of farmers around the city. The reservoir is also considered old; it was built in the 1960s and, as of 2005, had not been drained since then. For that reason, technical personnel from the state water agency, COGERH, believed that its visible water level was not reliable for making allocation decisions. In 2001, COGERH began a study to determine how much water the town's reservoir actually held. Activists and community leaders were eager to know the results. With a severe multiyear drought (1992–1998) fresh in their memories, residents had made it clear that they were not willing to risk their water supply for any reason. In May 2003, after two years of anxious waiting, the town was abuzz with news that the results were finally available. However, to everyone's surprise, including that of the local COGERH managers, it was announced that the results could not be used because technical difficulties of measuring soil density made the estimates untrustworthy. The study document, originally intended for circulation, remained at COGERH's central office in the state capital, and Feitiçeiro's residents never saw it. COGERH's managers tried in 2004 to hold a public water-allocation meeting. The effort did not go well; after striving to negotiate with residents protesting at the gates of the reservoir, managers cancelled the meeting before it even started. They returned to their offices, leaving behind a reservoir with a broken valve, an agitated protest that involved police presence, and another Brazilian town frustrated by the inability of the state to represent its interests. The conflict also meant that COGERH continued to manage the reservoir according to its own calculations but with no formal input from local residents.

One year later, in July 2005, after the rainy season had ended, state managers were making another attempt to hold an allocation meeting. We met at the local school in a classroom with three revolving ceiling fans and were given freshly brewed *cafezinho* (coffee) and *chá* (tea). In sweltering 115-degree heat, we sat in children's school chairs as the meeting began at 10:30 a.m. Martin, the head of the hydrological administrative region where Feitiçeiro is located, walked to the front of the classroom and began a short presentation. Using transparencies, he projected a table with ten columns and about twenty lines showing rainfall quantities and water availability for the preceding three years (figure 9.1). He explained the average and total rainfall quantities and emphasized that this information did not mean that the next three years were going to be identical, yet, he advised, residents should consider these numbers when making their decisions.

FIGURE 9.1

Martin presenting the results of the hydrological models and the proposed scenarios.

This use of probabilistic information is the norm in the participatory management program of COGERH. Having heard that explanation many times since I started doing fieldwork in Ceará in 2003, I continue to be fascinated by the injunction to consider information but not make any inferences or project that information directly into the future.

The next transparency Martin showed had three water-use scenarios for the upcoming year. They were calculated using COGERH's inventory of users and their water needs for agriculture and human consumption. The task at the meeting was to choose among the scenarios and adopt a decision that would govern the day-to-day opening and closing of the reservoir valve. After explaining the scenarios, Martin opened the floor for questions. For a few moments, silence filled the classroom as people looked inquisitively at one another, waiting to see who would speak first. Then, almost at once, a flood of complaints by schoolteachers, representatives of the women's organization, and residents took over the room. Their arguments went back to the 2001 study that had never left COGERH's headquarters and to the lack of certainty about water availability. The comments ignited an agitated discussion about models, water use, and predictions. Residents argued that the models were fraudulent because water volume data were not available, given the high level of sediments in the reservoir. They also posed that water use permits were untrustworthy because farmers never comply with the amount of water the permits authorize them to use. People claimed that the water in their reservoir was theirs and they were not going to pay the cost of giving it away to farmers or other communities to use.

After nearly forty minutes of comments and challenges from people in attendance, Martin explained that, although the water-level study finished in 2003 did not provide a definite number to calculate sedimentation, they had estimated its possible maximum level and used that number to make a conservative calculation of the water level in the reservoir. The message Martin was trying to convey was that the model had been run under the worst-case scenario of sedimentation, making the numbers extremely conservative, hence COGERH's confidence that any decision based on the scenarios would not pose any risk of water scarcity to Feitiçeiro. Clearly displeased with this line of reasoning, various members of the audience started interrupting Martin, voicing their concerns and explaining their opposition to the estimates. After about five minutes of many voices talking at the same time, a middle-aged schoolteacher managed to quiet the audience by speaking louder than anyone else. She then asked Martin, "Are these models that you are presenting here a reality, or are they only an estimate? Is it like here in the school, where we make estimates of how many students we will have the upcoming year? We come up with a number, and then we get fewer students or more students. Is it like that?" (fieldnotes, water allocation meeting, August 4, 2005). Perhaps foreseeing that he was going to end up in a tight spot, Martin answered with a tone of resignation, "Yes, it is an estimate like the one you do for the school." Then she said, "That is what I wanted to know. It is not a reality, and we cannot play with our water. We don't want to be drinking mud in a few months, because that is what happened in our neighboring town." After this intervention, Martin made a final attempt and asked the group whether it was willing to consider any estimate at all. The answer was a nearly unanimous, firm no. Recognizing that there was no room for immediate negotiation, Martin asked the audience to set a new date for holding another discussion, adjourned the meeting, and thanked everyone for coming.

In an unusual turn for the highly asymmetrical Brazil, during this meeting, the "state" ceded its authority after local residents challenged the expertise on which such authority is usually grounded. When I asked Martin why he had set a meeting for next month if it seemed that no agreement would be reached, he answered that they needed to continue talking to community residents regardless of the immediate outcome. With a shrug and a wan smile, he said, "We've got to keep going, right?" The schoolteacher who had asked the question about models was helping rearrange the chairs after the meeting when she told Martin how she expected him to come back on the agreed date so that the process could continue. After a brief pause, she said, "Somehow we'll understand each other. But if nothing works, you can always come for a cafezinho." The teacher's invitation was a symbol of the continuing relations between COGERH and Feitiçeiro, of their future engagements regardless of the histories of breakup, and of the uncertainty and continuity of those political relations.

In Feitiçeiro, COGERH managers could have imposed their expertise, as they historically had done in the region, yet they did not replicate that history and, without any certainty that in the future a "sensible" decision could be made, they embraced the lack of closure and committed to keep going. It is this "agonistic" set of relations between asymmetric actors who share a decision-making space that makes the arrangement stay open to the possibility of change. This form of relating cannot be understood as a zero-sum game of interests because it is experienced as a continuing engagement amidst the uncertainty the future brings. Political relations like these are closer to a form of faith than to the conventional oppositional model of liberal politics.

PUTTING FAITH IN THE REALM OF RELATIONS

All other chapters in this collection deal with religious forms of faith. I punctuate that unity by querying whether faith can be conceived only within a religious context. By decoupling faith and religion, I explore a nondoctrinaire form of faith that is based on the commitment to political action without relying on a metaphysical guarantor of morally good behavior. I have argued that this type of faith works to maintain relations across difference. In this sense, I take faith as a form of political commitment to social relations in settings where diverse forms of knowledge and interests need to be considered and where collective decisions need to be made. By taking this approach, I wish to pay attention to the oscillations and transactions that keep people, ideas, and artifacts entangled in political processes while de-emphasizing beliefs, interests, and positions as preexisting the social relations through which we recognize them. Seen from this perspective, faith is a form of political struggle in which politics are understood as a matter of forming and maintaining relationships (J. Robbins 2003:10). I want to propose three conditions that make the politics of water and knowledge, as experienced in these cases, resemble a form of faith: knowledge failure, pessimism, and openness to the future. The final part of this chapter briefly unpacks what they might mean with the aim of posing questions and directions that readers interested in nonreligious forms of faith might want to explore.

Governance models and their politics are deeply structured by epistemological contests in which experts play serious games of legitimizing and de-legitimizing knowledge claims (M. Fischer 2006; Jasanoff 2004b; Rose 1996). Historically, scientist and liberal-legal arguments and actors have dominated these contests. However, the privileged position that science and law have held is no longer taken for granted (Jasanoff 2004b; Nowotny 2003). Cases like the ones I presented partially challenge the supremacy of technoscientific knowledge and confront experts with the limits of their own knowledge. Yet what is of particular interest is that uncertainty or failure of knowledge is not quickly traversed on the way to new beginnings; rather, it is inhabited as an endpoint (Miyazaki and Riles 2005). Expediently traversing knowledge failure by bringing in "new" knowledge could make lawmakers in Costa Rica stop writing the text of the law until clear data on water quantities are available, or it could lead water managers in Brazil to circumvent the participatory process when local communities do not accept their technical data. Conversely, when inhabited as an endpoint, epistemological failure has the effect of making the terrain of politics uneasy for everyone. In this situation, a politics of failed knowledge is transformed into a commitment to retain connection across differences. The "inability to know" and the act of stripping away certainty from legal and technical knowledge create political hierarchies that are fragile and have the potential of fostering creative engagements and affecting alternative futures (see Scanlan Lyons, chapter 2, this volume, for a discussion of making religion work for conservation and social justice projects in which alternative futures can be imagined in the present). But what is most important in these cases is that it slows down business as usual. Not knowing creates a sense of precariousness that keeps difference in focus, rather than flatten it through the adoption of a single set of data. Lack of knowledge and predictability become their own forms of commitment to action and are sustained more by pessimism than by full and far-reaching optimism.

Although counterintuitive as an inspiration to sustain commitment to action, pessimism turns out to be crucial and is transformed from the dark and frustrating notion that we are more familiar with into a generative one. For the communities I worked with, faith does not translate into optimistic feelings and confidence. On the contrary, actors are profoundly pessimistic about the likelihood that their desired outcomes will be achieved. Eduardo really does not expect a "good" law to come out of the committee meetings. In Brazil, the total disagreement about a mathematical model breaks dialogue, and participants do not expect any consensus in the foreseeable future. Pessimism, in both cases, creates a sensation of lack of total control that surprisingly makes all participants develop a commitment to "keep going" despite the abundant evidence that the objectives they are working for might not be achieved. As Daneel (chapter 10, this volume) put it during the seminar, this faith is a disposition to find a solution even if there are no solutions, a commitment to work against the impossible odds of bringing together totally incompatible dimensions. Eagleton (2009:27) also suggests that by preserving a "steadfast fidelity to failure" and a "stonily disenchanted realism" about the improbability of the desired outcome one is working for (a "good" law or a decision based on "good" numbers), faith keeps alive the possibility that the unexpected might occur.

This commitment to retain connection through processes that at first glance do not seem to be moving in any direction is also possible because, alongside epistemological failure and pessimism, there is a sense of the future that highlights its open-endedness and its power to produce the unexpected. Troubled by an epochal change in the temporality of politics, Guyer (2007:410) has argued that "a double move, toward both very short and very long sightedness," has, through a multitude of "small ruptures," evacuated the near future as a site of political intervention. The two cases I present exemplify instances when the politics of the near future have not been fully evacuated but, instead, have morphed into open spaces and unplottable futures that cannot be rationally predicted or outlined but remain politically lively (Grosz 2004).

The inability to produce a detailed image of the near future is profoundly shaped by past histories of failure. In the case of Costa Rica, that history involves more than six years of activities to write a new law. In the case of Brazil, it can be glossed as at least one century of state control over water for political transactions. But regardless of these inauspicious pasts, my interlocutors still have faith that in a near future, which is unpredictable in the present (Grosz 2004), more democratic and sustainable politics will be possible. The future, as an unexpected event, will come on its own only if actors keep doing what they are doing, that is, if political relations keep being re-created. They are social arrangements in which "life is outrunning the pedagogies in which we have been trained" (M. Fischer 2003:37). Our technical pedagogies and theirs become inadequate, not because reality appears more complex and contingent than the pedagogies can manage but because the very instrumental logic of such pedagogies and tools cannot predict the middle-term futures they promise. Mathematical models do not facilitate a "participatory" decision. The law is no longer able to create predictabilities that are specific enough.

The temporality of the notion of faith I am exploring shows parallels with recent anthropological work on hope that suggests it is a method of temporal orientation and knowledge making that requires the holding of one's agency in abeyance (Miyazaki 2000, 2004). Faith and hope converge in their dynamic sense as methods, as forms of doing; they differ, however, to the extent that in the political contexts of Brazil and Costa Rica, faith has an orientation that does not aim to "replicate a past moment of hope" (Miyazaki 2004:139). In the cases at hand, the future is certainly at stake, at least in relation to water politics—a future that breaks with the past's unproductive, and perhaps morally wrong, chain of events through the creation and maintenance of relations across difference. These political relations speak to an ethical commitment for which the value is to attempt to do the right thing in the present, even though the future effects of such acts cannot be predicted or delineated (J. Robbins 2007). As a practical disposition to build cosmopolitical futures, the type of faith that these cases highlight does not emphasize its object in the way that having faith in a specific technical or legal solution to water problems does. This form of faith requires deferring one's agency when that agency involves anticipating and attempting to produce a detailed prescription of the right technical and legal solution, while maintaining a demanding commitment to continue cultivating one's relations.

CONCLUSION

In this chapter, I revisit two discrete moments in which faith as an assemblage of social relations enables a politics of change that embraces uncertainty. I argue that it is not the seamless articulation of means and ends, but the advent of the future and the unexpected, that creates the possibility of a radical politics in day-to-day water policies in Latin America. I do not imply that this openness is a guarantee for more democratic distribution of water, but I do suggest that, given the limits of rationalized and managerial political instruments, openness creates an opportunity to rearticulate meaning and value. My objective is not to provide an overarching theorization of the cultural meaning of faith but, instead, to experiment with faith as a way to understand contemporary "participatory" policy-making arrangements that are supposed to acknowledge difference without erasing it. In this guise, faith implies holding one's instrumental and managerial agencies in abeyance, which does not mean that faith is passive. Quite the opposite. Remaining committed to holding and maintaining relations while allowing for dispersion of knowledge, fragmentation of authority, and nonclosure of one's will is a highly demanding form of action.

By retaining relations that make political processes viable regardless of their failure to produce a desired result in the present, faith functions as a disposition to remain open to the future. It is experienced as a letting go of dreams and desires of control without abandoning politics and by preserving a commitment to continue working for one's dreams and desires. This is a future that is not linear or calculable, but one that allows for the advent of the unexpected. An awareness of the qualities that are constitutive of this type of faith—epistemological failure, pessimism, and openness to the future—can help us make sense of the day-to-day frustrations that being involved in water politics in Brazil, Costa Rica, and probably elsewhere entails. This type of engagement is similar to Daneel's experience with the Earthkeepers in Zimbabwe (chapter 10). In cases such as these, faith works when you do not believe that things will work the way you wish. This commitment to continue with the flow of the process is what, I argue, holds the potential for a transformation of the future, even against the odds of the present.

Acknowledgments

This chapter has benefited from the generosity of many people. First, I want to thank Robert Werth for patient, detailed, and multiple readings of this chapter. Participants of the dissertation writing seminar at UC Irvine helped me identify the blind spots of my argument. Bill Maurer and Michael Fischer gave me detailed and rigorous comments and suggestions on the connections between my manuscript and existing work in philosophy and anthropology, as well as feedback on my general argument. Finally, I want to thank all of the participants in the SAR seminar for the wonderful collegiality and conversations and the lovely time we spent in Santa Fe. Research for this chapter was funded by the Wenner Gren Foundation, the National Science Foundation, and the University of California, Irvine.

Notes

1. All names in this chapter have been changed to pseudonyms to respect anonymity agreements with informants.

2. See the website, http://www.gwp.org, accessed July 12, 2011.

10

Zimbabwe's Earthkeepers

When Green Warriors Enter the Valley of Shadows

Marthinus L. Daneel

When Professor Catherine Tucker invited me to participate in the seminar "Nature, Science, and Religion: Intersections Shaping Society and the Environment" at the School for Advanced Research, Santa Fe, New Mexico, my inclination was to decline the offer. The disappointment of observing the fragmentation and collapse of one of the most successful green movements in Africa, in which I had invested many years of my life, still rankled. For some years after the debacle, I had deliberately withdrawn from the green debate because I felt that the Zimbabwean story I had initiated, lived, and told had already shifted from historical day-to-day action to the realm of memories, myth, and myth making. Why should I rehash a story that has been dead and buried for several years? Yet I realized that due to the wide exposure the Zimbabwean "War of the Trees" had received (Daneel 1993, 1996a, 1996b, 1998, 1999, 2000, 2006; Sochaczewski 1996), I was obliged sooner or later to publish something on the movement's demise, for the sake of fellow Earthkeepers and academics who had shown interest in and identified in various ways with our work.

Perhaps the most inhibiting factor in my return to the green debate was the realization that I could no longer play to my strengths. I had thrived on mobilizing and fortifying the green struggle alongside African Earthkeepers in the field with an open-ended agenda that allowed for the adventure of tomorrow's creative ritualizing praxis, an emerging challenge that always held music for the future. My belief in the future and value of our ongoing struggle, given the immense need for Earthkeeping throughout Zimbabwe, Africa, and the entire world, had all along been such that I could hardly bear the thought of retelling a story that had somehow failed and died.

And yet there was the realization that my spiritual and activist commitment to Earthkeeping (Daneel 1998:17), which had preceded the official formation of our green movement, required ongoing involvement, even if it meant a return to the tree-planting experiences of yesteryear with a view to a recovery and reinterpretation of valuable insights obtained at the time for similar endeavors elsewhere. I had noticed, for instance, that the viewing of films on our tree-planting activities in Zimbabwe, after the movement's collapse, had inspirational value for my students at Boston University School of Theology. Thus, it happened that I showed up at the Santa Fe seminar as a somewhat reluctant participant, not with a paper but only with a short film on yesterday's War of the Trees in Zimbabwe.

I was pleasantly surprised at the warm welcome I received from the group of fellow participants, mainly anthropologists, all of whom shared a common interest in and dedication to the well-being of our planet Earth and the varied roles of religion and science they had studied regarding its protection. They did not seem to have a problem with the presence of a seventy-something old-timer theologian, and the encounter felt like a homecoming, an emergence into sunlight from the valley of shadows caused by the collapse of a treasured movement within the depressing and seemingly endless malaise of Mugabe's Zimbabwe.

Soon my reluctance made way for meaningful participation and positive reflection, not only on the impressive papers under discussion but also on those features in the Zimbabwean story that continue to have validity for future green endeavors in Africa and beyond, despite perplexities caused by human failure. It was, moreover, the encouraging and generous response of my seminar colleagues to the showing of the film that persuaded me to contribute this chapter.

The first section provides an overview of the organizational and ritual features of our green struggle of the War of the Trees as portrayed in the above-mentioned film. This includes a description of the interpretation of leading African-Instituted Church (AIC) Earthkeepers of their earth-healing activities as essentially a form of mission from within their churches. The second section contains a brief narrative of the factors that contributed to the collapse of the movement, followed by section three with concluding observations about the aftermath and the inspiration for an ongoing African-related green pilgrimage.

SECTION 1: PROFILE AND IMPACT OF ZIMBABWE'S EARTHKEEPING MOVEMENT: ORGANIZATION AND ACTIVITIES OF THE WAR OF THE TREES

The resolve in rural Zimbabwe to declare war on deforestation, soil erosion, and related forms of environmental destruction grew in the context of a research project conducted during the mid-1980s. I was probing the crucial role of religion in the mobilization of the *chimurenga* (liberation struggle) prior to independence. During extensive discussions with traditionalists and AIC leaders, most of them key players during the war, we agreed that the lost lands, which had been recaptured politically, were still being lost ecologically at an accelerating and alarming rate. Something massive and revolutionary was required to arrest the slide toward environmental bankruptcy and the mood of helplessness in rural society. We therefore decided to launch a new movement of "green fighters" as an extension of the pre-independence liberation struggle. In the subsequent drafting of constitutions and the mobilizing of a force of Earthkeepers, we declared the War of the Trees. Whereas the major concern to start with was nursery development and tree planting, the struggle, constitutionally, had three aims: afforestation, the protection of water resources, and wildlife conservation.

The organizational and financially empowering agency was the Zimbabwean Institute of Religious Research and Ecological Conservation (ZIRRCON), the institutionalized and extended version of my research team. Founded in 1984, this body took responsibility for the initiation and development of two affiliated organizations: the Association of Zimbabwean Traditional Ecologists (AZTREC), which comprised the majority of chiefs, headmen, spirit mediums, ex-combatants, and a large group of commoners in Masvingo Province; and the Association of African Earthkeeping Churches (AAEC), which at its peak included 180 AICs, mainly prophetic Zionist and Apostolic churches, then representing about two million adherents. During the 1990s, Zimbabwe's African Earthkeepers was the largest organization for environmental reform at the rural grassroots in southern Africa. According to internationally recognized ecological luminaries, such as Larry Rasmussen, Mary Evelyn Tucker, and John Grim, who visited us in Zimbabwe, ZIRRCON's inculturated and ritualized practices of earthcare also ranked as equally innovative as, if not more than, those of indigenous green movements they had observed elsewhere in the Two-Thirds World.

During ZIRRCON's first fifteen years, while I acted as director, we established fifteen to eighteen mother nurseries, some cultivating more than one hundred thousand seedlings yearly, and many small-scale satellite nurseries run by women and schools. An estimated twelve to fifteen million trees were planted in several thousand woodlots by AZTREC and AAEC peasant communities and by women and schoolchildren in the central and southeastern communal lands of Zimbabwe. The variety of trees planted included fruit trees in orchards for personal and commercial use; exotics like eucalyptus for building operations; indigenous trees for firewood and the restoration of denuded land; lucaena for cattle fodder, firewood, and nitrate fixing in arable lands; and indigenous hardwoods, like kiaat and pod mahogany, as a long-term investment for future generations. ZIRRCON's Earthkeepers became known for cultivating more indigenous fruit-tree seedlings, thorn trees, mountain acacias, and ancestor-related trees than any other institution in the country. Government officials, including President Mugabe, attended and participated in our annual tree-planting ceremonies.

A Women's Desk with several departments ably supervised the income-generating projects of eighty women's clubs that included cloth manufacturing, bakeries, soap production, the pressing and refining of sunflower oil, and vegetable and fruit production. These clubs also facilitated the struggle against soil erosion by filling erosion gullies with stones and planting vertiver grass in the affected areas. The spirit mediums and male tribal elders in turn assisted the chiefs by restoring the customary laws on the protection of trees and wildlife in the ancestral sanctuaries of holy groves. Offenders were apprehended and brought to chiefs' courts, where they were heavily fined and required to plant trees in denuded areas. Likewise, offenders who engaged in river bank cultivation and spoiling the veld's grass cover with sleighs were served with heavy fines by the "green chiefs."

Up to thirty youth clubs were developed at rural schools. The pupils were taken on bird- and tree-identification trips, and Parks and Wildlife personnel accompanied them to some of the larger game parks to teach them about big game and species of game no longer found in communal lands. They were also familiarized with issues of modern wildlife conservation. ZIRRCON proposed a conservation project for collective, interracial game farming that would incorporate about fifty farms to the east of Masvingo town. These plans had to be abandoned due to the farm invasions, allowed by Mugabe in the year 2000. A few years later, an estimated 85 percent of the entire game population on Zimbabwe's farms had been destroyed. So much for game conservation and protection of the country's natural resources!

A Ritualized Mission

All tree-planting ceremonies were ritualized in either traditionalist or Christian fashion. The ritual component shaped the green struggle as a holy war, directed by the Creator-God and forces from the spirit world. The rituals drew large contingents of rural participants, mobilized entire village and school communities, highlighted publicly the resolve and commitment of the green fighters, and united people in a common cause regardless of diverse religious persuasions and lingering conflicts of the past.

AZTREC's Traditionalist Rituals

AZTREC's ceremonies resembled the old rain-requesting rituals of the past, called *mukwerere* (Daneel 1998:chs. 4–6). Sacrificial finger-millet beer was brewed for the senior clan-ancestors, the *varidzi venyika* (ancestral guardians of the land), whose graves are in sacred groves on holy mountains. Sacrificial addresses of these ancestors, on the basis of traditional cosmology, entrusted the seedlings to be planted to their protective care and brought to the fore the neglected ecological obligations of old with appeals for their revival and implementation. The guardians were also requested to appeal to the African High-God, Mwari, for ample rain to sustain the newly planted woodlots of trees. Toward the end of each tree-planting season, a delegation of traditionalist tree planters was sent to the High-God shrines, 300 km away, to report to the oracle on the progress of the green struggle. This trek stemmed from the belief that Mwari and the senior clan-ancestors controlled all struggles in the country—for political and environmental liberation—from within a spirit war council.

Christian Earthkeepers of the AAEC also attended both traditional tree-planting and oracle-reporting ceremonies. They refrained from drinking sacrificial beer, to demonstrate the retention of their Christian identity, but assisted their non-Christian counterparts in planting the trees. Likewise, they refrained from full communion with the oracular deity, even as they engaged in close association and dialogue with cult officials at the shrines. Thus, in an ecumenical, open-ended movement, the bitter strife of the past between Zionist prophets and Mwari cultists made way for positive attitudes of understanding and tolerance in the execution of a common cause.

The AAEC's Tree-Planting Eucharist

AAEC's tree-planting eucharist integrated an Earthkeeping ministry with the sacrament of holy communion (Daneel 1999:ch. 2). This development was pivotal as it bound environmental stewardship into the heartbeat of church life and biblically based spirituality. In African agrarian society, this was a powerful way of witnessing a change of heart within the church, an illustration of revisioning the church at its core, for it to become a better vehicle for the missionary good news it wanted to convey. Moreover, this ceremony highlighted the characteristic trends of an emergent AIC theology of the environment, one not written in books but symbolized in budding trees sustaining a ravished countryside. Some of the key activities of the outdoor tree-planting sacrament were the following:

- Preparations of the woodlot included digging holes for the seedlings, fencing, and naming the woodlot "the Lord's Acre" as the Christian equivalent of the traditional sacred grove (*marambatemwa*).

- Dancing and singing around the stacked seedlings to praise God and inspire His Earthkeepers to engage in action.

- Sermons by AIC bishops and ZIRRCON staff, followed by speeches of representatives from the Forestry Commission and from Parks and Wildlife, government officials, and others, whereby the eucharist evolved into an inclusive public event rather than an exclusive in-group event.

- The sacrament itself was preceded by all Christian participants confessing publicly their ecological sins, such as felling trees without replanting, aggravating soil erosion through riverbank cultivating, and spoiling wildlife by poaching.

- After confession, each communicant carried a seedling to the table, where the bread and wine were administered. Thereby, nature was symbolically drawn into the inner circle of communion with Christ the Redeemer, through Whom the emergence of a new Heaven and Earth was anticipated and proclaimed.

- After bread and wine, the traditionalists, who were observing, joined the Christian communicants, and the green army moved together to the "Lord's Acre" to commit the seedlings to the soil.

- As they were planted, the seedlings were addressed as "relatives" by the planters and told of the care they would receive and the anticipated benefits they would bring to the planters.

- In conclusion, many of the tree planters knelt in queues in front of the prophetic healers for laying on of hands and prayer. Thus, the healing of the barren earth and of human beings blended into a single event that witnessed to Christ, the crucified and resurrected savior of all the Earth.

Ecumenical Sacrament and Mission Command

The Zimbabwean AICs traditionally have two mission-activating eucharists. First, the Easter Paschal eucharist festivities in Bishop Mutendi's Zion Christian Church (ZCC) became the springboard for the classic mission command as found in Matthew 28:19 (Daneel 1980). The sacramental good news of Christ's sacrificial death on the cross, blended with His call for mission after His resurrection, challenged the entire church to engage in countrywide campaigns culminating in mass conversions and baptisms. Such outreach was always planned during the Paschal celebrations and triggered immediately after the climactic eucharist administered by Mutendi. Second, the practice was extended in 1972 in the context of the first ecumenical movement of substance among the Zimbabwean AICs, popularly called *Fambidzano* (Church Cooperative) (Daneel 1989). To the member churches, the cornerstone texts of their movement, John 17:21–23, called for church unity as a condition for effective missionary witness. Their joint Paschal celebrations caused their former, individually conducted eucharists to be given a broader ecumenical base, although they did not trigger united missionary action of the same magnitude as that of the ZCC.

The AAEC capitalized on this twofold eucharistic tradition by building on both its ecumenical and its missionary dimensions. That the tree-planting eucharist itself was considered an empowered, earth-healing mission was reflected in the sermon of Bishop Wapendama, leader of the Signs of the Apostles Church, to a multichurch audience of tree planters:

> Mwari [God] saw the devastation of the land. So He called His envoys [ZIRRCON/AAEC leaders] to shoulder the task of delivering the earth....Deliverance, Mwari says, lies in the trees. Jesus said, "I leave you, my followers, to complete my work!" And that task is the one of healing! We, the followers of Jesus, have to continue with his healing ministry. We must all fight, clothing, healing the earth with trees! It is our task to strengthen this mission with our numbers of people. If all of us work with enthusiasm, we shall clothe and heal the entire land with trees and drive off affliction [the evil of destruction]. I believe we can change it! [Daneel 1999:39]

Wapendama implied that the union between Christ and his disciples (cutting across denominational boundaries) is sacramentally confirmed, with the mission of earth healing integral to it. God certainly takes the initiative to deliver and restore the ravaged earth, but responsibility to deliver the stricken earth from its malady lies with the Christian body of believers.

Implicit in Wapendama's words was the emerging AAEC image of Christ's church as keeper of creation. What the green church featured was the healing ministry of Christ extended through grace to the entire cosmos.

Features of Green Mission Churches

There can be little doubt that the AAEC's engagement in the War of the Trees has led to a breakthrough in AIC notions of the church as hospital. As propounded by Bishop Wapendama and as is generally true for most prophetic churches, the healing ministry of Christ was still focal in the church's mission. Healing of human affliction in the widest possible sense remained one of the most important recruitment devices of the AIC's prophetic ministry (Daneel 1974:186). But it now included more deliberately than before the holistic deliverance and salvation of Mwari's stricken earth. In healing the Earth, by reaching out beyond the physical and mental ailments of human beings, by setting internal leadership and interchurch conflicts aside for a higher God-given purpose, the Earthkeepers themselves were healed.

There was endless variation in the AAEC's tree-planting sermons, which bore out the strong theological undercurrent of understanding earthcare as *Missio Dei* and therefore as the mission of God's church. Rev. Davison Tawoneichi of the Evangelical Ministry of Christ Church, for instance, preached the following at a tree-planting ceremony: "Earthkeeping is part of the body of Christ.... Our destruction of nature is an offense against the body of Christ, and therefore the church should heal the wounded body of Christ." This view complemented the assertion of Bishop Wapendama about mission as an extension of Christ's healing ministry. Only, in this instance, Christ's body was understood as being, itself, afflicted by the abuse of nature (McFague 1987:69ff; D. Messer 1992:67ff). This statement underscored the growing tendency in AAEC tree-planting eucharists to view Christ's body in both its ecclesiastic and its cosmic connotations. Subsequently, Earthkeepers set out on their healing mission of afforestation to restore the cosmically wounded body of Christ.

Ecclesiological Shifts

How, then, did the green mission affect the life and shape of the Earthkeeping church? First, the healing ministry expanded. The black "Jerusalems," that is, prophetic church headquarters, were still healing colonies where the afflicted, the marginalized, and the poor could feel at home. But the concept visibly changed as dedicated Earthkeepers expanded their colonies into "environmental hospitals" to accommodate the wounded earth. The denuded land became a patient. The dispensary (the faith-healing arsenal of holy cords, holy water, staffs, paper, and related symbols of divine healing) became the nursery where the correct medicine—indigenous, exotic, and fruit trees—was cultivated. The entire church community, at religious headquarters and at outlying congregations, became the healing agent under the guidance of ZIRRCON-AAEC operational headquarters in Masvingo town. Consistent aftercare in new woodlots provided proof of the church's commitment in mission, the woodlot itself becoming the focus of witnessing sermons and the source of inspiration for an expanding ministry. The testimonies of healed human patients in the past had contributed both to a reaffirmation of belief in God's healing powers and to the church's recruitment of new members. Far from interfering with the church's worship and pastoral work, the earth-healing ministry appeared to provide new impetus and direction to church life, as well as church growth.

Second, a new generation of iconic church leaders emerged, environmental missionaries whose evangelical drive included good news for all creation. They replaced the prominent first-generation AIC icons, like Bishop Mutendi, who had been featured as "black Messiahs" (Daneel 1984). In this shift, it became evident that agroeconomic development and progress would be meaningless unless they included environmental sanctification and consciously struck a balance between exploitive agricultural progress and altruistic earth restoration. This was the true purpose of an expanded missionary mandate and message proclaimed by the AAEC's iconic missionaries. They were persistently present in village life; all people who wanted to participate were empowered to share a new dominion of service. All of the missionaries, whether they were staff members at AAEC headquarters, full-time nursery or woodlot keepers, bishops and prophets with "environmental hospitals," or women developing ministries of compassion, had their roots in peasant society and were well placed to demonstrate their churches' solidarity with nature. The tree planting was not obscuring Christ's lordship or saviorhood, as some evangelicals may be inclined to think, but unveiling and illuminating dimensions of the mystery of divine presence in nature that may have gone unnoticed by many believers and nonbelievers.

Third, the AAEC's afforestation programs stimulated a need for new ethical codes. Leading Earthkeepers felt strongly that clear environmental laws should be drafted on an ecumenical platform and that strict church discipline should be implemented in the green church against all trespassers of such laws. Bishop Farawo, who was managing a large nursery as a veritable Zion City of Trees, propagated court trials for tree fellers at church council level and punishment of offenders through extra duties of tree planting and aftercare in new woodlots to compensate for the damage done. Bishop Chimhangwa urged campaigns of "conscientization" to reinforce the gospel message of Earth's salvation. He considered general ignorance of the "gospel of the trees" to be the cause for unwarranted use of the destructive ax. The more radical exponents of the green struggle who identified the church's mission with environmental legislation and control insisted that trespassers be debarred from holy communion or even be excommunicated if they persisted in their evil ways. Evangelist Samuel Nhongo expressed such views: "The churches, the chiefs [AZTREC], and the government should sit down together and plan properly for this war. The church's new environmental laws should be universally known and respected! Otherwise, we will be merely chasing the wind." Seen as an institution with legislative and disciplinary powers, the church in this Earthkeeper's view also became the vehicle of uncompromising struggle. In this mission, the church was at risk, willing to be controversial, to suffer and sacrifice whatever discipleship in this realm required.

Fourth, the emergence of the green church meant the closing of ranks between Christian and traditionalist Earthkeepers in a common cause. The implied commitment of the church to a form of open ecumenism set the stage for regular and continuous interfaith dialogue in joint action. A great difference existed, however, between developing policies of antithesis to traditional religion from within the relative privacy of healer–patient consultations in healing colonies and the more open situation in which Earthkeeping required the conduct of joint religious ceremonies in the presence of large numbers of out-groups who in the past were the still-to-be converted heathen or at least the religious opposition. Much greater caution was required in the evaluation of another's religion when the "other" was always present in what had become religious brother- and sisterhoods bonded together in a common cause. The Earthkeeping brothers and sisters were no longer opponents, but fellow pilgrims in the quest for ecojustice. The green dialogue marked by interreligious tolerance and friendship by no means meant religious relativism. Yet it was as if the ecological struggle through the newly planted trees breathed the message "You cannot afford the luxury of religious conflict if it causes the wounded earth to suffocate!"

The shifts described above provide only a sampling of the wide range of activities ZIRRCON's contribution in earthcare had generated and a somewhat fleeting impression of the impact its green ministry had on the churches involved in the struggle. Nonetheless, I trust that even if only a fragment of the real story is told, it will portray something of the rich experience and legacy of Zimbabwe's Earthkeepers. Herein lies something of value: a history of struggle that does the rural poor of Africa proud; innovative green rituals, traditional and Christian, that can provide guidelines for grassroots ministries of nurturing a battered environment; and enacted patterns of earthcare that contain the building stones for future African theologies of creation and environmental ethics.

SECTION 2: THE DYNAMICS OF FAILURE
A Stable Organization?

As ZIRRCON, with headquarters in Masvingo town, was the administrative hub of our Earthkeepers' movement, great care was taken from the outset to provide organizational stability for its geographically far-flung and loosely knit constituencies. A legally drafted constitution defined the parameters of power and the interplay of governing bodies at the rural and headquarters levels. At headquarters, for instance, my duties and authority as founder-director, particularly in finance (fundraising abroad, salaries, and control of local expenditures), were subject to scrutiny and approval of an executive board. The board included representation of the main departments, such as the Women's Desk, Youth Work, Ecological Activities, Theological Education, Finance, and Transport, and full-time representatives of AZTREC and AAEC. The ultimate body of control with powers of assessing the performance of ZIRRCON and authorizing the appointment or dismissal of salaried workers, whether staff members in the office or field operators at tree nurseries, was the Annual General Meeting (AGM), which met on a rotation basis in rural districts. This body encompassed the widest possible representation of ZIRRCON staff and all senior stakeholders of its religious affiliates, AZTREC and AAEC. The safeguards for stability were constitutionally formulated, but written safeguards of course do not provide guarantees for stability if the coded guidelines are not fully backed up in practice.

Great care was also taken to establish relations of mutual trust between ZIRRCON and donor agencies abroad. As fundraiser, I insisted on total transparency and accountability by our finance department in the expenditure of the huge amounts received. This was accomplished through fully documented annual audits and, at my insistence, regular visits to our local projects by donor representatives for purposes of collaborative interaction and development of mutual trust. This policy led to financial stability and a considerable degree of mutual identification and satisfaction between donors and recipients, at least during the period when I was able to function as a hands-on director.

However, organizational effectiveness and consolidation were certainly not the accomplishment of a single individual. These were generated by a remarkable team effort and fed by the underlying vision and enthusiasm of a fast-growing people's movement. For once, the rural poor were walking tall! They had taken hold of something they were proud of. Through the public media, they were capturing the imagination of the nation. They were somehow directing their own destiny through the mobilization of school, village, church, and cult communities in a struggle beneficial to themselves and the earth community, which brought them a measure of self-esteem, dignity, national recognition, and a renewal of hope in a better future. But could it last in the face of ever-worsening economic conditions in the country?

Debilitating External Factors

One of the most serious problems ZIRRCON faced was the destabilizing effect of deteriorating political and economic conditions. The repeated devaluation of the local currency and the scarcity of foreign funds for individual use caused repeated revisions of salaries. At some point, it got so bad that salaries had to be revised and upgraded on a monthly basis. A degree of discontent among our salaried staff who barely could make ends meet was inevitable. Their salaries were generally much better than those of their relatives and friends with similar qualifications. But as they had made salaried progress, more members of their extended families became dependent on them. Thus, they were facing a perpetual no-win situation, a process well known in Africa.

As the economic situation worsened, corruption spread throughout society. The shared ideals of transparency and accountability in the use of donor funds in our movement appeared to be superseded by feelings of entitlement. The struggle for survival became an excuse to some key figures in our finance department for the slackening of moral standards, well hidden at first but escalating rapidly after my departure as director. What exacerbated this trend was the collapse of an independent judicial system in Zimbabwe. Success in court, it seemed, no longer depended on one's ability to provide conclusive evidence about wrongdoing but on connections with powerful politicians or other officials who were capable of having scheduled legal hearings aborted.

The classic example of this kind of maneuvering occurred toward the end of my directorship when an intensive investigation in Masvingo on the activities of senior officers in Fambidzano, the AIC ecumenical movement I had founded in 1972, had yielded sufficient evidence of mismanaged funds and related wrongdoing to warrant a trial in high court. But the interference of a senior government official resulted in the disappearance of the evidence and elimination of the case from the high court schedule: end of story, case closed! To those aware of what was happening, the writing for the ZIRRCON Earthkeepers was clearly on the wall. Justice for the people—the villagers operating at the rural grassroots—was certainly not on the agenda of the exploiters, who were enriching themselves by implementing hidden finance agendas.

External interference with our established field programs also damaged the internal equilibrium and unity between our rural and headquarters Earthkeepers. ZIRRCON's initial success and fundraising agenda drew the interest of an increasing number of donors and development agencies. Eventually, "too many cooks were spoiling the broth" and causing confusion in our constituencies at the expense of purpose and effective leadership. For example, a group of so-called "experts" on rural development arrived in Masvingo to teach "participant strategic planning," invited by the International Union for the Conservation of Nature's (IUCN) project office in Harare and my local successor-to-be. The "experts" were soon convincing villagers that they had to reinvent their own movement to introduce electrification schemes, dams, and other projects to uplift their communities, objectives that had never been on ZIRRCON's agenda. When all the "experts" left, feeling happy with themselves about their "hard work" in Zimbabwe, large numbers of starry-eyed Earthkeeping villagers were dreaming about the electrification and other wonderful things to come to their underdeveloped villages. What the "experts" conveniently forgot to tell them was where the money would come from for all their proposed schemes of progress. It became clear that my fellow Zimbabwean Earthkeepers had assumed that I, the "miracle maker," would land the resources for them. They were surprised and disappointed when I rejected that notion. They assumed that I had invited the "experts" and were ignorant of my opposition to foreigners who were misleadingly insinuating that participant strategic planning had not taken place at the outset of our movement. Many of our Earthkeepers did not realize that the so-called "experts" did not care about eroding our established patterns of local leadership or raising false expectations about rural development for which ZIRRCON had never undertaken any responsibility.

Leadership Issues

From the beginning, my fellow Earthkeepers and I had agreed that my role in building the Earthkeeping movement was a temporary one. I was to withdraw and continue with my academic concerns once the movement was solidly grounded and running on its own. The problem was how to determine the movement's maturity in terms of the three-self principle (self-governing, self-supporting, and self-propagating), a formula often used by church-planting mission churches to establish the ability of newly found indigenous churches to proceed on their own. No missionary institution was facilitating my decision making, other than the indigenous movement itself. As long as I managed to raise the basic funds for our work and controlled financial expenditure to the satisfaction of donors and Zimbabwean Earthkeepers, I remained as managing director. The challenge for me was to stay and facilitate the religious ritualization of our greening activities, stimulate the strategy of growth and religious interaction, and promote the consolidation of a fast-growing movement. Given the vast networks of contacts I had built and my ministry among Shona traditionalists (the Matonjeni cult in particular) and AICs, I was well placed for the challenge at hand and fascinated by an adventure in green praxis that complemented my academic work at the University of South Africa (UNISA).

However, a few crucial factors defined relations between my colleagues and me at ZIRRCON headquarters. First, I remained a privileged white African academic with a relatively high university salary and the built-in security of a pension scheme for retirement. My African colleagues, by contrast, had good salaries by local standards but without long-term pension prospects. Second, my academic contract and means allowed me flexibility to travel in and out of Zimbabwe. Thus, I was less captive in the deteriorating Zimbabwe situation than my fellow workers. I have little doubt that these discrepancies psychologically impacted staff relations and loyalties at ZIRRCON headquarters. It is possible, even likely, that comparison of our situations contributed to the eventual mismanagement of salary funds after my resignation.

Third, I moved to Boston University in the USA during the mid-1990s to teach as a part-time missiologist. This meant that I could spend only six months each year in southern Africa and had to relinquish my monthly visits from UNISA. The foundation of our movement held firm for several years as headquarters staff and Earthkeepers in the many villages kept working. Then, in 2000, the invasion of commercial and other white farms led to the breaking of Zimbabwe's economic backbone, the radical escalation of unemployment, and an increasing migration of laborers seeking better opportunities and a stable future elsewhere. The cracks in our own institution started appearing as the local leadership in Masvingo stumbled, compromising the strict discipline and work ethic of the past. The mismanagement of funds, buildings, vehicles, and other assets caused conflict and dissent, eroded the commitment to transparency and accountability, and dimmed the cherished vision of a greening Earth.

Entering the Valley of Shadows

The regular programs of our projects started faltering in late 2001, and matters came to a head after an investigation I requested by a bookkeeper representing one of our donors. The misuse and abuse of project vehicles, the discontinuation of keeping travel log books, the use of project fuel in private vehicles, and an unwillingness to provide the bookkeeper with full evidence of financial expenditure were clear pointers to abandonment of the ZIRRCON code of conduct we had all agreed to. With little influence after long absences, I had no option but to officially resign lest I be held responsible for the rot that had set in. During the subsequent change-of-leadership ceremony, I publicly mentioned five areas of administrative weaknesses that had to be addressed urgently for the movement to survive. My successor accordingly promised to address and mend them as he donned my robe, by way of symbolizing the Old Testament transfer of power from Moses to Joshua. The audience in turn shouted with raised fists, "Forward the War of the Trees!"

But, regardless of the dedication-binding rituals, the careful grooming of a successor with all the necessary credentials, the strength of a network carefully crafted on trust and mutuality, the built-in constitutional safeguards for future continuity and financial stability, and the boundless support by the vast majority of rural constituents for Joshua, the new director and successor of Bishop Moses, the end result was the same: mismanagement of funds, abuse and theft of the movement's assets, and the snatching away of future opportunities for millions of rural people. The valley of twilight we were entering soon turned into darkness.

Early in 2003, when ZIRRCON staff openly protested that the new director was ignoring his installation pledges, he fired twenty-eight salaried senior staff members working at headquarters. Thus, in one swoop, the nucleus of ZIRRCON, representing a fifteen-year investment in ecological experience and expertise, was wiped out. Some vacancies were filled by unqualified relatives and friends of the director who could not or would not maintain the former standards of Earthkeeping. Thereby, a people's movement of substance, national acclaim, and innovative diversity was turned into a faltering little kingdom of an extended family group.

During the next two years, delegations of dismissed staff members, AAEC bishops, and AZTREC chiefs visited me at my residence in Masvingo in search of a solution that would save our movement. But no solution was in sight as long as project funds were available to the man who held the purse, enabling him to arrange protection with town officials. For a short time, I had a judge of the high court in Harare freeze the main bank account of ZIRRCON, pending legal enquiry. But a junior local magistrate of Masvingo managed to overturn the judge's injunction, which left the account empty. The Earthkeeper delegations kept hoping against hope, but the darkness in the valley was the darkness of an entire country, which precluded from justice the faceless poor and the politically non-elect.

I attempted, on behalf of ZIRRCON's disgruntled Earthkeepers, to have a team of African lawyers in Masvingo and Harare prepare a court case against the man and his cohorts responsible for ZIRRCON's collapse. Lawyers' delays and fees kept escalating, and they appeared to be more interested in levying fees for work they never completed than orchestrating a fair trial for their clients. Ultimately, I came to the conclusion that in post-colonial Zimbabwe it was more important for the judiciary to overcome evil by obstructing a white man from embarrassing African colleagues through exposure of their destructive misuse of funds than to bring countrymen to justice who had deprived thousands of rural people from the opportunity and means to make economic progress for themselves and a meaningful ecological contribution to their country.

Meanwhile, my successor proceeded to also obstruct the AGM's ability to act. On the pretext of not receiving adequate funds for this annual event, he simply discontinued the meetings. Disappointed and disillusioned by the turn of events, our generous donors, who had committed themselves to sponsorship of the War of the Trees for the long haul, eventually walked away. As the funds dried up, the proud signposts of ZIRRCON, AZTREC, and AAEC came down, and the nurseries and women's and youth clubs disappeared.

In 2008, my former colleague, yesteryear's "man of promise," visited me in an attempt to restore our personal relations. But I told him I was not ready to talk about guilt and forgiveness while he was still wrongfully driving project vehicles and renting out ZIRRCON offices for personal gain. I insisted that he seek the forgiveness of former staff members whose careers he had ruined, publicly confess his betrayal of the rural poor, and empower the senior stakeholders of our green movement through prop-erly convened and representative AGM meetings. Stakeholders should be able to exercise their legitimate powers of determining what to do about the remaining ZIRRCON property, which they, not the movement's founder or executive director, owned. While I was still recognized as

Bishop Moses and as Muchakata (the Wild Cork Tree, a tree protected by the ancestors) by the Christian and traditionalist tree planters of AAEC and AZTREC, respectively, I felt I could not become party to a process of reconciliation with the guilty party before convincing signs of a complete change of heart were evident to all parties concerned.

It was sad to see the slumped shoulders of a former friend and confidant as he turned to leave. I was reminded of the biblical story of the rich young man who turned away from Christ because he could not face the cost of discipleship. It was my own shoulders I was looking at. For I, too, had often enough faltered and stumbled in the quest for true discipleship. Genuine forgiveness, I realized, could be realized only as a gift from beyond ourselves, from a merciful and caring God.

SECTION 3: RESUMPTION OF A GREEN PILGRIMAGE

Entanglement in disappointments, resentment at failures, feelings of helplessness to mend matters in the face of destructive forces, and the endless travail of the African dispossessed at your doorstep can cause one to no longer seek or see the light, to somehow stagnate in the anguish and despair of a twilight world. Surprisingly, then, the weight of it evaporates like mist before the sun when you surface into the lightness of being, celebration, and laughter—the spirit of which prevailed during the discussions at Santa Fe. I was impressed by the manner in which all team members took great interest in one another's papers and provided consistently penetrative evaluations of each individual contribution with a view to improvement of the envisaged joint publication. The atmosphere thus created also enabled me to relate meaningfully once more to the still challenging Earthkeepers' experience in Zimbabwe and to narrate aspects of the green struggle that still lives in its ground forces and towers above the unfortunate organizational failure and collapse.

Inspiration for a renewal of ecological commitment derived from discussions on the examples of religiously motivated or religion-related earth-care projects in various parts of the world. Hallum's (chapter 7, this volume) thorough examination of the role of Mayan religion in Guatemala in emphasizing the sacredness of nature and, as such, providing strong motivation for human protection of the environment, for instance, revealed a close parallel to the religiously driven work of the Zimbabwean Earthkeepers. She quotes Don Eladio, one of the former Mayan key figures working for the Alliance for International Reforestation. His words and the religious convictions behind them could just as well have been those of Bishop Wapendama (quoted earlier) and any of the AAEC bishops or a wisdom speech of one of our elderly traditionalist sages of AZTREC. Likewise, Scanlan Lyons's (chapter 2, this volume) arresting use of key words such as a "team of good Christians" and "servant leadership" to depict a growing awareness in Brazil of the crucial significance of religion as a "propulsion force" for the mobilization of nature-protecting initiatives resonates with the moral conviction and undergirding spirituality that moved the Zimbabwean forces of the War of the Trees.

Not that these parallel developments necessarily reflect predictable trends of homogeneity in the interface of religion and nature conservation. In Tucker's study of forestry management among Lenca coffee farmers in Honduras, (chapter 6, this volume), she mentions the decline of traditional beliefs. Moreover, traditional beliefs tend to see nature as self-renewing. Consequently, the traditional religious motivation for resource protection appears to be more limited than observed in some of the other case studies. Nonetheless, Tucker's clear analysis of the interplay between interfaith, environmental, and pragmatic economic considerations among the Lenca farmers provides us with profound insights about the kinds of complexities involved in the engagement of peasant societies in earthcare.

The point I wish to make, however, is that the general recognition during our discussions of the importance of religion for conservationist endeavors the world over reminded me of the ongoing validity in the global context of the Zimbabwean Earthkeeping experience and my responsibility to keep recounting it. For I realized afresh that the collapse of our movement and the bitterness it provoked were due to the moral failure of only a number of officers who misused their powers of control, and not a failure of all the rural Earthkeepers. Their dedication never flagged. Neither were the strategies of our green warfare flawed. The basic instincts and religious convictions that generated and maintained the momentum in the ranks of the green warriors for a massive seedling cultivation, tree planting, and a woodlot aftercare program were sound and genuine to the core. Having found an informed and creative soundboard among fellow stewards of the good earth, I felt ready to shake the inertia of the twilight valley and move on in a new phase of green pilgrimage, one that retains the positive message of Zimbabwe's Earthkeepers in the midst of facing new challenges.

Finally, I wish to acknowledge Ballestero's (chapter 9, this volume) understanding of faith as a generative power. In her Latin American study, such faith constitutes a willingness in an assortment of interest groups to engage in ongoing discourse, politics, and the preparation of legislation— on the use and control of water resources at national and multinational levels—even if the outcome over time remains uncertain. In a sense, she is signaling a faith against all odds, a "practical disposition" that factors in the possibility of failure. For, although such disposition is open to the possibility of positive resolution, it includes frustration and disbelief. According to Ballestero, "faith works when you do not believe things will work the way you wish."

When I first read Ballestero's paper, I was in a process of reorientation regarding the requirements of an ongoing pilgrimage beyond ZIRRCON. Touched by her remarkable exposition on faith, I realized to what extent I have operated in many fields on the basis of a faith that expected success at all costs and took success for granted. Conditioned by a Western performance culture and cast by my AIC friends in the role of a Moses figure, albeit reluctantly, I was focused rather one-sidedly on the positive and epic achievements of Israel's liberator figure. I attempted over thirty-five years to fortify their exodus from the white-led mission churches through a ministry of theological training for their leadership (Daneel 1989:chs. 5–7). It was only after the collapse and loss of two liberative movements that I was prepared to consider the flawed leadership of the prophet of Israel whose lapses in faith and quick temper eventually cost him an entry into the Promised Land. I recognized similar flaws in myself. For me, too, there was no promised land in terms of an ultimate achievement: no establishment of a permanent School of Theology for the AICs, as I had originally envisioned as end goal for Fambidzano, nor the introduction of ritually protected game sanctuaries on the basis of interracial reconciliation among the farming communities of Zimbabwe as ZIRRCON's ultimate contribution, next to the greening of Africa through afforestation. The Moses experience I had lived in Zimbabwe, in retrospect, had more to teach me on issues of humility and patience in faith than on the heroic deeds of success. After all, the investments made were in the people themselves rather than in the building of structures and organizations.

How, then, was Ballestero's understanding of a faith without predictable solutions for the future a faith against the odds, as I like to call it, relevant for our situation in the Zimbabwean valley of shadows? First, a comparative reflection enabled me to recognize in retrospect the positive features of a daring and open-ended faith I shared with traditionalist spirit mediums right at the start of our movement. They were hardened, former guerilla fighters of chimurenga, staying in my house during weekend-long sessions of planning a new offensive. They listened to my Old Testament readings about Israel's God promising afforestation and new waterways in the desert, and I listened to their addresses of guardian ancestors of the land as they dedicated their anticipated struggle for the renewal of the Earth to those guardians while pouring strong-odored, sacrificial snuff all over my floors. There was no guarantee of success, no sponsorship, no money, only a strong communal will to proceed, grounded in faith, gifted by the grace of our Creator. When we could see and feel the play of shiny leaves of seedlings between our fingers in our first nursery, situated in my backyard and nurtured by Lydia Chabata (Mafuranhunzi Gumbo 1995), a reputed spirit medium of the chimurenga war front, we knew that our War of the Trees was at hand.

Second, I was reminded of a bonding of different faiths in support of a common cause after the AICs joined the struggle. Misgivings about a possible loss of religious identity and Christian credibility in the mixing of religions and exposure to the so-called "demons" at the High-God shrines were overcome as the enemies of many years befriended each other and started planning for a joint campaign. There were no assurances that this kind of unprecedented venture in interreligious ecumenism could succeed and wax strong. Only a deep faith, combined with a willingness in the ranks of both groups to risk exposure, carried us forward when we started to break down the walls of partition and prejudice. Reflections on the regenerative faith that carried our earth stewards in the past revive those moments, clear away the clutter of despair, and provide momentum as I reach out (and as we all reach out) for a renewal of pilgrimage.

Third, the faith that holds no guarantees for future solutions, at least not those of our own designs, tells me that despite the collapse of ZIRRCON, the green fighters may yet again go to war in Zimbabwe. I mentioned this prospect during a discussion on the faith issue in Santa Fe with Ballestero and Tucker. Thousands upon thousands of rural-farmers-turned-Earthkeepers have invested in a successful movement and seen the benefits for themselves and for an abused Earth. They themselves were the creators of a proud new green tradition as a solid legacy of the rural poor. Their experience in itself represents the seeds that can germinate and grow unto renewal. One can dare, in faith, to hope that the shackles of dictatorship can be cast off to allow for another flowering of spiritual activism at the grassroots to heal the Earth. Should that happen while I am still around, I may be able to watch the greening of Gutu District, home area of my Rufura relatives, who have adopted me as a clansman of nomadic tradition—from the distant heights of the sacred Mount Rasa (my Mount Nebo?).

But, as I walk out of the darkened valley, feeling the warmth of the sun, I realize that God's time for what is to come can be as enigmatic and hidden from our understanding as the growth of some of the trees we planted. Once, we planted a fenced woodlot full of healthy red mahogany seedlings. Despite our care, all the young trees withered away and died. Disappointed, we left the fencing as we abandoned the woodlot. Several years later, to our surprise, young mahogany trees started breaking through the soil, showing excellent life and growth. We simply did not know that the young seedlings aboveground had to die while their root systems took several years to establish themselves in the good earth below before real tree growth could commence. Likewise, I did not expect the rekindling of the faith and hope that had gone down with ZIRRCON when I reluctantly traveled for a gathering in Santa Fe.

11

Religious (Re-)Turns in the Wake of Global Nature

Toward a Cosmopolitics

Adrian J. Ivakhiv

"God Is Back," exclaims the cover of the 2009 book by *Economist* journalists Micklethwaite and Wooldridge. It seems that what a minority of scholars had been quietly telling one another in the years following September 11, 2001, has now become something shouted from the rooftops: religion has not gone away as modernizers and secularization theorists—those who committed the deeds that contributed to God's removal and those who just observed and narrated them—assumed it would. No, it appears that religion has reawakened with a vengeance.

But is religion recuperating, or had it never really gone dormant, except among the secular intellectuals who prematurely announced its demise? Whatever the case with religion itself, it is less deniable that a religious turn has occurred among philosophers and social scientists, including some of the most prominent intellectuals of our time, from Derrida and Habermas to C. Taylor, Nancy, and Zizek (Davis, Milbank, and Zizek 2005; de Vries 2006, 2008; Latour and Weibel 2002). And while at least part of this theophilosophical turn preceded the events of September 11 (de Vries 1999), those events have surely contributed to the explosive charge that cultural and religious differences—civilizational differences, for some—have come to carry. This turn is no less the case in Western liberal democracies, where many fear the intrusive encroachment of "others" whose cultural values appear threateningly different from the mainstream, than in the parts of the world where foreign armies impose wars that are believed to be over religion as much as anything else.

If a "before" and an "after" are implicitly marked by the kinds of things described in this volume, this religious turn is a good candidate for such a moment. As suggested in the introductory chapter, at least two other before-and-after moments are lurking in the background of this collection, each related to the relationship between religion and nature. The first moment followed the publication of White's (1967) *Science* article, in which the historian famously argues that the Judaeo-Christian tradition shares a heavy burden of responsibility for the crisis in relations between humans and the natural world. The emergence and growth of the field of "religion and ecology" and the so-called "greening of religion" have been two expressions of this moment, which in the first chapter we term the *religious turn to ecology*. The other before-and-after moment, an environmentalist turn to religion, can be said to have commenced in the early 1980s when the World Wildlife Fund (WWF) invited leaders of the world's major religious traditions to gather in Assisi, Italy, home of the founder of the Franciscan monastic lineage, to discuss the role of religion in responding to the ecological crisis (WWF 1986). Tired of convincing with science alone and recognizing that religion is too potent a force to leave aside in the effort to raise environmental consciousness, some prominent scientists and environmentalists have since reached across the aisle to their religious peers, with varying results (Kellert and Farnham 2002; Oelschlaeger 1994; E. Wilson 2006). Besides the emergence of the religious-environmental alliance groups mentioned in the introduction and discussed in several chapters in this volume, significant international efforts have been initiated to collaborate across this religious-environmental divide: for instance, the Alliance of Religions and Conservation, which works with religious organizations around the world to assist and promote environmental protection efforts; Conservation International's Faith-Based Initiatives Program; the IUCN's World Commission on Protected Areas task force on cultural and spiritual values of protected sacred landscapes; and prominent statements and environmental pilgrimages of global religious leaders such as Ecumenical Orthodox Patriarch Bartholomeos I of Constantinople, Pope Benedict XVI, and His Holiness The Dalai Lama (Tenzin Gyatso) (ARC 2010; Dudley, Higgins-Zogib, and Mansourian 2005, 2009; Lee and Schaaf 2003; Posey 2002). At the same time, religious organizations can be notoriously slow to change, and resistance to environmentalism remains a powerful force among the world's major faith traditions, for a variety of reasons.

Together, these three moments—the turn to ecology within communities of faith, the turn to religion among environmentalists, and the return of philosophers to the full force and meaning of religion in the post–Cold War and post–September 11, 2001, worlds—frame a set of shifts in the relationship among religion, nature, and science, in light of which this volume's case studies are usefully seen and which I consider further in this closing chapter. While my focus here will be on religion, I would not wish to suggest that *science* and *nature* have remained free of controversy: the "science wars" of the 1990s are well known to anthropologists and others who study the social contexts of science, and at least a good part of what those so-called wars were over was the status of "nature"—considered as a social construct, an objective reality, or something in between (Chaloupka 2000; Ivakhiv 2002; Proctor, 1998, 2001, 2004, 2009; Soper 1995; Soulé and Lease 1995). Religion nevertheless can be said to function as a wild card in these discussions: it is, as I hope to show, the object that will least stand still and that calls most clearly for theorization. And the questions of science and of nature are intimately bound up with the thing that has most frequently been thought of as science's other, which is precisely what our society has called religion.

The argument I make here requires addressing four questions. The first two are the onto-epistemological and historical questions: *What is religion, and how is it related to what it is not? How did this set of relations between religion and nonreligion come about?* The onto-epistemological question has already been broached in the introduction. Here we are left mainly with the historical context that frames the second question and sets the stage for the third, which is the sociological or anthropological question: *What is happening with religion today?* Fourth and last comes the theoretical and strategic question: *What should we, as (engaged) scholars, do about these things?* In what follows, I proceed through each of these questions and propose some directions for thinking about the changing relationships among religion, science, nature, and politics in a world where each of these terms is fraught with uncertainties.

WHAT IS RELIGION, AND HOW IS IT RELATED TO WHAT IT *IS NOT*? HOW DID THIS SET OF RELATIONS ARISE?

Religion is notoriously difficult to define. As mentioned in the introduction, both *religion* and *the sacred* are terms that emerged historically as categories distinguishing certain things from others—religion from magic, superstition, science, and politics, the sacred from the secular and profane—and that served over time to fix and entrench the very differences they described (Ivakhiv 2006). Some, such as Karl Barth and Wilfred Cantwell Smith, have argued that the term *religion* is too humanistic and anthropocentric for what constitutes the religious domain for believers or that it is a modernist concept that enframes and reifies, and thus ultimately threatens, the most private and subjective domains of personal faith (Schussler Fiorenza 2000). Others have highlighted the role that the concept of religion has played in colonial, imperial, and missionizing projects: for instance, with indigenous people first described as lacking religion and later identified as in fact having religion, but of the basest kind (defined as fetishism, totemism, paganism, or animism). Their initial *lack* of religion signified their differences from colonizing Europeans; later it was precisely the *presence* of religion that came to signify that difference (Chidester 1996; Fitzgerald 2000; Masuzawa 2005; McCutcheon 1997; B. Saler 1993; J. Smith 1998). In Asad's (1993:29) influential genealogy of the modern anthropological concept of religion, he argues that the very notion of religion was the product of discursive processes of a European Christian world that separated religion from politics, law, science, and aesthetics and that distinguished between religion as a phenomenon and as a specific instance of that phenomenon. Others concur that this differentiation arose in part through developments internal to European colonial and Euro-Atlantic societies and in part through developments occurring at the borders of these societies and their non-Western—or, literally, their western, eastern, and southern—neighbors. Thinkers such as Luhmann (1995), Latour (1993), Beyer (2006), and Styers (2004) have variously considered this history as one of disembedding and functional differentiation: a process by which the religious has been separated from the political, the scientific, and the magical through some sort of carving up of spheres followed by an iterative consolidation of each in reference to the others (with the exception of the magical, which has ostensibly faded out as a remnant of the past).

Religion's differentiation from politics, for instance, emerged in the tug-of-war for authority between ecclesiastical houses and emerging national elites, with both taking advantage of the new print media: for purposes of political statecraft, for carving out a new space for religious alternatives (as with the Protestant reformers), and so on. Secularism, however, was not merely a result of *freeing* public space *from* religion, because it was profoundly influenced by medieval theological and canon law notions of the saeculum. Church-state separation, in time, also became the product not only of religion's antagonists but very much also of the activism of dissenting religious sectarians—as in the development of the American

Constitution. Similarly, demarcating science from religion was a goal of the new scientific societies that tried to establish their own authority with respect to the empirical, sensible world against the churches' authority over those things that were neither visible nor particularly powerful in the world.

In the end, however, what has been foregrounded, especially in Anglo-American contexts, is a view of religion as a matter of private beliefs—a view that is very much a product of Protestant Christianity and its relations with Catholicism, science, and capitalism. Arguments over secularization and its relationship to modernity have taken on a problematic and, at the very least, infinitely nuanced cast in recent years. Where the modern "secular myth" sees secularism as an achievement, one by which Europeans learned to separate religion, politics, and science following the religious wars of the seventeenth century (for example, Lilla 2008b), Casanova (2008:110) convincingly argues that the religious wars actually led to "state confessionalization and religious territorialization," with the Spanish Catholic state and its expulsion of Spanish Jews and Muslims as a paradigmatic model and the Polish-Lithuanian Commonwealth as a rare counterexample, the exception that proved the rule. "Ethno-religious cleansing, in this respect, stands at the very origin of the early modern European state," and for the next three hundred years or so, "European societies continued exporting all their religious minorities overseas" (Casanova 2008:110). The relationship between religion and politics took on different histories depending on their national circumstances, with histories of "collision" taking place in Latin American contexts and histories of "collusion" dominating in Anglo-Protestant contexts (Casanova 2008). But while all these developments describe the evolution of the *idea* of religion, we might say, with Latour (1993), that religion as a pure form, separate from politics, science, art, economics, and the rest, has *never existed*, because in practice we have "never been modern": we have always been hybrid and syncretic, *bricoleurs* and practical reasoners drawing on whatever is at hand to respond to the challenges facing us. Religion, like science and nature, is always both more and less than it claims to be.

In practice, then, religion remains difficult to separate from other cultural forms and activities, and the more appropriate question for scholars may in the end be this: What kinds of possibilities do the discourses of religion, sacredness, faith, spirituality, myth, enchantment, cosmovision, and the like, provide for theoretical engagement with situations in which religions, sciences, and nature encounter one another on the unstable grounds of a rapidly changing world?

WHAT IS HAPPENING WITH RELIGION TODAY?

The studies in this book focus closely on the social and ethnographic contours of the relationship among religion, science, and nature, that is, on what is happening on the ground at local sites where those things encounter one another in diverse and often ill-defined forms. They grapple with the issues I am raising here in contexts that reflect, to one degree or another, many of the themes that have become so prominent in cultural analysis of the past two decades: globalization, technological, "mediatization," neoliberalism, and the various hybridities and global flows, disjunctures and differences, border crossings and deterritorializations, millennial capitalisms and alternative modernities, conspiracies and spectralities, transcultures and transnational connections, and other ostensible features of the post–Cold War and post–September 11 worlds (Appadurai 1996; Canclini 1995; Comaroff and Comaroff 2001; Hannerz 1996; Inda and Rosaldo 2002; Meyer and Geschiere 1999; Meyer and Pels 2003; H. West and Sanders 2003; R. Wilson and Dissanayake 1996). Lurking somewhere in the background of each chapter is the question of the place of religion in all of it: What is happening with it today? Is religion resurgent, as many claim, or has it never gone away? Is secularization theory and its account of the progressive "disenchantment of the world" to be jettisoned, or are these models still relevant and useful? (On the last question, see also Bruce 2002; Dube 2002; Gauchet 1997; Norris and Inglehart 2004; Partridge 2004, 2005; M. Saler 2006; C. Taylor 2007.) How are global and local processes impin-ging on religion? How do global and local religiosities interact?

Scholars of religion have noted religion's resurgence around the world alongside its globalization and its seeming deprivatization (at least in Western contexts), but it is best considered alongside the ubiquity and persistence of religious practices and of the social forces through which it has always been expressed. One can see both faces in Christianity, which has undergone several waves of its own globalization, from its emergence as the unifying religion of the late Roman Empire through its colonial and missionary phases in the Americas, Africa, and the Far East, to its current transformations around the world. As Casanova (2008:115) observes, Catholicism has been dramatically reglobalizing since at least the 1880s, but the more recent spread of Pentecostalism has been taken as a paradigmatically "global religious culture," perhaps the "first truly global religion," that in its effects across the world both deterritorializes other religiosities and takes on deterritorialized forms of its own (Martin 2002). The broader picture of "deterritorialized transnational global imagined communities," of which Pentecostalism is just one example, might tempt one to speak of an "emerging global denominationalism" (Casanova 2008:118), but from ground level, the experience of religion may appear more like a "spiritual market-place" (Roof 2000) or, alternatively, a terrain of "spiritual warfare" (Robbins, chapter 3, this volume).

Introducing a volume on variable forms of "transnational transcendence," Csordas (2009) notes that religion takes on increasingly global forms that can be turned into "portable practices" and "transposable messages," which make use of the many channels available for such transit, including modern media, missionizing practices, and the flows of collective migration and individual mobility. This increased portability facilitates a movement in all directions: from the West outward, as one might speak of the McDonaldization of Christianity in its various forms, but also from the non-West to the West, as in the phenomena referred to as "Karma Cola" (Mehta 1991) and the "Easternisation of the West" (Campbell 2007), and within and between various "wests" and "non-wests." In the West, and perhaps nowhere more than in the comparatively religious hotbed of the USA, religion is both a fluid signifier and an elusive one to pin down with socio-logical accuracy. Many Americans are not easily classified today as members of a clearly defined religion, yet the vast majority would hesitate to call themselves *non*religious. Surveys have shown a growing preference for identifying oneself as spiritual rather than religious; or as polyconfessional, multireligious, nondenominational, or evolving; or as religious but of no single persuasion; and so on (Marler and Hadaway 2002; Roof 2000). In scholars' efforts to keep up with their data, they have proposed new notions of civil religion (Bellah 1967); diffuse, implicit, or deinstitutionalized reli-gion (Bailey 1983; Beyer 2003; Reader 1993; *Social Compass* 1990); nature religion (Albanese 1990); religious environmentalism (B. Taylor 2010); cultural religion (Alderman 2002); designer religion (Rountree 2002); self-spirituality (Heelas 1996; Ivakhiv 2003); and other such terms.

The chapters here refer to various encounters, meetings, mixtures, syn-cretisms, and hybridizations, especially of Christianities and non-Christian or traditional cultures, and one question we may ask is whether they follow recognizable patterns. Are there predictable differences, for instance, between the kinds of Catholic-traditional hybrids that one finds in Brazil (Scanlan Lyons, chapter 2, this volume) or in Mexico (Mathews and Norget, chapters 4 and 5, respectively, this volume) and the Evangelical-or Protestant-traditional hybrids found in Papua New Guinea (Robbins, chapter 3, this volume) or elsewhere in Brazil (Scanlan Lyons)? How do they map onto other processes, such as disenchantment–re-enchantment or secularization–post-secularization? Scanlan Lyons provides a set of contrasts between Catholicism and Evangelicalism in Bahia, Brazil, while Robbins demonstrates an instance of the global circulation of ideas being taken up locally and turned into something rather different from the original.

And how do religion and science, and religion and politics, interact both locally and globally? A range of negotiations can be seen around the demarcation of the respective spheres of authority of religion, science, and politics. Where environmentalism of one kind or another enters the picture, the demarcations of science and politics tend to become more fraught, since environmentalism typically operates in both domains, serving as expressions or interlocutors of one or the other and frequently, if problematically, crossing between the two. Are these negotiations to be thought of in terms of alternative or multiple modernities (Eisenstadt 2002; Gaonkar 2001), in which apparently modernizing processes take their own local forms, drawing in local beliefs and practices and mixing them with new ones, such as conservation, democratic or other kinds of political institutions, or capitalist market relations? What forms of hybridity manifest in these mixtures of the religious, the scientific, and the political?

Some of the hybrids seen herein might be regarded as *promising hybrids* insofar as they suggest a way in which activities that had previously been marked off from one another (local and state politics, indigenous religion, environmental conservation) come together in seemingly constructive re-engagements. TEK and ecotheology, as in the Zimbabwean example (Daneel, chapter 10, this volume), might be among these promising hybrids in the ways they bring together science (the "EK" of *TEK* and the "eco" of *ecotheology*), religion, and the sociopolitical sphere. So would the moral ecologies discussed by Norget (chapter 5, this volume), with their integration of "indigenous sacred-ecological conceptions and liberationist Catholic social justice and integral development." As scholarly interventions, these chapters suggest a fruitful attempt to broaden intellectual discourse toward a more inclusive understanding of religion, theology, and indigenous culture. The Brazilian interfaith spaces of "servant leadership, suffering, and justice," as described by Scanlan Lyons (chapter 2, this volume), and the open-space faith discussed in Ballestero's (chapter 9, this volume) account of water politics in Costa Rica may also be seen as sites in which promising hybrids or convergences might gestate.

Other kinds of hybrids, however, at least from an environmentalist perspective, would appear more unsettling. Robbins's (chapter 3, this volume) description of the church growth and Christian spiritual mapping/warfare movements presents them as unusual hybrids of social science and Evangelical Christianity: the first as a mixture of anthropology and missionizing, the second as an enlistment of sociological and cultural geographic research methods toward Evangelical demonology. And in the case of the Oaxacan millenarian movement described by Norget (chapter 5, this volume), one might wonder whether this hybrid better fits the pattern of creative and potentially transformative resistance movements or of fatalistic cargo cults. What of Oaxacan rural communities' use of desiccation theory (as described by Mathews, chapter 4, this volume), a scientific model that has been largely discarded by contemporary forest scientists, to promote forest protection and local control?

Evaluating such hybrids, however, may reveal little more than the biases of the evaluator, which brings us to the point at which we as scholars are implicated in our research and writing practices. If, as mentioned, there are three (or more) before-and-after moments within which our study of these topics finds its own contextual resonances, then each of them presumably shapes the ways in which we, as scholars, can align ourselves through our ethnographic and communicative practices. I turn to the question of our response in the next section.

WHAT, IF ANYTHING, SHOULD WE AS (ENGAGED) SCHOLARS DO ABOUT IT?

Amid these multiple contexts, what does it mean, and what might it add to our understanding, when we introduce language of the religious or the sacred into scholarly examination of culture and ecology? What happens when we call ecology "sacred," as Berkes (1999) does in the very title of his book on TEK? What are the implications of such redescriptions or rearticulations of the terms that, in a modern context, appear deeply, structurally opposed to one another: the scientific, the religious, the political, and the natural? If our redescriptions have the effect of hybridizing the discourses into which they are propelled, what are the possibilities they might open up or foreclose?

I have referred already to the functional differentiation of social systems or subsystems, such as science, politics, art, law, religion, and economics. Each of them, in Luhmann's (1995) analysis, has, over the course of the past few centuries in the West, become a relatively autonomous, self-defining, and self-organizing subsystem of society (although each in turn defines the others in its own terms). In Latour's (1993) account, different in emphasis but (for our purposes) loosely congruent with Luhmann's, modernity is underwritten by the "modern constitution," a tacit agreement by which nature and society have been identified as separate realms, to be studied, represented, and managed differently. In the case of nature, it is to be done dispassionately by the objective natural sciences. In the case of society, it is through the subjective politics of interest as governed by modern systems of political, legal, and philosophical representation. Religion, meanwhile, has become separated from both science and politics, becoming a matter of belief in the unproven and unprovable, a private and individual affair. Science takes care of the empirical and provable, and politics takes care of collective issues in the public sphere. In the process, as Latour puts it (1993:42, 33), a "bracketed" God "could descend into men's hearts without intervening in any way in their external affairs."

The picture in Latour's description is one of simultaneous purification and translation. As each system has been separated from the others through a series of displacements and delegations, it is granted its own proper space, its requisite institutions, procedures, and operational spaces—laboratories and journals for science, electoral representation for politics, the marketplace for economics, churches for religion, galleries for art, courts for law, schools for education, hospitals and clinics for medicine—and its standards of disciplinary judgment, such as objectivity or veracity for judging science, beauty for art, justice for law, health and normality for medicine. In this narrative anthropology of modernity, it appears, then, that "we" have proceeded from a state of premodern messiness to a clean separation of spheres. And yet, as Latour (1993) argues in the very title of his book, we have *never been* modern: politics and religion have commonly intermingled; art has been infused with religious impulses, political intent, or scientific knowledge; the exchange of objects has commonly been encumbered by social obligations or political expectations; and human subjectivity has arisen already entwined with places, landscapes, and material ecologies. The relations of the world, in other words, have always been messier and more hybrid than our communication about them today suggests, even if each human society may have its own categorizations by which it attempts to order those relations.

Similarly, nature and its representation by science have always been cultural products, just as culture has remained ecologically embedded. Not only has their interrelation *consisted* of hybrid relations, but also, under the modern configuration by which nature and society have been mutually purified of each other, we have created ever more powerful capabilities for *producing* new and more "monstrous" hybrids. The situation, for Latour (2002), is one in which a multiculturalism has been accompanied by a mononaturalism: that is, whereas *culture* is seen to be what differentiates people from other people and cultures are to be either treated equally or differentiated and evaluated based on commonly accepted standards of human rights or goods, *nature* is taken to be simply *there*, singular, lawful, invariable. Science, in turn, is the social force that has been delegated with the power to reveal nature for us and to speak on its behalf. But Latour rejects this division of labor: nature, he argues, does not provide a bedrock of reality against which our activities can be measured, because each culture is always already enacted within a particular set of ecological relations. Each is always already no less than a nature-culture.

The chapters in this book, in one way or another, tacitly agree with Latour in putting this "modern constitution" into question. At the very least, they do it to raise the possibility that *some* cultures, or cultural practices, or "knowledge-practice-belief complexes" may allow for a better or more sustainable relationship with nature than others (for example, Daneel, Hallum, Norget, Schnell, and Tucker, chapters 10, 7, 5, 8, and 6, respectively, this volume). This possibility, in turn, raises what can only become a more pressing question in cultural and ecological debates: How should we adjudicate among rival interpretations of the world and the human place within it? The options are several. One, as various ecotheologies have assumed, is that some ideas and beliefs are more ecological than others. Another is that some knowledge-belief-*practice* complexes are more ecological than others. Since the latter claim involves articulating the history by which such practices and complexes have evolved in specific places over time, it allows for the possibility that one such complex would be more appropriate than another *in a specific place*, but not necessarily in just *any* place, so it takes us out of the realm of abstract universality and emplaces us within a local context. This is the claim of TEK and of the proponents of "cosmovisions," "ecological ethnicities" (Parajuli 1998, 2001), "ecosystem people" (versus "biosphere people"; Dasmann 1988), and, implicitly or explicitly, many of the chapters in this volume.

But one could respond by arguing that history shows that such efforts are a losing battle. Valorizing the natural and primitive, whether through romantic poetics, anti-civilization polemics, or science (as one might argue that cultural ecologists have sometimes done), has a tendency to only strengthen the persistent dualism of pro- and anti-modernism. In describing the "indigenous sacred idiom" in which Oaxacan activism is cloaked, Norget (chapter 5, this volume) suggests that there are potential gains but also risks in the romanticization that attends such language, risks that should be clear from the history of ways in which indigenous cultures have been studied and managed by colonial authorities. Pursuing this line of critique, one might say instead that what is needed is to change the very grounds on which these arguments are made, so that the operative framework is no longer a single nature, represented by the universal language of science, posed against multiple cultures. We may need, as Latour (1993, 2002, 2004a, 2004c, 2009a) suggests, to give up our claim to nature via science and to opt instead for a meeting ground that is more hybrid and uncertain to start with, one on which not cultures but "naturecultures" meet. This shift would mean that both nature and culture become parts of the territory being struggled over, with no neutral arbiters available to fix the judgment in advance.

In the remainder of this chapter, I wish to think through the possibility that arises when we shift our conversation away from the frame of (multiple) cultures interacting with (a single) nature and toward a more open space where the goalposts are movable and the stakes unclear. This change takes us into the realm of what Latour (2004c) and Stengers (1996–97) call "cosmopolitics" and what Mol (1999) and Law (2004) refer to as "ontological politics"—a realm in which realities are not pregiven but are enacted and in which their enactment implicates us in an open-ended process by which their most foundational terms are to be negotiated step by step. But first, I detour through a notion that was not so long ago considered discredited, at least by anthropologists, whose own predecessors had been the ones to first articulate it: the notion of animism.

CLEARING A SPACE FOR THE COSMOPOLITICAL

While the term hardly appears in this volume, many of the case studies discussed refer to ways in which specific traditional cultural groups incorporate something like an animist set of conceptions and practices. *Animism*, like "primitive," "pagan," and "savage" but also like religion itself, is a term that has been used to classify cultural difference into a hierarchically valenced series: animists, for Tylor (1920) and other evolutionists, were thought to have maintained a "lower" and more "primitive" conception of the universe, one peopled by spirits and with objects being ascribed human characteristics. More recently, however, a loose coterie of anthropologists and scholars of religion has reappropriated the term to mean something rather more interesting (Bird-David 1999; Descola 2005, 2006, 2009; G. Harvey 2006; Ingold 2000; Viveiros de Castro 1992, 2004).

Descola (1996), whose work on Amazonian indigenous cultures presents one of the clearest cases disproving the notion that nature and culture constitute universal categories, develops a novel classification system for delineating the different kinds of relations one finds between humans and other entities. Descola's (2009:150) classification hinges on two sets of variables: whether a cultural group perceives a basic similarity or a fundamental

TABLE 11.1

Descola's four ontologies of human–nonhuman similarity and difference

	Similar in interiority (monoculturalism)	Dissimilar in interiority (multiculturalism)
Similar in physicality (mononaturalism)	Totemism	Naturalism
Dissimilar in physicality (multinaturalism)	Animism	Analogism

Adapted from Descola 2005, 2006, 2009.

dissimilarity between humans and nonhumans in two distinct dimensions: *interiority* ("intentionality, subjectivity, reflexivity, the aptitude to dream," and so on) and *physicality* ("form, substance, physiological, perceptual, sensory-motor, and proprioceptive processes, or even temperament as an expression of the influence of bodily humours"). When humans and non-human entities are considered to be similar in both mind and body (to use those rough approximations), we have what Descola calls *totemism*; when dissimilar in both, it is *analogism*; when similar in body but dissimilar in mind, *naturalism*; and when similar in mind but dissimilar in body, *animism* (table 11.1).

Both Descola and Latour have drawn on this series of classifications to argue that our modern worldview, or "modern constitution," presumes a *multi*culturalism set against a *mono*naturalism. In Descola's (2006:8) framework, it amounts to an ontology of "naturalism": accordingly, a "single unifying nature" coexists with "a multiplicity of cultures," and what, "for us, distinguishes humans from nonhumans is the mind, the soul, subjectivity, a moral conscience, language, and so forth, in the same way as human groups are distinguished from one another by a collective internal disposition" now known as culture. Animism, in Descola's scheme, is the reverse of naturalism: for animists, "all the classes of beings endowed with an interiority similar to that of humans reputedly live in collectives that possess the same kind of structure and properties," but "these collectives, that are all integrally social and cultural, are also distinguished from one another by the fact that their members have different morphologies and behavior" (Descola 2006:9). The "so-called natural and supernatural domains" are "peopled by collectives with which human collectives maintain relations according to norms that are deemed common to all" (Descola 2006:9). Among other things, they all "exchange signs," which sounds not unlike the central tenet of the emerging field of biosemiotics (Barbieri 2008; Hoffmeyer 1996).

Taking a cue from Amazonianist Viveiros de Castro (2004), Latour (2002, 2004a, 2004c, 2009a) makes the case that such mononaturalism is inadequate for a world of cultural-natural hybrids, which is the world he claims we live in. More appropriate would be something located partway between Descola's *animism*—where humans and nonhumans are perceived to share subjectivity and semiotic agency but to differ in their materialities—and an *analogism* that sees *both* interiority and materiality as multiple and different and, therefore, as bridgeable only through translation. (Since anthropologists are trained precisely in translation across cultural milieus, it should not surprise us that this notion appealed to them.) If we are no longer to rely on the singular foundation of a nature that speaks to us (through science), then we are thrown into a world in which humans are thought to resemble, in some measure, all other entities (think Darwin alongside Amazonian shamanism) *and* to differ radically, although in ways that are bridgeable through translation. This world would demand an ontological politics, or a cosmopolitics, by which the choices open to us with respect to the different ways we can entangle ourselves with places, nonhumans, technologies, and the material world as a whole become ethically inflected, open questions.

In the multivolume work *Cosmopolitiques* (1996–97) and publications that followed it, Stengers (2005) forwards a cosmopolitical proposal that, unlike most forms of cosmopolitan*ism*, does not presume the existence or even the possibility of a "good common world," an ecumenically peaceable cosmopolis. On the contrary, her proposal is intended to "slow down the construction of this common world, to create a space for hesitation regarding what it means to say 'good'" (Stengers 2005:994). The cosmos of her cosmopolitics "refers to the unknown constituted by [the] multiple, divergent worlds and to the articulations of which they could eventually be capable" (Stengers 2005:994). Such a cosmopolitics does not preassume what will count as common, whether it is human nature, cultural differences, or the laws and discoveries of science or, on the other hand, gods, souls, spirits, or anything else that anyone might bring to the table. Stengers's call is echoed by Latour (2004c), Mol (1999), and Law (2004), who argue in favor of a politics for building, enacting, or coproducing shared or common worlds—not worlds that posit nature as the "unique author of a single account" (Law 2004:123) propping up a "reality that is independent, prior, singular, and definite," but worlds in which "everything takes effort, continuing effort" (Law 2004:131–132). Such methods and modes of knowledge making recognize their own complicities in the worlds they enact, and they are political in the sense that they raise questions about how the world of associations—the society of humans and other entities—is to be organized. Seeing ourselves as cosmopolitically entwined with one another and the other others of the world means seeing ourselves as actively practicing ways of "worlding" or "world-making" (R. Wilson and Connery 2007).

What, in the concrete instances described in this book, might this mean? Is such world making not already in progress all around us, and is religion not already in the thick of so much of it? Borrowing and reformulating Miyazaki's (2004) notion of hope, Ballestero (chapter 9, this volume) suggests that a kind of faith, in the highly indeterminate context of water politics in Costa Rica, works to fill an uncertainty gap between science's deferred promise of predictability and the day-to-day need to coexist and to maintain relationships across social and existential gaps. Several other chapters here depict their own uncertainty gaps: uncertainty connected to ecological risks, as Beck (1992) famously laid out in his *Risk Society*, to matters of cultural survival, and to individuals' and groups' abilities to comprehend global changes and their likely local impacts. Uncertainties unfold within the power relations between insiders and outsiders, locals and globals, and issue from the gap between the viscerally experienced power provided by religion and the subjectifying, distance-making forces of the state or of science, as Mathews (chapter 4, this volume) suggests in his discussion of the latter's knowledge making and the former's state-making practices. Uncertainty also arises in the opening up of politics when, for instance, modern notions of ownership and property encounter traditional understandings of land as owned by spirits (among the Urapmin of Papua New Guinea, in Robbins's chapter 3, this volume) or the rather common perception of land as communal or ancestral property.

Ballestero's Miyazakian notion of faith (chapter 9, this volume), like Schnell's proposed "affective belief" (chapter 8, this volume), begins to nudge us in the direction that political philosopher Connolly (1995, 1999, 2005, 2011) outlines as a "deep pluralism." Connolly calls for the cultivation of a set of dispositions that would deepen and radically democratize the kind of limited pluralism that is taken for granted in liberal societies. They include an openness to a "pluralistic universe" in James's (1920) terms, in which not everything is knowable, and to the emergence of novelty in conditions not entirely under the control of any single party to the proceedings. Echoing this kind of thought at our SAR seminar, Ballestero described the faith that holds together Costa Rican water politics as a "holding in abeyance of agency," a "subjacent disposition" of "confidence that puts conflicting visions against one another and bestows them with a future." Such faith is productive and generative, affective and rational. It provides a sense of constraints but also enables for a course of events to unfold while holding in abeyance the requirements of, in the Costa Rican case, rational or managerial decision making.

One might wonder, however, whether this faith is just another word for a shared framework or sensibility, the glue that holds a society together and that allows disparate groups within it to engage one another across differences. In the United States of the Bush II and Obama eras, any kind of common civil faith as such—faith, for instance, in democratic and liberal institutions—seems to have broken down into a deeply polarized body politic. Is this kind of common faith something that can only emerge through the deep internal massage of nation building (typically accompanied by civil wars and other purifications, its eventual positive results having long ago elapsed in the USA) or in the kinds of bounded local contexts in which different sides to a conflict can be trusted to return to the table and to continue returning despite the lack, as Ballestero (chapter 9, this volume) demonstrates, of any tangible progress? What does this element of faith or trust depend on, and to what extent does it require face-to-face community of the sort that Ostrom's (1990) and others' work on communal property regimes suggests may be crucial for sustainable management of local resources?

This idea of faith also brings to mind Bateson's (1987) argument that sometimes it is better *not* to be conscious of certain things—better, for instance, to let a ritual do its work than to overthink its efficacy or inefficacy. We can think of this as the self-reflexive cyberneticists' paradox: we want to know how the system works, but we do not want our knowledge of its details to negatively affect the way it works. The sacred, Bateson suggests, is something that may have to be maintained by some kind of noncommunication—a prohibition, silence, or taboo—or the recognition that something might be incommunicable not just because it is unknown and uncertain, but also because if we try to talk about it, in the terms that are available to us, we are bound to mess it up. In a Luhmannian sense (Luhmann 1995), one might say that each social subsystem, being its own communicative system and made up of informational messages circling around a set of fundamental binary terms, has its blind spots, places where it dare not venture. The world today might even be thought of as offering huge expanses of uncertainty, about which we might not be able to communicate very well, in part because of the risk that if we do, our efforts will be drawn into powerful hegemonic logics—managerial, market-rational, or technocratic ones—that may close off the possibility of the more radical openings they call for.

To come back to the notion of a "before" and an "after" framing the cases examined in this volume, we might answer the question "What comes after?" by saying that the *after* is a space open to novel co-articulations, global-local visions (or cosmovisions), and moral ecologies, the status of which is always a "not yet." The contours of this "after" are to be worked out in an open, emergent space that is not dominated or predetermined by a single party, vision, project, discourse, or even, in Stengers's (1996–97) terms, a single cosmos. What is called for in this space is something like a Gramscian "politics of articulation," an effort to forge new alliances across gaps (Clifford 2007; Hall 1986; Slack 1996), but one that is less sure than ever of its beginnings and more open to thinking worlds differently.

Several of the chapters here provide useful insights into the question of how such alliances and co-articulations may develop, how they negotiate points of tension, and how they may succeed or fail to sustain their movements over time. We see variations on this process in Scanlan Lyons's work on servant leadership, justice, suffering, and environmental action based on positive commonalities as opposed to co-belligerences (chapter 2, this volume); in Mathews's account of rural Mexican communities' use of desiccation theory to co-articulate with environmentalists (chapter 4, this volume); in Robbins's discussion of the Urapmin, who remain seemingly unable to become the market entrepreneurs they wish to be, despite their efforts to rescind their obligations to the nature spirits (chapter 3, this volume); and in Daneel's Zimbabwean work, which shows the deep fragility of coalition building across environmental–religious fissures (chapter 10, this volume). When such fragile coalitions fail, is it because of the persistence of material factors, or an overreliance on singular leaders and a persistence of their social or familial obligations? What solidifies connections across gaps, and what makes them break down? What is the role of theoretical or communicative innovation, for instance, by theologians like Leonardo Boff in Brazil, scientists like E. O. Wilson, and scholars like John Grim and Mary Evelyn Tucker (of the religion and ecology movement) or by the rural communities described in this volume by Matthews, Scanlan Lyons, and others? And at what point does the theoretical and articulatory become insufficient and the need arise for something more purely affective—something that can only emerge from the mutual shaping of sensibilities that occurs through the coexistence of communities over time?

This book's introduction mentions two ways in which White's (1967) challenge was addressed by scholars and intellectuals: a strategic one that, in cosmopolitical retrospect, we might say preassumed its goals too readily and an empirical one that is valuable but does not take us far enough. At this point, we can try to formulate a third option, a moral and cosmopolitical one. Such an option would entail experimentation and a willingness to act without specific outcomes in mind. It would engage with new audiences and actors in a search for common principles, potential co-articulatory threads, but without presuming to provide the language for those principles in advance (say, conservation or nature protection) or a final means of measuring the outcomes (such as a count of acres or species protected). This is not to say that it could not propose variations on existing themes—for instance, justice, commons, faith, creation care, solidarity, sustainability, and blessedness. To open ourselves to a *multinaturalism*, we would have to take seriously the propositions that nature is neither stable nor certain; that science speaks for nature not as a ventriloquist, but as an active and effective generator of ways of doing things; that neither science, nor religion, nor environmentalism eludes judgment on the grounds of morals, knowledge, or politics; and that culture is always something more akin to nature-culture, with ontological and cosmopolitical propositions deeply embedded in the very ways it is enacted into practice.

To pick up again the thread from Ballestero (chapter 9, this volume), if faith is seen as an affective subtext for articulatory politics in frictional (Tsing 2005) and uncertain contexts, the question becomes how, and with whom, to produce that affective subtext. Through what kinds of activities are the conditions for co-articulation generated? If the case studies presented here help move our thinking in this direction, they will have fulfilled a valuable function because the kinds of hybrid and uncertain processes, in which religion, science, and nature are scrambled and thrown together without a clear referee or even a stable playing field, are certain to increase over the years to come.

Acknowledgments

I wish to express my gratitude to Catherine Tucker for inviting me to participate in this seminar as a collaborator and respondent to the others' work and for masterfully steering the ship through its course—it has indeed come a long way; to the other participants for their rich insight, enthusiasm, persistence, and friendship; and to SAR for making it all possible.

References

Adriance, Madeleine Cousineau
1995   Promised Land: Base Christian Communities and the Struggle for the Amazon. Albany: State University of New York Press.

Agamben, Giorgio
2004   The Open: Man and Animal. K. Attell, trans. Stanford: Stanford University Press.

Aguilar Schramm, Alejandra, Xinia Alvarado Zeledón, Yamileth Astorga Espeleta, Sonia Avendaño Mata, Carlos Blanco Obando, Jorge Mora-Portuguez, Guiselle Rodríguez Villalobos, Haydée Rodríguez Romero, Daniel Vartanián Alarcón, and José Miguel Zeledón
2004   Hacia una nueva ley del agua: Memoria de un proceso de construcción participativa [Toward a new water law: Report of a participatory design process]. San Jose, Costa Rica: Grupo Tecnico del Agua Costa Rica. http://www.gwpcentroamerica.org/uploaded/content/article/2044558305.pdf, accessed March 3, 2011.

Alaimo, Stacy
1994   Cyborg and Ecofeminist Interventions: Challenges for an Environmental Feminism. Feminist Studies 20(1):133–152.

Albanese, Catherine
1990   Nature Religion in America: From the Algonkian Indians to the New Age. Chicago: University of Chicago Press.

Alderman, Derek H.
2002   Writing on the Graceland Wall: On the Importance of Authorship in Pilgrimage Landscapes. Tourism Recreation Research 27(2):27–33.

Anderies, John M.
1998   Culture and Human Agro-Ecosystem Dynamics: The Tsembaga of New Guinea. Journal of Theoretical Biology 192:515–530.

REFERENCES

Anderson, Eugene N.

1996   Ecologies of the Heart: Emotion, Belief, and the Environment. New York: Oxford University Press.

2004   Valuing the Maya Forests. *In* Rights, Resources, Culture and Conservation in the Land of the Maya. Betty B. Faust, E. N. Anderson, and John G. Frazier, eds. Pp. 117–130. Westport: Praeger.

Andréassian, Vazken

2004   Waters and Forests: From Historical Controversy to Scientific Debate. Journal of Hydrology 291:1–27.

Ansell, Aaron

2010   Auctioning Patronage in Northeast Brazil. American Anthropologist 112(2):283–294.

Anta Fonseca, Salvador, and Leticia Merino

2003   Community Management of Natural Resources in Oaxaca. The Common Property Resource Digest 66(September):3–5.

Appadurai, Arjun

1996   Modernity at Large: Cultural Dimensions of Globalization. Minneapolis: University of Minnesota Press.

ARC (Alliance of Religions and Conservation)

2010   Green Pilgrim Cities. http://www.arcworld.org/downloads/Green-Cities -Leaflet.pdf, accessed December 15, 2010.

Ardón Mejía, Mario

1989   Panorama de la Alfarería Tradicional de La Campa, Honduras. Folklore Americano 48:69–80.

Arons, Nicholas Gabriel

2004   Waiting for Rain: The Politics and Poetry of Drought in Northeast Brazil. Tucson: University of Arizona Press.

Asad, Talal

1993   Genealogies of Religion: Discipline and Reasons of Power in Christianity and Islam. Baltimore: Johns Hopkins University Press.

Ascher, William

1999   Why Governments Waste Natural Resources: Policy Failures in Developing Countries. Baltimore: Johns Hopkins University Press.

Ataroff, Michele, and Fermín Rada

2000   Deforestation Impact on Water Dynamics in a Venezuelan Andean Cloud Forest. Ambio 29(7):440–444.

Ayres, Ed

2003   Mapping the Nature of Diversity. World Watch 16(2):30.

Bailey, Edward

1983   The Implicit Religion of Contemporary Society: An Orientation and a Plea for Its Study. Religion 13:69–83.

Baland, Jean-Marie, and Jean-Philippe Platteau

1996   Halting Degradation of Natural Resources: Is There a Role for Rural Communities? New York: Oxford University Press.

Balée, William

1985   Ka'apor Ritual Hunting. Human Ecology 13(4):485–510.

Balée, William, and Clark L. Erickson

2006   Time and Complexity in Historical Ecology: Studies in the Neotropical Lowlands. New York: Columbia University Press.

Ballestero, Andrea

2004   Institutional Adaptation and Water Reform in Ceará: Revisiting Structures for Social Participation at the Local Level. M.A. thesis, School of Natural Resources and Environment, University of Michigan.

2006   Construcción del espacio político a través de las prácticas locales: Bajo Jaguaribe y la Política de Recursos Hídricos [Construction of political space through local practices: Lower Jaguaribe and water policy]. *In* Economía política da urbanização do Baixo Jaguaribe (CE) [The political economy of Lower Jaguaribe Urbanization Processes (CE)]. D. Elias, R. Pequeno, and E. Pereira Junior, eds. Pp. 116–139. Fortaleza, Brazil: UECE.

Barabas, Alicia Mabel

1977   Chinantec Messianism: Mediator of the Divine. *In* Western Expansion and Indigenous Peoples: The Heritage of Las Casas. Elías Sevilla-Casas, ed. Pp. 221–254. World Anthropology Series. The Hague, Netherlands: Mouton.

1994   El Aparicionismo en America Latina: Religión, territorio e identidad [Apparitionism in Latin America: Religion, territory and identity]. La Palabra y el Hombre 89:2–12.

2006   Dones, dueños y santos [Gifts, gods and saints]. México, DF: Instituto Nacional de Antropología e Historia and Miguel Angel Porrua.

2008   Cosmovisiones y etnoterritorialidad en las culturas indígenas de Oaxaca [Cosmovisions and ethnoterritoriality in the indigenous cultures of Oaxaca]. Antipoda: Revista de Antropología y Arqueología 7:119–139.

Barabas, Alicia, and Miguel de Bartolomé

1973   Hydraulic Development and Ethnocide: The Mazatec and Chinantec People of Oaxaca, Mexico. IWGIA Document No.15. Copenhagen, Denmark: International Work Group for Indigenous Affairs (IWGIA).

1984   El Rey Cono hoy: tradición mesiánica y privación social entre los Mixes de Oaxaca [The King Cono today: Messianic tradition and social deprivation among the Mixes of Oaxaca]. Oaxaca, Mexico: Instituto Nacional de Antropología e Historia.

1992   Antropología y relocalizaciones [Anthropology and relocalizations]. Alteridades 2(4):5–15.

Barbieri, Marcello

2008   Introduction to Biosemiotics: The New Biological Synthesis. Dordrecht, the Netherlands: Springer.

Barrera-Bassols, Narciso, and Victor M. Toledo

2005   Ethnoecology of the Yucatec Maya: Symbolism, Knowledge and Management of Natural Resources. Journal of Latin American Geography 4(1):9–41.

Barrionuevo, Alexi

2009   Fight Nights and Reggae Pack Brazilian Churches. The New York Times, September 14, Americas.

Bastide, Roger

2007   The African Religions of Brazil: Toward a Sociology of the Interpenetration of Civilizations. Baltimore: Johns Hopkins University Press.

Bateson, Gregory

1987   Let Not Thy Left Hand Know. *In* Angels Fear: Towards an Epistemology of the Sacred. Gregory Bateson and Mary Catherine Bateson, eds. Pp. 69–81. New York: Macmillan.

2000   Steps to an Ecology of Mind. Chicago: University of Chicago Press.

Beck, Ulrich

1992   Risk Society: Towards a New Modernity. London: Sage.

Bellah, Robert

1967   Civil Religion in America. Dædalus 96(1):1–21.

Berger, Peter L.

1967   The Sacred Canopy: Elements of a Sociological Theory of Religion. New York: Doubleday.

Berk, Gerald, and Dennis Galvan

2009   How People Experience and Change Institutions: A Field Guide to Creative Syncretism. Theory and Society 38(6):543–580.

Berkes, Fikret

1999   Sacred Ecology: Traditional Ecological Knowledge and Resource Management. Philadelphia: Taylor and Francis.

2001   Religious Traditions and Biodiversity. *In* Encyclopedia of Biodiversity, vol. 5. Simon A. Levin, ed. Pp. 109–120. San Diego: Academic Press.

2008a   Community Conserved Areas Policy Issues in Historic and Contemporary Context. Conservation Letters (2008):1–6.

2008b   Sacred Ecology. 2nd edition. New York: Routledge.

Berkes, Fikret, Johan Colding, and Carl Folke

2000   Rediscovery of Traditional Ecological Knowledge as Adaptive Management. Ecological Applications 10(5):1251–1262.

Beyer, Peter

2003   Conceptions of Religion: On Distinguishing Scientific, Theological, and "Official" Meanings. Social Compass 50(2):141–160.

2006   Religions in Global Society. London: Routledge.

Bird-David, Nurit

1999   "Animism" Revisited: Personhood, Environment, and Relational Epistemology. Current Anthropology 40:S67–S91.

Birman, Patricia

2006   Future in the Mirror: Media, Evangelicals, and Politics in Rio de Janeiro. *In* Religion, Media, and the Public Sphere. Birgit Memyer and Annelies Moors, eds. Pp. 52–72. Bloomington: Indiana University Press.

Blackman, Allen, Heidi Albers, Beatriz Ávalos-Sartorio, and Lisa Crooks

2005   Deforestation and Shade Coffee in Oaxaca, Mexico: Key Research Findings. Discussion Paper 05-39. Washington, DC: Resources for the Future.

Boff, Leonardo

1986   Liberation Theology: From Dialogue to Confrontation. New York: Harper and Row.

1995   Ecology and Liberation: A New Paradigm. Maryknoll: Orbis Books.

1997   Cry of the Earth, Cry of the Poor. Maryknoll: Orbis Books.

Bonilla-Carrion, Roger, and Luis Rosero-Bixby

2004   Presión demográfica sobre los bosques y áreas protegidas, Costa Rica 2000 [Population pressure on forests and protected areas, Costa Rica 2000]. *In* Costa Rica a la luz del censo 2000 [Costa Rica in light of the 2000 census]. L. Rosero-Bixby, ed. Pp. 564–582. Proyecto Estado de la Nación e Instituto de Estadística y Censos, Centro Centroamericano de Población de la Universidad de Costa Rica, San José.

Botkin, Daniel

1990   Discordant Harmonies: A New Ecology for the Twenty-First Century. New York: Oxford University Press.

Brandon, Katrina, Kent H. Redford, and Steven E. Sanderson

1998   Parks in Peril: People, Politics and Protected Areas. Washington, DC: Island Press.

Bray, David Barton

1991   The Struggle for the Forest: Conservation and Development in the Sierra Juarez. Grassroots Development 15(3):13–25.

Bray, David Barton, Leticia Merino-Pérez, Patricia Negreros-Castillo, Gerardo Segura-Warnholtz, Juan Manuel Torres-Rojo, and Henricus F. M. Vester

2003   Mexico's Community Managed Forests as a Global Model for Sustainable Landscapes. Conservation Biology 17(3):672–677.

Brechin, Steven R.

2003   Preface. *In* Contested Nature: Promoting International Biodiversity Conservation with Social Justice in the Twenty-First Century. Steven R. Brechin, Peter R. Wilshusen, Crystal L. Fortwangler, and Patrick C. West, eds. Pp. x–xiv. Albany: State University of New York Press.

REFERENCES

Brightman, Robert A.

1987   Conservation and Resource Depletion: The Case of the Boreal Forest
        Algonquins. *In* The Question of the Commons: The Culture and Ecology of
        Communal Resources. B. J. McCay and J. M. Acheson, eds. Pp. 121–141.
        Tucson: University of Arizona Press.

Brockington, Dan

2002   Fortress Conservation: The Preservation of the Mkomazi Game Reserve,
        Tanzania. Oxford: James Currey.

Brosius, J. Peter, Anna Lowenhaupt Tsing, and Charles Zerner, eds.

2005   Communities and Conservation: Histories and Politics of Community-Based
        Natural Resource Management. Walnut Creek: AltaMira Press.

Bruce, Steve, ed.

2002   Religion and Modernization: Sociologists and Historians Debate the
        Secularization Thesis. Oxford: Oxford University Press.

Bruijnzeel, L. A.

2004   Hydrological Functions of Tropical Forests: Not Seeing the Soil for the
        Trees? Agriculture, Ecosystems & Environment 104(1):185–228.

Bunzl, Matti

2004   Boas, Foucault, and the "Native Anthropologist": Notes toward a Neo-
        Boasian Anthropology. American Anthropologist 106(3):435–442.

Burdick, John

1993   Looking for God in Brazil: The Progressive Catholic Church in Urban
        Brazil's Religious Arena. Berkeley: University of California Press.

2004   Legacies of Liberation: The Progressive Catholic Church in Brazil at the
        Start of a New Millenium. Surrey, UK: Ashgate.

Burdick, John, and Warren Edward Hewitt, eds.

2000   The Church at the Grassroots in Latin America: Perspectives on Thirty Years
        of Activism. Westport: Praeger.

Burkert, Walter

1996   Creation of the Sacred: Tracks of Biology in Early Religions. Cambridge:
        Harvard University Press.

Burridge, K.

1969   New Heaven, New Earth. New York: Schocken.

Caddy, J. F., and J. C. Seijo

2005   This Is More Difficult Than We Thought! The Responsibility of Scientists,
        Managers and Stakeholders to Mitigate the Unsustainability of Marine
        Fisheries. Philosophical Transactions: Biological Sciences 360(1453):59–75.

Caldeira, Teresa P. R.

2000   City of Walls: Crime, Segregation, and Citizenship in Sao Paulo. Berkeley:
        University of California Press.

Callicott, J. Baird
1994   Toward a Global Environmental Ethic. *In* Worldviews and Ecology.
        M. E. Tucker and J. A. Grim, eds. Pp. 30–40. Cranbury: Associated
        University Publishers.

Callicott, J. Baird, and Michael P. Nelson
2004   American Indian Environmental Ethics: An Ojibwa Case Study. Basic Ethics
        in Action Series. Upper Saddle River: Prentice Hall.

Camacho Torres, Jimena
2004   Lumbre en el monte: La historia de Rodolfo Montiel y la lucha de los
        campesinos ecologistas de Guerrero [Fire on the mountain: The history of
        Rodolfo Montiel and the fight of the rural ecologists of Guerrero]. Mexico
        City: La Jornada Ediciones, Editorial Itaca, Demos, Desarrollo de
        Medios.Campbell, Colin
2007   The Easternization of the West: A Thematic Account of Cultural Change in
        the Modern Era. London: Paradigm.

Canclini, Nestor Garcia
1995   Hybrid Cultures: Strategies for Entering and Leaving Modernity.
        Minneapolis: University of Minnesota Press.

Carmagnani, Marcello
1988   El regreso de los dioses [The return of the gods]. México, DF: Fondo de
        Cultura Económica.

Carr, David
2004   Ladino and Q'echi' Maya Land Use and Land Clearing in the Sierra de
        Lacandon National Park, Petén, Guatemala. Agriculture and Human Values
        21:171–179.

Carroll, John E.
2004   Sustainability and Spirituality. Albany: State University of New York Press.

Carruthers, David V.
1996   Indigenous Ecology and the Politics of Linkage in Mexican Social
        Movements. Third World Quarterly 17(5):1007–1028.

Casanova, José
2008   Public Religions Revisited. *In* Religion: Beyond a Concept. Hent de Vries, ed.
        Pp. 101–119. New York: Fordham University Press.

Casey, Edward
1996   How to Get from Space to Place in a Fairly Short Stretch of Time:
        Phenomenological Prolegomena. *In* Senses of Place. Steven Feld and Keith
        Basso, eds. Pp.13–52. Santa Fe: SAR Press.

CEPAL (Comisión Económica para América Latina y el Caribe)
2002   Centroamérica: El impacto de la caída de los precios del café en 2001
        [Central America: The impact of the fall in coffee prices in 2001]. Document
        LC/MEX/R.822. México, DF: Comisión Económica para América Latina y el
        Caribe, Naciones Unidas.

REFERENCES

Chaloupka, William

2000   Jagged Terrain: Cronon, Soule, and the Struggle over Nature and
        Deconstruction in Environmental Theory. Strategies 13(1):23–29.

Chapin, Mac

2004   A Challenge to Conservationists. World Watch 17(6):17–32.

Chapman, Anne

1986   Los Hijos del Copal y la Candela: Tradición católica de los lencas de
        Honduras [Children of copal and flame: Catholic tradition among the
        Lencas of Honduras]. México, DF: Universidad Nacional Autónoma de
        México.

1992   Los Hijos del Copal y la Candela: Ritos Agrarios y Tradición Oral de los
        Lencas de Honduras [Children of copal and flame: Agrarian rituals and oral
        tradition among the Lencas of Honduras]. 2nd edition. México, DF:
        Universidad Nacional Autónoma de México.

Chidester, David

1996   The Church of Baseball, the Fetish of Coca-Cola, and the Potlatch of Rock
        'n' Roll: Theoretical Models for the Study of Religion in American Popular
        Culture. Journal of the American Academy of Religion 64(4):743–765.

Choy, Timothy K.

2005   Articulated Knowledges: Environmental Forms after Universality's Demise.
        American Anthropologist 107(1):5–18.

CI (Conservation International)

2007   Biodiversity Hotspots. http://www.biodiversityhotspots.org/Pages/default
        .aspx, accessed July 14, 2009.

Clarke, Peter B., ed.

2006   Encyclopedia of New Religious Movements. New York: Routledge.

Clifford, James

2007   Indigenous Articulations. *In* The Worlding Project. Rob Wilson and
        Christopher Leigh Connery, eds. Pp. 13–36. Berkeley: North Atlantic Books.

Cocks, Michelle

2006   Biocultural Diversity: Moving beyond the Realm of "Indigenous" and
        "Local" People. Human Ecology 34(2):185–200.

Colding, Johan, and Carl Folke

1997   The Relations among Threatened Species, Their Protection, and Taboos.
        Conservation Ecology 1(1): art. 6 [online]. http://www.ecologyandsociety
        .org/v011/iss1/art6/, accessed September 25, 2009.

Comaroff, Jean, and John L. Comaroff, eds.

2001   Millennial Capitalism and the Culture of Neoliberalism. Durham: Duke
        University Press.

Conklin, Beth, and Laura Graham
1996   The Shifting Middle Ground: Amazonian Indians and Eco-Politics. American Anthropologist 97(4):695–710.

Connolly, William E.
1995   The Ethos of Pluralization. Minneapolis: University of Minnesota Press.
1999   Why I Am Not a Secularist. Minneapolis: University of Minnesota Press.
2005   Pluralism. Durham: Duke University Press.
2011   A World of Becoming. Durham: Duke University Press.

Contaminação por urânio na Bahia: Relatório do Greenpeace exige investigação sobre as condições de saúde da população local [Uranium contamination in Bahia: Greenpeace report calls for research on the health of local people]
2009   domtotal [online], June 2: Especiais. http://www.domtotal.com/especiais /artigo_detalhes.php?espId=267&espId_art=271, accessed July 17, 2009.

Coward, Harold, and Daniel C. Maguire, eds.
2000   Visions of a New Earth: Religious Perspectives on Population, Consumption, and Ecology. Albany: State University of New York Press.

Cronon, William, ed.
1996   Uncommon Ground: Rethinking the Human Place in Nature. New York: Norton.

Csordas, Thomas J.
2009   Introduction: Modalities of Transnational Transcendence. *In* Transnational Transcendence: Essays on Religion and Globalization. Thomas J. Csordas, ed. Pp. 1–29. Berkeley: University of California Press.

Daneel, Marthinus L.
1974   Old and New in Southern Shona Independent Churches, vol. 2: Church Growth: Causative Factors and Recruitment Techniques. The Hague, Netherlands: Mouton.
1980   The Missionary Outreach of African Independent Churches. Missionalia 8(3):105–120.
1984   Black Messianism: Corruption or Contextualization? Theologia Evangelica 17(1):40–77.
1989   Fambidzano: Ecumenical Movement of Zimbabwean Independent Churches. Gweru, Zimbabwe: Mambo Press.
1993   Healing the Earth: Traditional and Christian Initiatives in Southern Africa. Journal for the Study of Religion 6(1):3–30.
1996a   Earthkeeping in Missiological Perspective: An African Challenge. Mission Studies 13(25–26):130–188.
1996b   Environmental Reform: A New Venture of Zimbabwe's Traditional Custodians of the Land. Journal of Legal Pluralism and Unofficial Law 37–38:347–376. http://www.jlp.bham.ac.uk/volumes/37–38/daneel-art.pdf, accessed July 12, 2011.

1998   African Earthkeepers, vol. 1: Interfaith Mission in Earth Care. Pretoria,
        South Africa: Unisa Press.

1999   African Earthkeepers, vol. 2: Environmental Mission and Liberation in
        Christian Perspective. Pretoria, South Africa: Unisa Press.

2000   Earthkeeping Churches at the African Grass Roots. *In* Christianity and
        Ecology: Seeking the Well-Being of Earth and Humans. Dieter T. Hessel and
        Rosemary Radford Ruether, eds. Pp. 531–558. Religions of the World and
        Ecology Series. Cambridge: Harvard University Center for the Study of
        World Religions.

2001   African Earthkeepers: Wholistic Interfaith Mission. Maryknoll: Orbis Books.

2006   African Initiated Churches as Vehicles of Earth-Care in Africa. *In* Oxford
        Handbook of Religion and Ecology. Roger S. Gottlieb, ed. Pp. 535–567.
        Oxford: Oxford University Press.

Dasmann, Raymond F.

1988   Toward a Biosphere Consciousness. *In* The Ends of the Earth: Perspectives
        on Modern Environmental History. Donald Worster, ed. Pp. 277–288. New
        York: Cambridge University Press.

Davis, Creston, John Milbank, and Slavoj Zizek, eds.

2005   Theology and the Political: The New Debate. Durham: Duke University
        Press.

Dawkins, Richard

2006   The God Delusion. Boston: Houghton Mifflin.

Dawson, Andrew

2007   New Era, New Religions: Religious Transformation in Contemporary Brazil.
        Ashgate New Critical Thinking in Religion, Theology and Biblical Studies.
        Surrey, UK: Ashgate.

De la Fuente, Julio

1949   Yalalag, una villa Zapoteca serrana [Yalalag, a Zapoteca serrana village].
        Mexico City: Museo Nacional de Antropologia.

De la Vega, Ricardo

1933   El fuego y la expansión agraria hacia el bosque como principales motivos de
        la desforestación del territorio patrio [Fire and agrarian expansion toward
        the forest as principal motives of deforestation of native territory]. Mexico
        Forestal XI(11–12):205–209.

De Vries, Hent

1999   Philosophy and the Turn to Religion. Baltimore: Johns Hopkins University
        Press.

De Vries, Hent, ed.

2006   Political Theologies: Public Religions in a Post-secular World. New York:
        Fordham University Press.

2008   Religion: Beyond a Concept. New York: Fordham University Press.

Denevan, William
1992   The Pristine Myth: The Landscape of the Americas in 1492. Annals of the Association of American Geographers 82(3):369–385.

Derr, Thomas Sieger
1975   Religion's Responsibility for the Ecological Crisis. Worldview 18(1):39–45.

Descola, Philippe
1996   In the Society of Nature: A Native Ecology of Amazonia. Nora Scott, trans. New York: Cambridge University Press.

2005   Par-dela nature et culture [Beyond nature and culture]. Paris: Gallimard.

2006   Beyond Nature and Culture. Proceedings of the British Academy 139:137–155. Reprinted online at old.eu.spb.ru/news/files2007/descola.pdf, accessed January 20, 2012. Pp. 1–14.

2009   Human Natures. Social Anthropology/Anthropologie Sociale 17(2):145–157.

Dessai, Suraje, Karen O'Brien, and Mike Hulme
2007   Editorial: On Uncertainty and Climate Change. Global Environmental Change 17(1):1–3.

Diamond, Jared
2005   Collapse: How Societies Choose to Fail or Succeed. New York: Penguin.

Diegues, Antonio Carlos, coord.
1995   Conflitos entre populações humanas e unidades de conservação [d]e Mata Atlântica [Conflicts between human populations and Atlantic Forest conservation units]. São Paulo, Brazil: Núcleo de Apoio à Pesquisa Sobre Populações Humanas e Áreas Úmidas.

Dietz, Thomas, Elinor Ostrom, and Paul C. Stern
2003   The Struggle to Govern the Commons. Science 302:1907–1912.

Dorm-Adzobu, Clement, and Peter G. Veit
1991   Religious Beliefs and Environmental Protection: The Malshegu Sacred Grove in Northern Ghana. Nairobi, Kenya: World Resources Institute.

Douglas, Mary
1966   Purity and Danger: An Analysis of Concepts of Pollution and Taboo. London: Routledge and Kegan Paul.

1975   Implicit Meanings: Essays in Anthropology. London: Routledge and Kegan Paul.

Dube, Saurabh
2002   Introduction: Enchantments of Modernity. South Pacific Quarterly 101(4):729–755.

Dubuisson, Daniel
2003   The Western Construction of Religion: Myths, Knowledge, and Ideology. William Sayers, trans. Baltimore: Johns Hopkins University Press.

Dudley, Nigel, Liza Higgins-Zogib, and Stephanie Mansourian
2005   Beyond Belief: Linking Faiths and Protected Areas to Support Biodiversity Conservation. Gland, Switzerland: World Wide Fund for Nature (WWF) / Alliance of Religions and Conservation.

2009   The Links between Protected Areas, Faiths, and Sacred Natural Sites. Conservation Biology 23(3):568–577.

Durkheim, Emile
1915   The Elementary Forms of the Religious Life. London: G. Allen & Unwin.
1976[1912] The Elementary Forms of the Religious Life. J. W. Swain, trans. London: Allen & Unwin.

Eagleton, Terry
2009   Reason, Faith, and Revolution: Reflections on the God Debate. New Haven: Yale University Press.

Eakin, Hallie, Catherine Tucker, and Edwin Castellanos
2006   Responding to the Coffee Crisis: A Pilot Study of Farmers' Adaptations in Mexico, Guatemala and Honduras. The Geographical Journal 172(2):156–171.

Eisenstadt, Shmuel N.
2002   Multiple Modernities. New Brunswick: Transaction.

ELI (Environmental Literacy Council)
2008   Hotspots of Biodiversity. http://www.enviroliteracy.org/subcategory.php/202.html, accessed March 9, 2009.

Escobar, Arturo
1998   Whose Knowledge, Whose Nature? Biodiversity, Conservation, and the Political Ecology of Social Movements. Journal of Political Ecology 5:53–82.
2008   Territories of Difference: Place, Movements, Life, *Redes*. Durham: Duke University Press.

Escobar, Arturo, and Sonia Alvarez, eds.
1992   The Making of Social Movements in Latin America. Boulder: Westview Press.

Esterci, Neide, and Raul Silva Telles do Valle
2003   Reforma agrária e meio ambiente [Agrarian reform and the environment]. Special Document of the II World Social Forum. Brasilia, Brasil: Instituto Socioambiental. http://www.socioambiental.org/inst/pub/, accessed December 10, 2009.

Evans-Pritchard, Edward Evan
1937   Witchcraft, Magic, and Oracles among the Azande. Oxford: Clarendon Press.

Evernden, Neil
1992   The Social Creation of Nature. Baltimore: Johns Hopkins University Press.

Farriss, Nancy
1984   Maya Society under Colonial Rule. Princeton: Princeton University Press.

Fischer, Edward, and Peter Benson
2005   Something Better: Hegemony, Development, and Desire in Guatemalan

Export Agriculture. Social Analysis 49(1):3–20.

Fischer, Michael M. J.

2007   Four Genealogies for a Recombinant Anthropology of Science and Technology. Cultural Anthropology 22(4):539–615.

Fischer, Michael

2003   Emergent Forms of Life and the Anthropological Voice. Durham: Duke University Press.

2006   Changing Palestine-Israel Ecologies: Narratives of Water, Land, Conflict, and Political Economy, Then and Now, and Life to Come. Cultural Politics 2(2):159–191.

Fisher, Frank

2000   Citizens, Experts, and the Environment: The Politics of Local Knowledge. Durham: Duke University Press.

Fitzgerald, Timothy

1997   A Critique of "Religion" as a Cross-cultural Category. Method and Theory in the Study of Religion 9(2):91–110.

2000   The Ideology of Religious Studies. Oxford: Oxford University Press.

Fitzgerald, Timothy, ed.

2007   Religion and the Secular: Historical and Colonial Formations. London: Equinox.

Floresta Viva

2008   Diagnóstico participativo e fortalecimento comunitário de comunidades quilombolas em Itacaré, Sul da Bahia [Participatory appraisal and community empowerment of maroon communities in Itacaré, Southern Bahia]. Final project report. Ilhéus, Brazil: Floresta Viva.

Foltz, Richard C., ed.

2003   Worldviews, Religion, and the Environment: A Global Anthology. Belmont: Wadsworth / Thomson Learning.

2005   Environmentalism in the Muslim World. Hauppage, NY: Nova Science.

Foltz, Richard C., Frederick M. Denny, and Azizan Baharuddin, eds.

2003   Islam and Ecology: A Bestowed Trust. Cambridge: Harvard University Press.

Forsyth, Tim

2005   Land Use Impacts on Water Resources: Science, Social and Political Factors. *In* Encyclopedia of Hydrological Sciences. Malcolm G. Anderson, ed. Pp. 2915–2928. Hoboken: Wiley.

Franklin, Adrian

2001   Nature and Social Theory. London: Sage.

Frazer, James G.

1890   The Golden Bough: A Study in Comparative Religion. London: Macmillan.

REFERENCES

Freire, Paulo
1972   Pedagogy of the Oppressed. New York: Continuum.

Freud, Sigmund
1927   The Future of an Illusion. London: Hogarth Press.

Freudenburg, William R., and Violetta Muselli
2010   Global Warming Estimates, Media Expectations, and the Asymmetry of
        Scientific Challenge. Global Environmental Change 20(3):483–491.

Friedlingstein, Pierre, and Susan Solomon
2005   Contributions of Past and Present Human Generations to Committed
        Warming Caused by Carbon Dioxide. Proceedings of the National Academy
        of Sciences of the United States of America 102(31):10832–10836.

Gaonkar, Dilip P.
2001   Alternative Modernities. Durham: Duke University Press.

Gardner, Gary T.
2006   Inspiring Progress: Religion's Contributions to Sustainable Development.
        New York: W. W. Norton.

Gauchet, Marcel
1997   The Disenchantment of the World: A Political History of Religion. Oscar
        Burge, trans. New Brunswick: Princeton University Press.

Geertz, Clifford
1965   Religion as a Cultural System. In Anthropological Approaches to the Study
        of Religion. Michael Banton, ed. Pp. 1–46. London: Tavistock Publications.
1973   The Interpretation of Cultures: Selected Essays. New York: Basic Books.

Geist, Helmut J., and Eric F. Lambin
2001   What Drives Tropical Deforestation? LUCC Report Series, No. 4. Louvain la
        Neuve, Belgium: LUCC International Project Office.

Gezon, Lisa L.
1999   Of Shrimps and Spirit Possession: Toward a Political Ecology of Resource
        Management in Northern Madagascar. American Ethnologist 101(1):58–67.

Gibson, Clark C.
2001   Forest Resources: Institutions for Local Governance in Guatemala. In
        Protecting the Commons: A Framework for Resource Management in the
        Americas. J. Burger, E. Ostrom, R. B. Norgaard, D. Policansky, and B.
        Goldstein, eds. Pp. 71–89. Washington, DC: Island Press.

Gieryn, Thomas F.
1995   The Boundaries of Science. In Handbook of Science and Technology
        Studies. Rev. edition. Sheila Jasanoff, Gerald E. Markle, James C. Petersen,
        and Trevor Pinch, eds. Pp. 393–443. Thousand Oaks: Sage.

Gill, Sam D.
1991   Mother Earth. Chicago: University of Chicago Press.

Glacken, Clarence
1967   Traces on the Rhodian Shore: Nature and Culture in Western Thought from Ancient Times to the End of the Eighteenth Century. Berkeley: University of California Press.

Godoy, Ricardo, Victoria Reyes-Garcia, Elizabeth Byron, William R. Leonard, and Vincent Vadez
2005   The Effect of Market Economies on the Well-Being of Indigenous Peoples and on Their Use of Renewable Natural Resources. Annual Review of Anthropology 34(1):121–138.

Godoy, Ricardo, David Wilkie, and Jeffrey Franks
1997   The Effects of Markets on Neotropical Deforestation: A Comparative Study of Four Amerindian Societies. Current Anthropology 38(5):875–878.

Goloubinoff, Marina, Esther Katz, and Annamaria Lammel
1997   Antropología del clima en el mundo Hispanoamericano, tomo I [Climate anthropology in the Spanish-American world, vol. I]. Quito, Ecuador: Ediciones Abya-Yala.

Gomez-Pompa, Arturo, and Andrea Kaus
1992   Taming the Wilderness Myth. BioScience 42:271–279.
1999   From Pre-Hispanic to Future Conservation Alternatives: Lessons from Mexico. Proceedings of the National Academy of Sciences of the United States of America 96(11):5982–5986.

González, Roberto J.
2001   Zapotec Science: Farming and Food in the Northern Sierra of Oaxaca. Austin: University of Texas Press.

Goody, Jack
1962   Death, Property and the Ancestors: A Study of the Mortuary Customs of the Lodagaa of West Africa. Stanford: Stanford University Press.

Gottlieb, Roger S.
2006a   A Greener Faith: Religious Environmentalism and Our Planet's Future. New York: Oxford University Press.

Gottlieb, Roger S., ed.
2004   This Sacred Earth: Religion, Nature, Environment. 2nd edition. New York: Routledge.
2006b   Oxford Handbook of Religion and Ecology. Oxford: Oxford University Press.

Greenberg, James
1989   Blood Ties. Tucson: University of Arizona Press.

Greenfield, Sidney M., and André Droogers
2005   Reinventing Religions: Syncretism and Transformation in Africa and the Americas. Lanham: Rowman & Littlefield.

Greenleaf, Robert K.
1977   Servant Leadership: A Journey into the Nature of Legitimate Power and Greatness. Mahwah: Paulist Press.

Grim, John A.
2006   Indigenous Traditions: Religion and Ecology. *In* The Oxford Handbook of Religion and Ecology. Roger S. Gottlieb, ed. Pp. 283–309. Oxford: Oxford University Press.

Grim, John A., ed.
2001   Indigenous Traditions and Ecology: The Interconnections of Cosmology and Community. Cambridge: Harvard University Press.

Gross, Daniel R., George Eiten, Nancy M. Flowers, Francisca Leoi, Madeline Lattman Ritter, and Dennis W. Werner
1979   Ecology and Acculturation Among Native Peoples of Central Brazil. Science 206(4422):1043–1050.

Grosz, Elizabeth
2004   The Nick of Time: Politics, Evolution, and the Untimely. Durham: Duke University Press.

Grove, Richard H.
1995   Green Imperialism. New York: Cambridge University Press.

Gruzinski, Serge
1993   The Conquest of Mexico. Eileen Corrigan, trans. Cambridge, UK: Polity.

Gurung, Barun
1997   The Perceived Environment as a System of Knowledge and Meaning: A Study of the Mewahang Rai of Eastern Nepal. *In* Nature Is Culture: Indigenous Knowledge and Socio-cultural Aspects of Trees and Forests in Non-European Cultures. K. Seeland, ed. Pp. 19–27. London: Intermediate Technology Publications.

Guthrie, Stewart E.
1993   Faces in the Clouds: A New Theory of Religion. New York: Oxford University Press.

Gutiérrez, Gustavo
1988   A Theology of Liberation: History, Politics and Salvation. Maryknoll. 15th anniv. edition with new introduction by author. Maryknoll: Orbis Books.

Guyer, Jane I.
2007   Prophecy and the Near Future: Thoughts on Macroeconomic, Evangelical, and Punctuated Time. American Ethnologist 34(3):409–421.

Guyer, Jane I., Naveeda Khan, and Juan Obarrio
2010   Introduction. Anthropological Theory 10(1–2):36–61.

Haenn, Nora
2005   Fields of Power, Forests of Discontent: Culture, Conservation, and the State

in Mexico. Tuscon: University of Arizona Press.

Hale, Charles A.

1985 El gran debate de libros de texto en 1880 y el Krausismo en México [The great debate of textbooks in 1880 and Krausism in Mexico]. Historia Mexicana 35(2):275–298.

Hall, Stuart

1986 Gramsci's Relevance for the Study of Race and Ethnicity. Journal of Communication Inquiry 10(2):5–27.

1996 Gramsci's Relevance for the Study of Race and Ethnicity. *In* Stuart Hall: Critical Dialogues in Cultural Studies. David Morley and Kuan-Hsing Chen, eds. Pp. 411–441. London: Routledge.

Hall, Stuart, and Lawrence Grossberg

1996 On Postmodernism and Articulation: An Interview with Stuart Hall. *In* Stuart Hall: Critical Dialogues in Cultural Studies. David Morley and Kuan-Hsing Chen, eds. Pp. 131–150. London: Routledge.

Hallum, Anne Motley

1996 Beyond Missionaries: Toward an Understanding of the Protestant Movement in Central America. Lanham: Rowman and Littlefield.

2003 Ecotheology and Environmental Praxis in Guatemala. Nova Religio: The Journal of Alternative and Emergent Religions 7(2):55–70.

Hames, Raymond

1987 Game Conservation or Efficient Hunting? *In* The Question of the Commons: The Culture and Ecology of Communal Resources. B. J. McCay and J. M. Acheson, eds. Pp. 92–107. Tucson: University of Arizona Press.

Hamilton, Lawrence S.

1995 Mountain Cloud Forest Conservation and Research: A Synopsis. Mountain Research and Development 15(3):259–266.

Hamp, Eric P.

1976 The Last Lenca. International Journal of American Linguistics 42(1):73–79.

Hannerz, Ulf

1996 Transnational Connections: Culture, People, Places. London: Routledge.

Harding, Rachel

2003 A Refuge in Thunder: Candomblé and Alternative Spaces of Blackness. Bloomington: Indiana University Press.

Harkin, Michael E., and David Rich Lewis, eds.

2007 Native Americans and the Environment: Perspectives on the Ecological Indian. Lincoln: University of Nebraska Press.

Harrison, Peter

1998 The Bible, Protestantism, and the Rise of Natural Science. Cambridge: Cambridge University Press.

REFERENCES

Harvey, David
2007   Neoliberalism as Creative Destruction. The Annals of the American
         Academy of Political and Social Science 610(1):21–44.

Harvey, Graham
2006   Animism: Respecting the Living World. New York: Columbia University
         Press.

Harvey, Neil
1996   The Reshaping of Agrarian Policy in Mexico. *In* Changing Structure of
         Mexico: Political, Social, and Economic Prospects. Laura Randall, ed. Pp.
         103–110. Armonk: M. E. Sharpe.

Hayden, Cori
2003   When Nature Goes Public: The Making and Unmaking of Bioprospecting in
         Mexico. Princeton: Princeton University Press.

Heelas, Paul
1996   The New Age Movement. Oxford: Blackwell.

Henrich, Joseph
1997   Market Incorporation, Agricultural Change, and Sustainability among the
         Machiguenga Indians of the Peruvian Amazon. Human Ecology
         25(2):319–351.

Hervieu-Léger, Danièle
2001   Religion as a Chain of Memory. Simon Lee, trans. New Brunswick: Rutgers
         University Press.

Hessel, Deiter T., and Rosemary Radford Reuther, eds.
2000   Christianity and Ecology: Seeking the Well-Being of Earth and Humans.
         Cambridge: Harvard University Press.

Hewitt, W. E.
2000   Introduction: The Legacy of the Progressive Church in Latin America. *In*
         The Church at the Grassroots in Latin America: Perspectives on Thirty Years
         of Activism. John Burdick and Warren E. Hewitt, eds. Pp. vii–xx. Westport:
         Praeger.

Hobbes, Thomas
1651   Leviathan. London: Andrew Crooke.

Hochstetler, Kathryn, and Margaret E. Keck
2007   Greening Brazil: Environmental Activism in State and Society. Durham:
         Duke University Press.

Hoffmeyer, Jesper
1996   Signs of Meaning in the Universe. Barbara J. Haveland, trans. Bloomington:
         Indiana University Press.

Hokari, Misuo, and Sadao Hokari
1997   Yarigatake kaizan Banryū [Banryū, who opened Mount Yari]. Tokyo:
         Taishūkan Shoten.

Holmes, Douglas R., and George Marcus
2005   Cultures of Expertise and the Management of Globalization: Toward a Re-functioning of Ethnography. *In* Global Assemblages: Technology, Politics and Ethics as Anthropological Problems. A. Ong and S. J. Collier, eds. Pp. 235–252. Malden: Blackwell.

Holvast, René
2009   Spiritual Mapping in the United States and Argentina, 1989–2005. Leiden, Netherlands: Brill.

Horigan, Stephen
1988   Nature and Culture in Western Discourses. New York: Routledge.

Houtzager, Peter
1997   Caught between Church and State: Popular Movements in the Brazilian Countryside 1964–1989. Ph.D. dissertation, University of California, Berkeley.

Humphries, Sally
1993   The Intensification of Traditional Agriculture among Yucatec Maya Farmers: Facing Up to the Dilemma of Livelihood Sustainability. Human Ecology 21(1):87–102.

Hunn, Eugene
2006   Meeting of Minds: How Do We Share Our Appreciation of Traditional Environmental Knowledge? Journal of the Royal Anthropological Institute 12(1):143–160.

Hunn, Eugene S., Darryll R. Johnson, Priscilla N. Russell, and Thomas F. Thornton
2003   Huna Tlingit Traditional Environmental Knowledge, Conservation, and the Management of a "Wilderness" Park. Current Anthropology 44(S5):S79–S103.

IBGE (Instituto Brasileiro de Geografia e Estatística)
N.d.   Banco de dados agregados: Censo demográfico e contagem da população [Database of households: Census and population count]. http://www.sidra .ibge.gov.br/bda/tabela/listabl.asp?z=cd&o=7&i=P&c=2102, accessed December 10, 2009.

IDB-USAID-World Bank (Inter-American Development Bank, United States Agency for International Development, and World Bank)
2002   Discussion Document: The Competitive Transition of the Coffee Sector in Central America. Antigua, Guatemala: IDB, USAID, and World Bank.

Igoe, Jim, and Tim Kelsall
2005   Between a Rock and a Hard Place: African NGOs, Donors and the State. Durham: Carolina Academic Press.

Inda, Jonathan Xavier, and Renato Rosaldo, eds.
2002   The Anthropology of Globalization: A Reader. Oxford: Wiley-Blackwell.

Ingold, Tim
2000   The Perception of the Environment: Essays in Livelihood, Dwelling and Skill. London: Routledge.

References

Ion, A. Hamish
1999 Introduction. *In* Collected Works of Walter Weston. Walter Weston, author. Pp. v–xiv. Tokyo: Ganesha Publishing.

Ireland, Kenneth R.
1993 Westonization in Japan: The Topos of the Mountain in Yasushi Inoue's *Hyoheki*. Comparative Literature Studies 30(1):16–31.

Ivakhiv, Adrian
2001 Claiming Sacred Ground: Pilgrims and Politics at Glastonbury and Sedona. Bloomington: Indiana University Press.
2002 Toward a Multicultural Ecology. Organization & Environment 15(4):389–409.
2003 Nature and Self in New Age Pilgrimage. Culture and Religion 4(1):93–118.
2006 Toward a Geography of "Religion": Mapping the Distribution of an Unstable Signifier. Annals of the Association of American Geographers 96(1):169–175.
2007 Religion, Nature, and Culture: Theorizing the Field. Journal for the Study of Religion, Nature and Culture 1(1):47–57.

Jacka, Jerry K.
2010 The Spirits of Conservation: Ecology, Christianity, and Resource Management in Highlands Papua New Guinea. Journal for the Study of Religion, Nature and Culture 4(1):24–47.

James, William
1920 A Pluralistic Universe. New York: Longmans, Green, and Company.

Jasanoff, Sheila
2004a Ordering Knowledge, Ordering Society. *In* States of Knowledge: The Co-production of Knowledge and Social Order. Sheila Jasanoff, ed. Pp. 13–42. London: Routledge.
2005 Designs on Nature. Princeton: Princeton University Press.

Jasanoff, Sheila, ed.
2004b States of Knowledge: The Co-production of Science and Social Order. New York: Routledge.

Jasanoff, Sheila, and Marybeth Long Martello, eds.
2004 Earthly Politics: Local and Global Environmental Governance. Cambridge: MIT Press.

Jennings, Theodore W., Jr.
1982 On Ritual Knowledge. Journal of Religion 62(2):111–127.

Johnson, Mark
1993 Moral Imagination. Chicago: Chicago University Press.

Johnson, Paul Christopher
2005 Secrets, Gossip, and Gods: The Transformation of Brazilian Candomble. Oxford: Oxford University Press.

Jordan, William R., III
2003   The Sunflower Forest: Ecological Restoration and the New Communion with Nature. Berkeley: University of California Press.

Jorgensen, Dan
2005   Third Wave Evangelism and the Politics of the Global in Papua New Guinea: Spiritual Warfare and the Recreation of Place in Telefolmin. Oceania 75(4):444–461.

Joseph, Gilbert M., and Daniel Nugent
1994   Everyday Forms of State Formation: Revolution and the Negotiation of Rule in Modern Mexico. Durham: Duke University Press.

Kaimowitz, David
2004   The Great Flood Myth. New Scientist 182(2452):18.

Keck, Margaret E., and Kathryn Sikkink
1998   Activists beyond Borders: Advocacy Networks in International Politics. Ithaca: Cornell University Press.

Kellert, Stephen R., and Timothy J. Farnham, eds.
2002   The Good in Nature and Humanity: Connecting Science, Religion, and Spirituality with the Natural World. Washington, DC: Island Press.

Kempton, Willett, James S. Boster, and Jennifer A. Hartley
1995   Environmental Values in American Culture. Cambridge: MIT Press.

Kinsley, David
1995   Ecology and Religion: Ecological Spirituality in Cross-Cultural Perspective. Englewood Cliffs: Prentice-Hall.

Klooster, Dan
2003   Campesinos and Mexican Forest Policy during the Twentieth Century. Latin American Research Review 38(2):94–126.

Kraft, Charles H.
2000a   Two Kingdoms in Conflict. *In* Behind Enemy Lines: An Advanced Guide to Spiritual Warfare. Charles H. Kraft with Mark White, eds. Pp. 17–29. Eugene: Wipf and Stock.
2000b   Spiritual Power: Principles and Observations. *In* Behind Enemy Lines: An Advanced Guide to Spiritual Warfare. Charles H. Kraft with Mark White, eds. Pp. 31–62. Eugene: Wipf and Stock.

Kraft, Siv Ellen
2002   "To Mix or Not to Mix": Syncretism/Anti-syncretism in the History of Theosophy. Numen 49(2):142–177.

Krech, Shepard, III
1999   The Ecological Indian: Myth and History. New York: Norton.
2005   Reflections on Conservation, Sustainability and Environmentalism in Indigenous North America. American Anthropologist 107(1):78–86.

REFERENCES

Kuhn, Thomas
1970   The Structure of Scientific Revolutions. 2nd edition. Chicago: University of Chicago Press.

Kurono, Kōki
1997   Yarigatake kaizan Banryū Shonin no ashiato-ten (Special exhibition on the traces of Banryū Shonin, opener of Mount Yari). Mitake, Gifu prefecture: Nakasendō Mitake-kan.

Lambek, Michael
2008   Provincializing God? Provocations from an Anthropology of Religion. *In* Religion: Beyond a Concept. Hent de Vries, ed. Pp. 120–138. New York: Fordham University Press.

Lansing, J. Stephen
1991   Priests and Programmers: Technologies of Power in the Engineered Landscape of Bali. Princeton: Princeton University Press.
2006   Perfect Order: Recognizing Complexity in Bali. Princeton: Princeton University Press.

Latour, Bruno
1993   We Have Never Been Modern. Cambridge: Harvard University Press.
2002   War of the Worlds: What about Peace? Chicago: Prickly Paradigm Press.
2004a   The Politics of Nature: How to Bring the Sciences into Democracy. Cambridge: Harvard University Press.
2004b   Scientific Objects and Legal Objectivity. *In* Law, Anthropology, and the Constitution of the Social: Making Persons and Things. A. Pottage and M. Mundy, eds. Pp. 73–114. Cambridge: Cambridge University Press.
2004c   Whose Cosmos? Which Cosmopolitics? Comments on the Peace Terms of Ulrich Beck. Common Knowledge 10(3):450–462.
2009a   Perspectivism: "Type" or "Bomb"? Anthropology Today 25(2):1–2.
2009b   Will Non-humans Be Saved? An Argument in Ecotheology. Journal of the Royal Anthropological Institute, n.s., 15:459–475.

Latour, Bruno, and Peter Weibel, eds.
2002   Iconoclash: Beyond the Image Wars in Science, Religion, and Art. Cambridge: MIT Press.

Law, John
2004   After Method: Mess in Social Science Research. New York: Routledge.

Leal, Carlos Galindo, and Ibsen de Gusmao Câmara
2003   The Atlantic Forest of South America: Biodiversity Status, Threats, and Outlook. Washington, DC: Island Press.

Lee, C., and T. Schaaf, eds.
2003   The Importance of Sacred Natural Sites for Biodiversity Conservation. Paris: United Nations Educational, Social and Cultural Organization (UNESCO).

Lee, Cathy, and Thomas Schaaf, eds.
2003   The Importance of Sacred Natural Sites for Biodiversity Conservation. Paris: United Nations Educational, Social and Cultural Organization (UNESCO).

Leite, Ilka Boaventura
2000   Os Quilombos no Brasil: questoes conceituais e normativas [Quilombos in Brazil: Conceptual and normative questions]. Etnográfica IV(2):333–354.

Lemos, Maria Carmen
2003   A Tale of Two Policies: The Politics of Climate Forecasting and Drought Relief in Ceará, Brazil. Policy Sciences 36:101–123.

Lemos, Maria Carmen, and Joao Lucio Farias de Oliveira
2004   Can Water Reform Survive Politics? Institutional Change and River Basin Management in Ceará, Northeast Brazil. World Development 32(12):2121–2137.

Leopold, Aldo
1970   A Sand County Almanac with Essays on Conservation from Round River. Exp. edition. New York: Ballantine Books. Compilation from A Sand County Almanac, 1949, and Round River, 1953, Oxford University Press, London.

Li, Tanya Murray
2000   Articulating Indigenous Identity in Indonesia: Resource Politics and the Tribal Slot. Comparative Study of Society and History 42:149–179.

Libert, Antoine
2003   Religiosity in Tlahuitoltepec. Research report. Montreal, Canada: Department of Anthropology, McGill University.

Lilla, Mark
2008a   The Persistence of Political Theology. Current History 107(705):41–46.
2008b   The Stillborn God: Religion, Politics, and the Modern West. New York: Random House.

Livingstone, David N.
1994   The Historical Roots of Our Ecological Crisis: A Reassessment. Fides et Historia 26:38–55.

Loaiza, Vanessa
2005   Plan impide a agricultores sembrar en el 75% del país [Plan prohibits agriculture in 75 percent of the territory]. La Nación, http://www.nacion.com/ln_ee/2005/agosto/25/pais0.html, accessed June, 23, 2010.

Lopez, Barry
1978   Of Wolves and Men. New York: Touchstone.
1996   from "Arctic Dreams: Imagination and Desire in a Northern Landscape." *In* This Sacred Earth: Religion, Nature, Environment. Roger S. Gottlieb, ed. Pp. 21–22. New York: Routledge.
2001[1986] Arctic Dreams. New York: Vintage Books.

López Austin, Alfredo
1988   The Human Body and Ideology: Concepts of the Ancient Nahuas. Thelma
        Ortiz de Montellano and Bernard Ortiz de Montellano, trans. Salt Lake City:
        University of Utah Press.

Lorentzen, Lois Ann, and Salvador Leavitt-Alcantara
2006   Religion and Environmental Struggles in Latin America. In The Oxford
        Handbook of Religion and Ecology. Roger S. Gottlieb, ed. Pp. 510–534.
        Oxford: Oxford University Press.

Lovgren, Stefan
2003   Map Links Healthier Ecosystems, Indigenous Peoples. National Geographic
        News, February 27:1–2.

Luhmann, Niklas
1995   Social Systems. Stanford: Stanford University Press.

Mafuranhunzi Gumbo (pseudonym of M. L. Daneel)
1995   Guerilla Snuff. Harare, Zimbabwe: Baobab Books.

Mainwaring, Scott
1986   The Catholic Church and Politics in Brazil, 1916–1985. Stanford: Stanford
        University Press.

Malhi, Yadvinder, J. Timmons Roberts, Richard A. Betts, Timothy J. Killeen, Wenhong
Li, and Carlos A. Nobre
2008   Climate Change, Deforestation, and the Fate of the Amazon. Science
        319(5860):169–172.

Malinowski, Bronislaw
1992[1925] Magic, Science, Religion, and Other Essays. Long Grove: Waveland Press.

Marler, Penny L., and C. Kirk Hadaway
2002   "Being Religious" or "Being Spiritual" in America: A Zero-Sum Proposition?
        Journal for the Scientific Study of Religion 41(2):289–300.

Marroquín, Enrique
1989   La cruz messiánica [The messianic cross]. Oaxaca, Mexico: Universidad
        Autónoma de Benito Juárez–Palabras Ediciones.

Marsden, George M.
1995   Reforming Fundamentalism: Fuller Seminary and the New Evangelicalism.
        Grand Rapids: William B. Eerdman's Publishing.

Martin, David
2002   Pentecostalism: The World Their Parish. Oxford: Blackwell.

Martini, Adriana Maria Zanforlin, Raul Fiaschi, André M. Amorim, and
José Lima da Paixão
2007   A Hot-Point within a Hot-Spot: A High Diversity Site in Brazil's Atlantic
        Forest. Biodiversity and Conservation 16(11):3111–3128.

Masuzawa, Tomoko
2005   The Invention of World Religions: Or, How European Universalism Was

Preserved in the Language of Pluralism. Chicago: University of Chicago Press.

Mathews, Andrew Salvador

2003   Suppressing Fire and Memory: Environmental Degradation and Political Restoration in the Sierra Juárez of Oaxaca 1887–2001. Environmental History 8(1):77–108.

2008   Statemaking, Knowledge and Ignorance: Translation and Concealment in Mexican Forestry Institutions. American Anthropologist 110(4):484–494.

2009   Unlikely Alliances: Encounters between State Science, Nature Spirits, and Indigenous Industrial Forestry in Mexico, 1926–2008. Current Anthropology 50(1):75–101.

Maurer, Bill

2005   Mutual Life Limited: Islamic Banking, Alternative Currencies, Lateral Reason. Princeton: Princeton University Press.

McCutcheon, Russell T.

1997   Manufacturing Religion: The Discourse on Sui Generis Religion and the Politics of Nostalgia. Oxford: Oxford University Press.

McFague, Sallie

1987   Models of God. Minneapolis: Fortress Press.

2008   A New Climate for Theology: God, the World, and Global Warming. Minneapolis: Fortress Press.

McGee, Gary B., and B. A. Pavia

2002   Wagner, Charles Peter. *In* The New International Dictionary of Pentecostal and Charismatic Movements. Rev. and exp. edition. Stanley M. Burgess and Eduard M. van der Maas, eds. P. 1181. Grand Rapids: Zondervan.

McGrath, Alister

2002   The Reenchantment of Nature: The Denial of Religion and the Ecological Crisis. New York: Doubleday.

McIntosh, Gary L.

2004   Introduction: Why Church Growth Can't Be Ignored. *In* Evaluating the Church Growth Movement: 5 Views. Paul E. Engle and Gary L. McIntosh, eds. Pp. 7–28. Grand Rapids: Zondervan.

McKinley, Andrew

2008   Hope in a Hopeless Age: Environmentalism's Crisis. Environmentalist 28:319–326.

Mehta, G.

1991   Karma Cola: Marketing the Mystical East. New York: Ballantine.

Menchú, Rigoberta

1984   I, Rigoberta Menchú: An Indian Woman in Guatemala. Elisabeth Burtos-Debray, trans. London: Verso Press.

Merchant, Carolyn

1989   The Death of Nature: Women, Ecology, and the Scientific Revolution. New York: Harper & Row.

Messer, Donald E.

1992   A Conspiracy of Goodness: Contemporary Images of Christian Mission. Nashville: Abingdon Press.

Messer, Ellen, and Michael Lambek, eds.

2001   Ecology and the Sacred: Engaging the Anthropology of Roy A. Rappaport. Ann Arbor: University of Michigan Press.

Meyer, Brigit, and Peter Geschiere

1999   Globalization and Identity: Dialectics of Flow and Closure. Oxford: Blackwell.

Meyer, Brigit, and Peter Pels

2003   Magic and Modernity: Interfaces of Revelation and Concealment. Stanford: Stanford University Press.

Michaelson, Evalyn Jacobson, and Walter Goldschmidt

1976   Family and Land in Peasant Ritual. American Ethnologist 3(1):87–96.

Micklethwait, John, and Adrian Wooldridge

2009   God Is Back: How the Global Revival of Faith Is Changing the World. New York: Penguin.

Mignolo, Walter D.

2000   Local Histories/Global Designs: Coloniality, Subaltern Knowledges, and Border Thinking. Princeton: Princeton University Press.

Milton, Kay

1999   Nature Is Already Sacred. Environmental Values 8(4):437–449.

Minteer, Ben A., and Robert E. Manning

2003   Pragmatism in Environmental Ethics: Democracy, Pluralism, and the Management of Nature. In Environmental Ethics: An Anthology. Andrew Light and Holmes Rolston III, eds. Pp. 319–330. London: Wiley-Blackwell.

2005   An Appraisal of the Critique of Anthropocentrism and Three Lesser Known Themes in Lynn White's "The Historical Roots of Our Ecologic Crisis." Organization & Environment 18(2):163–176.

Miyazaki, Hirokazu

2000   Faith and Its Fulfillment: Agency, Exchange, and the Fijian Aesthetics of Completion. American Ethnologist 27(1):31–51.

2004   The Method of Hope: Anthropology, Philosophy, and Fijian Knowledge. Stanford: Stanford University Press.

Miyazaki, Hirokazu, and Annelise Riles

2005   Failure as Endpoint. In Global Assemblages: Technology, Politics, and Ethics as Anthropological Problems. A. Ong and S. J. Collier, eds. Pp. 320–332. Malden: Blackwell.

Moguel, Patricia, and Victor M. Toledo
1999   Biodiversity Conservation in Traditional Coffee Systems of Mexico.
         Conservation Biology 13(1):11–21.

Mol, Annemarie
1999   Ontological Politics: A Word and Some Questions. *In* Actor Network Theory
         and After. John Law and John Hassard, eds. Pp. 74–89. Oxford: Blackwell.

Monaghan, John
1995   The Covenants with Earth and Rain: Exchange, Sacrifice and Revelation in
         Mixtec Sociality. The Civilization of the American Indian Series, vol. 219.
         Norman: University of Oklahoma Press.

Montejo, Victor
2001   The Road to Heaven: Jakaltek Maya Beliefs, Religion, and the Ecology. *In*
         Indigenous Traditions and Ecology: The Interbeing of Cosmology and
         Community. John A. Grim, ed. Pp. 175–195. Religions of the World and
         Ecology Series. Cambridge: Harvard University Press.

Moran, Emilio F., and Elinor Ostrom, eds.
2005   Seeing the Forest and the Trees: Human–Environment Interactions in Forest
         Ecosystems. Cambridge: MIT Press.

Moran, Katy
1999   Toward Compensation: Returning Benefits from Ethnobotanical Drug
         Discovery to Native Peoples. *In* Ethnoecology: Situated Knowledge/Located
         Lives. V. D. Nazarea, ed. Pp. 249–262. Tucson: University of Arizona Press.

Morellato, L. Patricia C., and Célio F. B. Haddad
2000   Introduction: The Brazilian Atlantic Forest. Biotropica 32(4b):786–792.

Muñoz Piña, Carlos, Alejandro Guevara, Juan Manuel Torres, and Josefina Brana
2008   Paying for the Hydrological Services of Mexico's Forests: Analysis,
         Negotiations and Results. Ecological Economics 65(4):725–736.

Myers, Norman
1988   Threatened Biotas: "Hotspots" in Tropical Forests. The Environmentalist
         8:187–208.

Myers, Norman, Russell A. Mittermeier, Cristina G. Mittermeier,
Gustavo A. B. da Fonseca, and Jennifer Kent
2000   Biodiversity Hotspots for Conservation Priorities. Nature 403:853–858.

Nadasdy, Paul
2007   The Gift in the Animal: The Ontology of Hunting and Human–Animal
         Sociality. American Ethnologist 34(1):25–43.

Nader, Laura
1996   Naked Knowledge: Anthropological Inquiry into Boundaries, Power, and
         Knowledge. New York: Routledge.

REFERENCES

Nash, June C.
2001   Mayan Visions: The Quest for Autonomy in an Age of Globalization. New York: Routledge.

Nash, Roderick
1996   The Greening of Religion. *In* This Sacred Earth: Religion, Nature, Environment. Roger S. Gottlieb, ed. Pp. 194–229. New York: Routledge.

Nasr, Seyyed Hossein
2003   The Spiritual and Religious Dimensions of the Environmental Crisis. *In* Seeing God Everywhere: Essays on Nature and the Sacred. Barry McDonald, ed. Pp. 73–100. Bloomington: World Wisdom.

Nazarea, Virginia D., ed.
2003   Ethnoecology: Situated Knowledge/Located Lives. Tucson: University of Arizona Press.

Nazarea, Virginia, Robert Rhoades, Erla Bontoyan, and Gabriela Flora
1998   Defining Indicators Which Make Sense to Local People: Intra-cultural Variation in Perception of Natural Resources. Human Organization 57(2):159–170.

Nelson, Donald R., and Timothy J. Finan
2009   Praying for Drought: Persistent Vulnerability and the Politics of Patronage in Ceará, Northeast Brazil. American Anthropologist 111(3):302–316.

Nelson, Richard K.
1983   Make Prayers to the Raven: A Koyukon View of the Northern Forest. Chicago: University of Chicago Press.

Netting, Robert McC., M. Priscilla Stone, and Glenn D. Stone
1989   Kofyar Cash-Cropping: Choice and Change in Indigenous Agricultural Development. Human Ecology 17(3):299–319.

Newson, Linda
1986   The Costs of Conquest: Indian Decline in Honduras under Spanish Rule. Boulder: Westview Press.

Norgaard, Richard B.
2002   Can Science and Religion Better Save Nature Together? Bioscience 52(9):842–846.

Norget, Kristin
1997   The Politics of "Liberation": The Popular Church, Indigenous Theology and Grassroots Mobilization in Oaxaca, Mexico. Latin American Perspectives 24(5):96–127.

2004   "Knowing Where We Enter": Indigenous Theology and the Catholic Church in Oaxaca, México. *In* Resurgent Voice in Latin America: Indigenous Peoples, Political Mobilization, and Religious Change. Edward Cleary and Tim Steigenga, eds. Pp.154–186. New Brunswick: Rutgers University Press.

2006   Days of Death, Days of Life: Ritual in Oaxacan Popular Culture. New York: Columbia University Press.

2010   A Cacophony of Autochthony: Representing Indigeneity in Oaxacan Popular Mobilization. Journal of Latin American and Caribbean Anthropology 15(1):115–143.

Norris, Pippa, and Ronald Inglehart
2004   Sacred and Secular: Religion and Politics Worldwide. Cambridge: Cambridge University Press.

Northcott, Michael S.
1996   The Environment and Christian Ethics. London: Cambridge University Press.

Nowotny, Helga
2003   Dilemma of Expertise: Democratising Expertise and Socially Robust Knowledge. Science and Public Policy 30(3):151–156.

Ntiamoa-Baidu, Yaa
2008   Indigenous Beliefs and Biodiversity Conservation: The Effectiveness of Sacred Groves, Taboos and Totems in Ghana for Habitat and Species Conservation. Journal for the Study of Religion, Nature and Culture 2(3):309–326.

Oelschlaeger, Max
1994   Caring for Creation: An Ecumenical Approach to the Environmental Crisis. New Haven: Yale University Press.

Orr, David
2005   Armageddon versus Extinction. Conservation Biology 19:290–292.

Ostrom, Elinor
1990   Governing the Commons: The Evolution of Institutions for Collective Action. New York: Cambridge University Press.
2005   Understanding Institutional Diversity. Princeton: Princeton University Press.

Ostrom, Elinor, Thomas Dietz, Nives Dolšak, Paul C. Stern, Susan Stonich, and Elke U. Weber, eds.
2002   The Drama of the Commons. Washington, DC: National Academies Press.

Otis, George, Jr.
1999   Informed Intercession: Transforming Your Community Through Spiritual Mapping and Strategic Prayer. Ventura: Renew.

Otto, Rudolph
1958   The Idea of the Holy. 2nd edition. John W. Harvey, trans. Oxford: Oxford University Press.

Pacheco, Ana Patrícia Bastos
2009   Moradores do sudoeste baiano se posicionam contra a instalação da BAMIN. http://www.acaoilheus.org/news/1109-moradores-do-sudoeste-baiano-se -posicionam-contra-a-instalacao-da-bamin, accessed August 30, 2011.

REFERENCES

Page, Joseph
1996   The Brazilians. New York: De Capo Press.

Palmer, Martin, and Victoria Finlay
2003   Faith in Conservation: New Approaches to Religion and Environment. Washington, DC: World Bank.

Pals, Daniel L.
2006   Eight Theories of Religion. 2nd edition. New York: Oxford University Press.

Parajuli, Pramod
1998   Beyond Capitalized Nature: Ecological Ethnicity as an Arena of Conflict in the Regime of Globalization. Ecumene 5(2):186–217.
2001   Learning from Ecological Ethnicities: Towards a Plural Political Ecology of Knowledge. *In* Indigenous Traditions and Ecology. John Grim, ed. Pp. 559–589. Cambridge: Harvard University Press.

Partridge, Christopher
2004   The Re-enchantment of the West, vol. 1. London: T. & T. Clark.
2005   The Re-enchantment of the West, vol. 2. London: T. & T. Clark.

Peet, Richard, and Michael Watts
1996   Liberation Ecologies: Environment, Development, Social Movements. New York: Routledge.

Perfecto, Ivette, Robert A. Rice, Russell Greenberg, and Martha E. van der Voort
1996   Shade Coffee: A Disappearing Refuge for Biodiversity. BioScience 46(8):598–608.

Peters, Debra P. C., Brandon T. Bestelmeyer, Jeffrey E. Herrick, Ed L. Fredrickson, H. Curtis Monger, and Kris M. Havstad
2006   Disentangling Complex Landscapes: New Insights into Arid and Semiarid System Dynamics. Bioscience 56(6):491–501.

Petras, James, and Henry Veltmeyer
2005   Social Movements and State Power: Argentina, Brazil, Bolivia, Ecuador. London: Pluto Press.

Pierucci, António Flávio, and Reginaldo Prandi
2000   Religious Diversity in Brazil. International Sociology 15(4):629–639.

Porter, Theodore M.
1995   Trust in Numbers: The Pursuit of Objectivity in Science and Public Life. Princeton: Princeton University Press.

Posey, Darrell A., ed.
2002   Cultural and Spiritual Values of Biodiversity. Reading, UK: UN Environment Programme and Intermediate Technology Publications.

Presidencia de la República
1958a   Codigo Forestal: Decreto que declara de utilidad publica la constitucion de una unidad industrial de explotacion forestal en favor de la empresa denominada Fabricas de Papel Tuxtepec, S.A. de C.V. [Forest Code: Decree

that declares a public interest in constituting an industrial forestry exploitation unit in favor of the company Tuxtepec Paper Factories]. *In* Diario Oficial. Pp. 691–719. Mexico.

1958b   Codigo Forestal: Decreto que establece una Unidad Industrial de Explotacion Forestal a favor de la Compañia Forestal de Oaxaca S. de R.L., en predios boscosos enclavados en los Distritos de Zimatlan, Sola de Vega, Miahuatlan y Yautepec, en el Estado de Oaxaca [Forest Code: Decree that declares a public interest in constituting an industrial forestry exploitation unit in favor of the Oaxaca Forestry Company S.R.L.]. *In* Diario Oficial. Pp. 736–753. Mexico.

Proctor, James D.

1998   The Social Construction of Nature: Relativist Accusations, Pragmatist and Critical Realist Responses. Annals of the Association of American Geographers 88(3):362–376.

2001   Concepts of Nature, Environmental/Ecological. *In* International Encyclopedia of the Social and Behavioral Sciences. Neil J. Smelser and Paul B. Bates, eds. Pp. 10400–10406. Oxford: Elsevier Science.

2004   Resolving Multiple Visions of Nature, Science, and Religion. Zygon 39(3):637–657.

Proctor, James D., ed.

2009   Envisioning Nature, Science, and Religion. West Conshohocken: Templeton Press.

Proctor, James D., and Evan Berry

2005   Social Science on Religion and Nature. *In* Encyclopedia of Religion and Nature, vol. 2. Bron R. Taylor, ed. Pp. 1571–1577. London: Thames Continuum.

Pryke, Michael

2007   Geomoney: An Option on Frost, Going Long on Clouds. Geoforum 38(3):576–588.

Pulido, Laura

1998   The Sacredness of "Mother Earth": Spirituality, Activism and Social Justice. *Review of* Justice, Nature and the Geography of Difference by David Harvey. Annals of the Association of American Geographers 88(4):719–723.

Pyne, S. J.

1997   Fire in America: A Cultural History of Wildland and Rural Fire. Seattle: University of Washington Press.

Quevedo, Miguel Angel de

1930   La preservación de los bosques comunales y ejidales [The preservation of communal and ejidal forests]. Mexico Forestal VIII(4):73–74.

1935[1910]   El origen de la cuestión forestal en México. [Origin of the forestry question in Mexico]. Mexico Forestal XIII(11–12):105–116.

1943   Relato de mi vida [Story of my life]. Mexico City: private publisher.

REFERENCES

Rajan, S. Ravi

2006   Modernizing Nature: Forestry and Imperial Eco-development 1800–1950. Oxford: Oxford University Press.

Rappaport, Roy A.

1984   Pigs for the Ancestors: Ritual in the Ecology of a New Guinea People. Exp. edition. New Haven: Yale University Press.

1993[1979] Ecology, Meaning & Religion. New York and Berkeley: North Atlantic Books.

1999   Ritual and Religion in the Making of Humanity. London: Cambridge University Press.

Reader, Ian

1993   Introduction. *In* Pilgrimage in Popular Culture. Ian Reader and Tony Walter, eds. Pp. 1–25. London: Macmillan Press.

1995   Cleaning Floors and Sweeping the Mind. *In* Ceremony and Ritual in Japan: Religious Practices in an Industrial Society. Jan van Bremen and D. P. Martinez, eds. Pp. 227–245. New York: Routledge.

Reader, Ian, and George J. Tanabe, Jr.

1998   Practically Religious: Worldly Benefits and the Common Religion of Japan. Honolulu: University of Hawai'i Press.

Redford, Kent H., and Steven E. Sanderson

2000   Extracting Humans from Nature. Conservation Biology 14(5):1362–1364.

Redman, Charles L.

1999   Human Impact on Ancient Environments. Tucson: University of Arizona Press.

Reichel-Dolmatoff, Gerardo

1976   Cosmology as Ecological Analysis: A View from the Rainforest. Man 11:307–318.

Ribeiro, Darcy

2000   The Brazilian People: The Formation and Meaning of Brazil. Gregory Rabassa, trans. Gainesville: University Press of Florida.

Rivas, Ramón D.

1993   Pueblos Indígenas y Garífuna de Honduras [Indigenas pueblos and Garífuna of Honduras]. Tegucigalpa, Honduras: Editorial Guaymuras.

Roach, Catherine M.

2003   Mother/Nature: Popular Culture and Environmental Ethics. Bloomington: Indiana University Press.

Robbins, Joel

1995   Dispossessing the Spirits: Christian Transformations of Desire and Ecology among the Urapmin of Papua New Guinea. Ethnology 34(3):211–224.

1998   On Reading "World News": Apocalyptic Narrative, Negative Nationalism, and Transnational Christianity in a Papua New Guinea Society. Social Analysis 42(2):103–130.

2003   Properties of Nature, Properties of Culture: Possession, Recognition, and the Substance of Politics in a Papua New Guinea Society. Journal of the Finnish Anthropological Society (Suomen Antropologi) 28(1):9–28.

2004   Becoming Sinners: Christianity and Moral Torment in a Papua New Guinea Society. Berkeley: University of California Press.

2007   Causality, Ethics and the Near Future. American Ethnologist 34(3):433–436.

2009   Conversion, Hierarchy, and Cultural Change: Value and Syncretism in the Globalization of Pentecostal and Charismatic Christianity. *In* Hierarchy: Persistence and Transformation in Social Formations. Knut M. Rio and Olaf H. Smedal, eds. Pp. 65–88. New York: Berghahn.

Robbins, Paul
2004   Political Ecology: A Critical Introduction. Oxford: Blackwell.

Roof, Wade Clark
2000   Spiritual Marketplace: Baby Boomers and the Remaking of American Religion. Princeton: Princeton University Press.

Rose, Nikolas
1996   Governing "Advanced" Liberal Democracies. *In* Foucault and Political Reason: Liberalism, Neo-liberalism and Rationalities of Government. A. Barry, T. Osborne, and N. Rose, eds. Pp. 37–64. Chicago: University of Chicago Press.

Ross, Eric Barry, Margaret L. Arnott, Ellen B. Basso, Stephen Beckerman, Robert L. Carneiro, Richard G. Forbis, Kenneth R. Good, Knud-Erik Jensen, Allen Johnson, Jaan Kaplinski, R. S. Khare, Olga F. Linares, Paul S. Martin, Bernard Nietschmann, G. T. Nurse, Nancy J. Pollock, Indu Sahai, Taylor Kenneth Clarkson, David Turton, William T. Vickers, and Wilma E. Wetterstrom
1978   Food Taboos, Diet, and Hunting Strategy: The Adaptation to Animals in Amazon Cultural Ecology [and Comments and Reply]. Current Anthropology 19(1):1–36.

Rountree, Kathryn
2002   Goddess Pilgrims as Tourists: Inscribing the Body through Sacred Travel. Sociology of Religion 63(4):475–496.

Rudel, Thomas K.
2002   Paths of Destruction and Regeneration: Globalization and Forests in the Tropics. Rural Sociology 67(4):622–636.

Saatchi, S., D. Agosti, K. Alger, J. Delabie, and J. Musinsky
2001   Examining Fragmentation and Loss of Primary Forest in the Southern Bahian Atlantic Forest of Brazil with Radar Imagery. Conservation Biology 15(4):867–875.

REFERENCES

Saberwal, Vasant K.
1998   Science and the Desiccationist Discourse of the 20th Century. Environment
        and History 4:309–343.

Sahr, Wolf Dietrich Gustav Johannes
2001   Religion and Scientificism in Brazil: Towards a Regional Geography of
        Knowledge—A Geographical Essay. Revista de Historia Regional 6(2):43–74.

Saler, Benson
1993   Conceptualizing Religion: Immanent Anthropologists, Transcendent
        Natives, and Unbounded Categories. New York: Brill Academic.

Saler, Michael
2006   Modernity and Enchantment: A Historiographic Review. The American
        Historical Review 111(3):692–716. http://www.historycooperative.org
        /journals/ahr/111.3/saler.html, accessed July 12, 2011.

Salmon, Enrique
2000   Kincentric Ecology: Indigenous Perceptions of the Human–Nature
        Relationship. Ecological Applications 10(5):1327–1332.

Samaddar, Arindam
2006   Traditional and Posttraditional: A Study of Agricultural Rituals in Relation
        to Technological Complexity among Rice Producers in Two Zones of West
        Bengal, India. Culture & Agriculture 28(2):108–121.

Santilli, Juliana
2005   Socioambientalismo e novos direitos [Socioenvironmentalism and new
        rights]. São Paulo, Brazil: Peiropolis.

Schmitt, Karl M.
1962   Catholic Adjustment to the Secular State: The Case of Mexico, 1867–1911.
        The Catholic Historical Review 48(July):182–204.

Schnell, Scott
2007   Are Mountain Gods Vindictive? Competing Images of the Japanese
        Alpine Landscape. Journal of the Royal Anthropological Institute, n.s.,
        13(4):863–880.

Schussler Fiorenza, Francis
2000   Religion: A Contested Site in Theology and the Study of Religion. Harvard
        Theological Review 93(1):7–34.

Scott, James C.
1998   Seeing like a State: How Certain Schemes to Improve the Human Condition
        Have Failed. New Haven: Yale University Press.

SEI (Scientists and Evangelicals Initiative)
2007   An Urgent Call to Action: Scientists and Evangelicals Unite to Protect
        Creation. News release, National Press Club, January 17. Boston: Center for
        Health and Global Environment, Harvard Medical School. http://www.pbs
        .org/now/shows/343/letter.pdf, accessed August 7, 2011.

Shapin, Steven, and Simon Schaffer
1985   Leviathan and the Air-Pump: Hobbes, Boyle and the Experimental Life. Princeton: Princeton University Press.

Shellenberger, Michael, and Ted Nordhaus
2004   The Death of Environmentalism: Global Warming Politics in a Post-Environmental World. http://www.thebreakthrough.org/PDF /Death_of_Environmentalism.pdf, accessed July 14, 2009.

Simpson, Larry D.
2003   Integrated Water Resources Management, Ceara, Brazil. Washington, DC: World Bank.

Slack, Jennifer Daryl
1996   The Theory and Method of Articulation in Cultural Studies. *In* Stuart Hall: Critical Dialogues in Cultural Studies. David Morley and Kuan Hsing-Chen, eds. Pp. 112–129. London: Routledge.

Smith, Christian, and Joshua Prokopy
1999   Latin American Religion in Motion. New York: Routledge.

Smith, Eric Alden, and Mark Wishnie
2000   Conservation and Subsistence in Small-Scale Societies. Annual Review of Anthropology 29:493–524.

Smith, Jonathan Z.
1998   Religion, Religions, Religious. In Critical Terms for Religious Studies. Mark C. Taylor, ed. Pp. 269–284. Chicago: University of Chicago Press.

Sochaczewski, Paul Spencer
1996   Zimbabwe's "War of the Trees" Fights on Holy Ground: People Wage Holy War on Drought. Gemini News Service (no longer operational). http://www.sochaczewski.com/ARTtzirrcon.html, accessed July 12, 2011.

Social Compass
1990   Special issue on implicit religion. December; 37(4).

Soper, Kate
1995   What is Nature? Culture, Politics and the non-Human. Oxford: Blackwell.

Soulé, Michael, and Gary Lease, eds.
1995   Reinventing Nature? Responses to Postmodern Deconstruction. Washington, DC: Island Press.

Southworth, Jane, and Catherine M. Tucker
2001   The Roles of Accessibility, Local Institutions and Socioeconomic Factors Influencing Forest Cover Change in the Mountains of Western Honduras. Mountain Research and Development 21(3):276–283.

Souza, Carlos M., Jr.
2006   Mapping Land Use of Tropical Regions from Space. Proceedings of the National Academy of Sciences of the United States of America 103(39):14261–14262.

REFERENCES

Sponsel, Leslie E.
2007   Religion, Nature and Environmentalism. David Casagrande, topic ed. *In* Encyclopedia of Earth. Cutler J. Cleveland, ed. Washington, DC: Environmental Information Coalition, National Council for Science and the Environment. http://www.eoearth.org/article/Religion,_nature_and _environmentalism, accessed December 2, 2009.

Steigenga, Timothy, and Edward L. Cleary
2008   Conversion of a Continent: Contemporary Religious Change in Latin America. New Brunswick: Rutgers University Press.

Stengers, Isabelle
1996–97 Cosmopolitiques [Cosmopolitics], 7 vols. Paris: La découverte.
2005   The Cosmopolitical Proposal. *In* Making Things Public: Atmospheres of Democracy. B. Latour and P. Weibel, eds. Pp. 994–1003. Cambridge: MIT Press.

Stephenson, David J., Jr.
1999   A Practical Primer on Intellectual Property Rights in a Contemporary Ethnoecological Context. *In* Ethnoecology: Situation Knowledge/Located Lives. V. D. Nazarea, ed. Pp. 230–248. Tucson: University of Arizona Press.

Stepp, John Richard, Hector Castaneda, and Sarah Cervone
2005   Mountains and Biocultural Diversity. Mountain Research and Development 25(3):223–227.

Steward, Julian
1955   Theory of Culture Change. Urbana: University of Illinois Press.

Stoll, David
1990   Is Latin America Turning Protestant? The Politics of Evangelical Growth. Berkeley: University of California Press.

Styers, Randall
2004   Making Magic: Religion, Magic, and Science in the Modern World. Oxford: Oxford University Press.

Tabarelli, Marcelo, Luiz Paulo Pinto, Jose M. C. Silva, Marcia Horotas, and Lucio Bede
2005   Challenges and Opportunities for Biodiversity Conservation in the Brazilian Atlantic Forest. *Conservation Biology* 19(3):695–700.

Tavera, Gloria, and Rocio Heredía
2002   Community Protected Areas: A Gift to the Earth (WWF-Programa Oaxaca). *In* ParksWatch, "News From the Field." http://www.parkswatch.org /news.php?1=eng&id=45, accessed December15, 2009.

Taylor, Bron
2010   Dark Green Religion: Nature Spirituality and the Planetary Future. Berkeley: University of California Press.

Taylor, Bron, ed.
2005   Encyclopedia of Religion and Nature, 2 vols. London: Continuum International.

Taylor, Charles

2007   A Secular Age. Cambridge: Harvard University Press / Belknap.

Tedlock, Dennis, trans.

1985   Popol Vuh: The Definitive Edition of the Mayan Book of the Dawn of Life and the Glories of Gods and Kings. New York: Simon and Schuster.

Terborgh, John

1999   Requiem for Nature. Washington, DC: Island Press.

Terraciano, Kevin

2001   The Mixtecs of Colonial Oaxaca. Stanford: Stanford University Press.

Theije, Marjo, and Cecília L. Mariz

2008   Localizing and Globalizing Processes in Brazilian Catholicism: Comparing Inculturation in Liberationist and Charismatic Catholic Cultures. Latin American Research Review 43(1):33–53.

Thoreau, Henry David

1995[1854] Walden, or, Life in the Woods. New York: Dover.

TIASA (Técnica Informática Aplicada, S.A.)

1993   Programa de manejo forestal, Ixtlan de Juarez, Oax, 1993–2000 [Forest management program, Ixtlan de Juarez, Oaxaca, 1993–2000], 4 vols. Texcoco, Mexico: TIASA.

Tiedje, Kristina

2008   Situating the Corn-Child: Articulating Animism and Conservation from a Nahua Perspective. Journal for the Study of Religion, Nature and Culture 2(1):93–115.

Tillich, Paul

1959   Theology of Culture. New York: Oxford University Press.

Tippett, Alan R.

1971   People Movements in Southern Polynesia. Chicago: Moody Press.

Toledo, Victor M.

2001   Indigenous Peoples and Biodiversity . In Encyclopedia of Biodiversity, S. Levin, ed. Pp. 451–463. San Diego: Academic Press.

Tsing, Anna Lowenhaupt

2005   Friction: An Ethnography of Global Connections. Princeton: Princeton University Press.

Tuan, Yi-Fu

1968   Discrepancies between Environmental Attitude and Behaviour: Examples from Europe and China. Canadian Geographer 12:176–191.

Tucker, Catherine M.

1999   Common Property Design Principles and Development in a Honduran Community. Praxis: The Fletcher Journal of Development Studies 15:47–76.

2008   Changing Forests: Collective Action, Common Property and Coffee in Honduras. Dordrecht: Springer.

2010 Private Goods and Common Property: Pottery Production in a Honduran Lenca Community. Human Organization 69(1):43–53.

Tucker, Catherine M., Hallie Eakin, and Edwin Castellanos
2010 Perceptions of Risk and Adaptations: Coffee Producers, Market Shocks and Extreme Weather in Central America and Mexico. Global Environmental Change 20:23–32.

Tucker, Mary Evelyn
2003 Worldly Wonder: Religions Enter Their Ecological Phase. Chicago: Open Court.
2009 The Sacred Universe: Earth, Spirituality and Religion in the Twenty-First Century. New York: Columbia University Press.

Tucker, Mary Evelyn, and John Grim
2007 The Greening of the World's Religions. The Chronicle of Higher Education 53(23):B9–B10.

Tucker, Mary Evelyn, and John Grim, eds.
2001 Religion and Ecology: Can the Climate Change? Daedalus: Journal of the American Academy of Arts and Sciences 130(4):1–306.

Tucker, Mary Evelyn, and Duncan Ryuken Williams, eds.
1997 Buddhism and Ecology: The Interconnection of Dharma and Deeds. Cambridge: Harvard University Press.

Turner, Nancy J., and Fikret Berkes
2006 Coming to Understanding: Developing Conservation through Incremental Learning in the Pacific Northwest. Human Ecology 34(4):495–513.

Tylor, Edward B.
1920[1871] Primitive Culture: Researches into the Development of Mythology, Philosophy, Religion, Language, Art, and Custom. London: John Murray.

Umlas, Elizabeth
1996 Non-governmental Organizations and Environmental Policy. *In* Changing Structure of Mexico: Political, Social, and Economic Prospects. Laura Randall, ed. Pp. 243–251. Armonk: M. E. Sharpe.

UNDP (United Nations Development Programme)
2003 Informe sobre desarrollo humano, Honduras 2003 [Human development report, Honduras 2003]. San José, Costa Rica: Editorama, SA.

UNESCO (United Nations Educational, Scientific, and Cultural Organization)
2008 The MAB Programme: Mata Atlântica (Including Sao Paulo Green Belt). http://www.unesco.org/mabdb/br/brdir/directory/biores.asp?code=BRA+01&mode=all, accessed January 18, 2010.

Urry, John, and Phil Macnaghten
1996 Contested Natures. London: Sage.

Van Dyke, Fred
2005   Between Heaven and Earth—Evangelical Engagement in Conservation. Conservation Biology 19(6):1693–1696.

Van Houtan, Kyle S.
2006   Conservation as Virtue: A Scientific and Social Process for Conservation Ethics. Conservation Biology 20(5):1367–1372.

Varese, Stefano
1996   The Ethnopolitics of Indian Resistance in Latin America. Latin American Perspectives 89(2):58–71.

Vayda, Andrew
1969   An ecological approach to cultural anthropology. Bucknell Review 17:112–119.

Verran, Helen
2001   Science and an African Logic. Chicago: University of Chicago Press.

Viola, Eduardo
1992   From Preservationism to Sustainable Development: A Challenge for the Environmental Movement in Brazil. International Journal of Sociology and Social Policy 12(4):129–150.
1997   The Environmental Movement in Brazil: Institutionalization, Sustainable Development and Crisis of Governance since 1987. *In* Latin American Environmental Policy in International Perspective. Gordon J. MacDonald, Daniel L. Nielson, and Marc A. Stern, eds. Pp. 88–110. Latin America in Global Perspective Series. Boulder: Westview Press.

Viveiros de Castro, Eduardo
1992   From the Enemy's Point of View: Humanity and Divinity in an Amazonian Society. Chicago: University of Chicago Press.
2004   Exchanging Perspectives: The Transformation of Objects into Subjects in Amerindian Ontologies. Common Knowledge 10(3):463–484.

Voeks, Robert
1997   Sacred Leaves of Candomblé: African Magic, Medicine, and Religion in Brazil. Austin: University of Texas Press.

Vogel, Steven
1996   Against Nature: The Concept of Nature in Critical Theory. Albany: State University of New York Press.

Wakild, Emily
2007   Naturalizing Modernity: Urban Parks, Public Gardens and Drainage Projects in Porfirian Mexico City. Mexican Studies/Estudios Mexicanos 23(1):101–123.

Walker, David, John Paul Jones III, Susan M. Roberts, and Oliver R. Frohling

2007   When Participation Meets Empowerment: The WWF and the Politics of Invitation in the Chimalapas, Mexico. Annals of the Association of American Geographers 97(2):423–444.

Wang, Jingfeng, Frederic J. F. Chagnon, Earle R. Williams, Alan K. Betts, Nilton O. Renno, Luiz A. T. Machado, Gautam Bisht, Ryan Knox, and Rafael L. Bras

2009   Impact of Deforestation in the Amazon Basin on Cloud Climatology. Proceedings of the National Academy of Sciences of the United States of America 106(10):3670–3674.

Warren, Kay B.

1998   Indigenous Movements and Their Critics: Pan-Maya Activism in Guatemala. Princeton: Princeton University Press.

Watanabe, John M., and Barbara B. Smuts

1999   Explaining Religion without Explaining It Away: Trust, Truth, and the Evolution of Cooperation in Roy A. Rappaport's "The Obvious Aspects of Ritual." American Anthropologist 101(1):98–112.

Watling, Tony

2008   The Field of Religion and Ecology: Addressing the Environmental Crisis and Challenging Faiths. In Religion: Beyond a Concept. Hent de Vries, ed. Pp. 473–488. New York: Fordham University Press.

Weber, Max

1946   From Max Weber: Essays in Sociology. H. H. Gerth and C. W. Mills, trans. and eds. New York: Oxford University Press.

West, Harry G., and Todd Sanders, eds.

2003   Transparency and Conspiracy: Ethnographies of Suspicion in the New World Order. Durham: Duke University Press.

West, Paige

2006   Conservation Is Our Government Now: The Politics of Ecology in Papua New Guinea. Durham: Duke University Press.

Weston, Walter

1896a   Exploration in the Japanese Alps, 1891–1894. The Geographical Journal 7(2):125–146.

1896b   Mountaineering and Exploration in the Japanese Alps. London: John Murray.

1918   The Playground of the Far East. London: John Murray.

White, Lynn, Jr.

1967   The Historical Roots of Our Ecologic Crisis. Science 155(3767):1203–1207.

Whitney, Elspeth

1993   Lynn White, Ecotheology, and History. Environmental Ethics 15(2):151–169.

Wigen, Kären

2005   Discovering the Japanese Alps: Meiji Mountaineering and the Quest for
Geographical Enlightenment. Journal of Japanese Studies 31(1):1–26.

Willems, Emilio

2008   Followers of the New Faith: Cultural Change and the Rise of Protestantism in
Brazil and Chile. *In* Latin American Religions: Histories and Documents in
Context. Anna L. Peterson and Manuel Vásquez, eds. Pp. 183–190. New
York: New York University Press.

Williams, Michael

2003   Deforesting the Earth: From Prehistory to the Global Crisis. Chicago:
University of Chicago Press.

Williams, Raymond

1976   Keywords: A Vocabulary of Culture and Society. London: Fontana.

Wilson, Bruce M.

1998   Costa Rica: Politics, Economics, and Democracy. London: Lynne Rienner.

Wilson, E. O.

2006   The Creation: An Appeal to Save Life on Earth. New York: W. W. Norton.

Wilson, Richard

1995   Maya Resurgence in Guatemala. Norman: University of Oklahoma Press.

Wilson, Rob, and Christopher Leigh Connery, eds.

2007   The Worlding Project. Berkeley: North Atlantic Books.

Wilson, Rob, and Wimal Dissanayake, eds.

1996   Global/Local: Cultural Production and the Transnational Imaginary.
Durham: Duke University Press.

Worster, Donald

1996[1994] Nature's Economy: A History of Ecological Ideas. 2nd edition.
Cambridge: Cambridge University Press.

1997   The Ecology of Order and Chaos. *In* Out of the Woods: Essays in
Environmental History. Char Miller and Hal Rothman, eds. Pp. 3–17.
Pittsburgh: University of Pittsburgh Press.

Wright, Angus, and Wendy Wolford

2003   To Inherit the Earth: The Landless Movement and the Struggle for a New
Brazil. Oakland: Food First.

WWF (World Wildlife Fund)

1986   The Assisi Declarations: Messages on Man and Nature from Buddhism,
Christianity, Hinduism, Islam and Judaism. Gland, Switzerland: WWF.

Yavesia (Autoridades Comunales de Yavesia)

1999   Letter to Salvador Anta Fonseca asking for a suspension of logging in
Yavesia. Unpublished letter, Yavesia, Oaxaca, Mexico.

REFERENCES

Yomiuri Shimbun
2004 Evening edition, November 8, 3.

Young, Robert
1972 The Anthropology of Science. New Humanist 88(3):102–105.

Index

School for Advanced Research Advanced Seminar Series
Published by SAR Press

GRAY AREAS: ETHNOGRAPHIC ENCOUNTERS
WITH NURSING HOME CULTURE
Philip B. Stafford, ed.

PLURALIZING ETHNOGRAPHY: COMPARISON
AND REPRESENTATION IN MAYA CULTURES,
HISTORIES, AND IDENTITIES
John M. Watanabe & Edward F. Fischer, eds.

AMERICAN ARRIVALS: ANTHROPOLOGY
ENGAGES THE NEW IMMIGRATION
Nancy Foner, ed.

VIOLENCE
Neil L. Whitehead, ed.

LAW & EMPIRE IN THE PACIFIC:
FIJI AND HAWAI'I
Sally Engle Merry & Donald Brenneis, eds.

ANTHROPOLOGY IN THE MARGINS
OF THE STATE
Veena Das & Deborah Poole, eds.

THE ARCHAEOLOGY OF COLONIAL
ENCOUNTERS: COMPARATIVE PERSPECTIVES
Gil J. Stein, ed.

GLOBALIZATION, WATER, & HEALTH:
RESOURCE MANAGEMENT IN TIMES OF
SCARCITY
Linda Whiteford & Scott Whiteford, eds.

A CATALYST FOR IDEAS: ANTHROPOLOGICAL
ARCHAEOLOGY AND THE LEGACY OF
DOUGLAS W. SCHWARTZ
Vernon L. Scarborough, ed.

THE ARCHAEOLOGY OF CHACO CANYON: AN
ELEVENTH-CENTURY PUEBLO REGIONAL
CENTER
Stephen H. Lekson, ed.

COMMUNITY BUILDING IN THE TWENTY-
FIRST CENTURY
Stanley E. Hyland, ed.

AFRO-ATLANTIC DIALOGUES:
ANTHROPOLOGY IN THE DIASPORA
Kevin A. Yelvington, ed.

COPÁN: THE HISTORY OF AN ANCIENT MAYA
KINGDOM
E. Wyllys Andrews & William L. Fash, eds.

THE EVOLUTION OF HUMAN LIFE HISTORY
Kristen Hawkes & Richard R. Paine, eds.

THE SEDUCTIONS OF COMMUNITY:
EMANCIPATIONS, OPPRESSIONS, QUANDARIES
Gerald W. Creed, ed.

THE GENDER OF GLOBALIZATION: WOMEN
NAVIGATING CULTURAL AND ECONOMIC
MARGINALITIES
Nandini Gunewardena & Ann Kingsolver, eds.

NEW LANDSCAPES OF INEQUALITY:
NEOLIBERALISM AND THE EROSION OF
DEMOCRACY IN AMERICA
*Jane L. Collins, Micaela di Leonardo,
& Brett Williams, eds.*

IMPERIAL FORMATIONS
*Ann Laura Stoler, Carole McGranahan,
& Peter C. Perdue, eds.*

OPENING ARCHAEOLOGY: REPATRIATION'S
IMPACT ON CONTEMPORARY RESEARCH AND
PRACTICE
Thomas W. Killion, ed.

SMALL WORLDS: METHOD, MEANING, &
NARRATIVE IN MICROHISTORY
*James F. Brooks, Christopher R. N. DeCorse,
& John Walton, eds.*

MEMORY WORK: ARCHAEOLOGIES OF
MATERIAL PRACTICES
Barbara J. Mills & William H. Walker, eds.

FIGURING THE FUTURE: GLOBALIZATION
AND THE TEMPORALITIES OF CHILDREN AND
YOUTH
Jennifer Cole & Deborah Durham, eds.

TIMELY ASSETS: THE POLITICS OF
RESOURCES AND THEIR TEMPORALITIES
*Elizabeth Emma Ferry &
Mandana E. Limbert, eds.*

DEMOCRACY: ANTHROPOLOGICAL
APPROACHES
Julia Paley, ed.

CONFRONTING CANCER: METAPHORS,
INEQUALITY, AND ADVOCACY
Juliet McMullin & Diane Weiner, eds.

Participants in the School for Advanced Research advanced seminar "Nature, Science, and Religion: Intersections Shaping Society and the Environment" chaired by Catherine M. Tucker, August 17–21, 2009. *Standing, from left:* Andrea Ballestero, Kristin Norget, Andrew S. Mathews, Anne Motley Hallum, Joel Robbins, Marthinus L. Daneel; *seated, from left:* Colleen M. Scanlan Lyons, Adrian J. Ivakhiv, Scott Schnell, Catherine M. Tucker.
Photograph by Jason S. Ordaz.